My Undercover Vendetta
to Take Down the
VAGOS OUTLAW
MOTORCYCLE GANG

GODS of MISCHIEF

GEORGE ROWE

A TOUCHSTONE BOOK

Published by Simon & Schuster

New York   London   Toronto   Sydney   New Delhi

Touchstone
A Division of Simon & Schuster, Inc.
1230 Avenue of the Americas
New York, NY 10020

First Touchstone hardcover edition February 2013

TOUCHSTONE and colophon are registered trademarks of Simon & Schuster, Inc.

For information about special discounts for bulk purchases, please contact Simon & Schuster Special Sales at 1-866-506-1949 or business@simonand schuster.com.

The Simon & Schuster Speakers Bureau can bring authors to your live event. For more information or to book an event contact the Simon & Schuster Speakers Bureau at 866-248-3049 or visit our website at www.simon speakers.com.

Designed by Joy O'Meara

Manufactured in the United States of America

10 9 8 7 6 5 4 3 2 1

Library of Congress Cataloging-in-Publication Data
Rowe, George.
   The gods of mischief : my undercover vendetta to take down the Vagos outlaw motorcycle gang / George Rowe.
      pages   cm
   1. Motorcycle gangs—California.   2. Outlaws—California.   I. Title.
HV6489.C2R69   2013
361.406'6—dc23   2012041994

ISBN 978-1-4516-6734-9
ISBN 978-1-4516-6736-3 (ebook)

To my father . . . who loved me unconditionally.

Lightning flashes anger, and thunder sounds my rage.
My heart screams to be out of this hell-bound cage.
My soul cries out and yearns to be free far from this place.

CONTENTS

GODS of MISCHIEF

PROLOGUE

Hemet, California; Thursday, March 9, 2006

few hours before dawn I'm wide awake and skittish as hell, waiting for the shitstorm. My fiancée lies asleep beside me, nine months pregnant and blissfully unaware her world is about to shatter. For three tense years I've been living on the edge as a federal informant, operating deep undercover to gather criminal evidence against one of this country's most violent motorcycle gangs—evidence that will lock my brothers away. My fiancée knows me as a patched member of the Vagos Motorcycle Club, but that's only half the story. I wonder how she'll take it when she learns the rest: that the man she loves is a man she never really knew . . . that our time together was a lie.

Talk about a rude awakening.

Too restless to stay in bed, I head into the kitchen for coffee and cigarettes. Leaning against the counter, chain-smoking Marlboros while the coffee drips, I check the clock on the microwave.

5:36 a.m.

Almost time.

In less than thirty minutes there's no turning back. At precisely 6:00 a.m. (PST), more than seven hundred heavily armed law enforcement officers will sweep through Southern California in one of the largest gang busts in United States history.

And it all starts with me.

In the winter of 2003, the year I went undercover, my hometown was under siege, its citizens terrorized by a group of crank-fueled outlaws no one could control. I was a local businessman with a shameful history—a one-time drug dealer and two-time felon haunted by the sins of my past. Though I'd spent much of my life in the company of Harley-riding outcasts like the Hells Angels, for the sake of the community I turned against the brotherhood and vowed to end their violence and intimidation.

When I volunteered for that thankless mission, shaking hands with Special Agent John Carr in Bee Canyon, my path seemed clear enough; a few months riding with the Vagos and wham-bam-thank-you-ma'am, I'd have my hometown cleaned up and those fuckers in cages.

Dumb bastard. What the hell were you thinking?

Before that handshake I had the world by the balls, brother. Ol' George Rowe was sitting pretty. Now everything's gone to shit. The life I knew, like the man I was, is slipping away—and there's not a damn thing I can do about it.

Guess I should have known where this was headed. I might have been three years under, but it's taken a lifetime to get here. I've been riding a hell wave, and there's no breaking free. Nothing to do but let the waters take me.

1

A Banging Place

inety miles east of Los Angeles, out beyond the San Bernardino Mountains and down into the scorching heat of the San Jacinto Valley, you'll find the city of Hemet, California. My old hometown was still a ranch and farming community when Mother forced it down my throat in the summer of '71—nothing but potato fields, low buildings and a few flat streets skirting the western edge of the Mojave Desert. But with Californians migrating inland from the coast in search of affordable property, the valley's population was booming.

From the Santa Rosa Hills on Hemet's south flank to the city of San Jacinto, which shares the valley floor to the north, came a growing flood of retirement communities, trailer parks and stucco subdivisions. In just ten years—from 1970 to 1980—the city's population nearly doubled, creating opportunities for anyone looking to make a buck . . . legal or otherwise.

For the lawless few, geography was the key to scoring big money. Hemet's founding fathers would have shit their Levis had they known their little start-up would become the ass-end of a pipeline delivering marijuana, cocaine and heroin from Mexico, one hundred miles to the south. Starting in the 1960s, Hemet became a banging place for outlaw biker gangs hungry for a slice of that Mexican drug connection, many rolling in from neighboring cities like Riverside and San Bernardino, birthplace of the Hells Angels.

As a boy, I grew accustomed to the roar of their straight pipes blasting through the valley—iron horses farting thunder, ridden by barbarians with wild manes, greasy leathers and fuck-you attitudes. I wanted some of that. I too raised my middle finger to authority and shared a passion for motorcycles, which I'd been riding since I was seven years old, barely tall enough to reach the shift lever of the little Hodaka my father bought me before he died.

He was tough, my old man, a full-blooded Yaqui Indian and decorated Korean War veteran. But the warrior was no match for malaria and alcohol, a one-two punch that fried his brain and ravaged his liver. Terminally ill, Dad wanted to spend his last years teaching his boy how to hunt and fish in the mountains, but for that he needed custody from Mother, a mean-spirited drunk with a face like leather, ridden hard and put away wet by more men than I can remember. When I was a toddler I swear I spent more time napping in bars while Mommy trolled for bed partners than I did sleeping in my own room.

Warren Road in Hemet, biker paradise.

Custody was hard fought and harder won by fathers in those days, but when I jumped to my feet at the juvenile court hearing and screamed, "I don't want to live with her, I want to live with my dad!" the judge heard me loud and clear. Mother got my sisters, Carol and Lin Ann, while Dad pulled me from kindergarten and took me into the Cascades up near the California-Oregon border.

Those were special years we shared in the high country, the absolute best of my life. But watching your father wither away from cirrhosis and thrash on the ground in fits of epilepsy, eyes rolling in their sockets, was asking a lot from a ten-year-old. So in 1970, with the end near, the old man packed our belongings and came down from the mountain, returning to Southern California to die.

Dad was forty-one when his wasted body finally quit. In my mind's eye I can still picture the end like it happened this morning. We were sitting on a couch watching television when he slumped sideways and fell across my lap. At first I thought he'd passed out—it had happened before—but as his

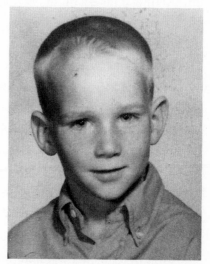

Me at five years old, just before dropping out of kindergarten.

skin grew cold I realized there was no waking him up again. Four hours later my uncle stopped by and found me still pinned beneath Dad's stiffening body. Truth is, I didn't want to let go. I was ten years old and terrified of a future without him. Afraid of being alone.

I became a ward of the state, bounced between foster homes until a kind woman from Buena Park took me under her wing and tried teaching me how to read and write, lessons this kindergarten dropout had missed while learning survival skills in the Cascades. The world turns unexpectedly, and certainly nothing is guaranteed in life, but I believe my future would have been different had I stayed with that woman. I really do.

But then Mother returned, looking for custody of the Social Security checks I'd been collecting since my old man passed away, and once they were hers I was dragged into the backseat of her Oldsmobile 88 and shanghaied to Hemet. I still remember heading east on the San Bernardino Freeway, desperately trying to memorize the road signs that would lead me back to that foster home in Buena Park. Instead the bitch dumped my ass on the county, and I ended up in a cage at juvenile hall trying to figure out what "incorrigible" meant.

The couple that rescued me owned the Hemet property where Mother was shacking up. With her blessing, they adopted me a few months later. Guess I should have been grateful for a roof over my head and three squares on the table, but life was never easy with that dysfunctional crew. There was a shitload of drinking and fighting in that house, with much of the anger directed at me.

My new dad was a tough little sonofabitch, strong and tanned from working with the town's park and recreation department. Pat was a firm believer in old-fashioned "spare the rod, spoil the child" discipline. And when that man doled out punishment, the lessons came hard. To be fair, I was never a choirboy and probably deserved the occasional buttkicking, but Pat's brand of abuse was an entirely new experience. The dad I'd lost had raised his hand to me only once.

This one broke my arm.

Had my old man been alive, I know how he would have handled things. When my uncle back in the San Fernando Valley gave me a black eye, dad gave him two. When a perfect stranger in a Burbank mall slapped me upside the head for mouthing off, my father lifted him up and dropped him on his skull.

"Son," he said as he knelt before me, "don't ever let anyone push you around."

Later in life I took Dad's advice to heart, but when you're an eleven-year-old getting pounded by a grown man, it's easier said than done. For now my best defense against my adoptive father was vaulting the six-foot backyard fence whenever he was after me.

"That boy sure can jump," Pat would boast to his drinking buddies.

Tough as he was, though, my new dad was no match for his 250-pound wife. Pat might have worn the pants in the family, but no one messed with Mama Cass—that's what I called her when she was safely out of earshot. Pat came through the door shitfaced one night and mouthed off as his wife was in the middle of ironing. Big mistake. Dodi pinned him to the wall and ironed her hubby's chest. Swear to God, that woman had a heart as big as her appetite, but piss her off and you'd best run for cover. Whatever Dodi had in her hands you'd get clobbered with. Garden tools, spatulas, skillets—you name it, she'd wing it. I saw more spaghetti on the walls than in the pots.

In the back bedroom of the house, my alcoholic mother was shacking up with Pat's brother, John, the town drunk with a heart of gold. Down the hall lived my little sister, Lin Ann, and my older sister, Carol, fifteen years old, knocked up and soon to be married. In the basement slept my adoptive brother, Keith, a machinist in town who was good friends with a couple of biker brothers from the neighborhood—one who rode with the Vagos Motorcycle Club, and the other a patched member of the Hells Angels, named Freight Train. Vagos and Angels mix like oil and water, but in the brothers' case blood was thicker than club loyalty.

Keith's half brother, Gary, the only family member missing from that Hemet nuthouse, was a twenty-four-year-old roughneck who'd lost his foot in a Texas oil field accident. As gangrene crept in, the doctors chased the infection up his leg, amputating it one chunk at a time. Wasn't long before the poor bastard lost that entire limb, followed by his wife and kids. Homesick and depressed, Gary came limping home on a prosthetic leg, rented a house with Freight Train and got busy drinking himself to death.

Freight Train had earned his road name with the Hells Angels for good reason. The man was a four-hundred-pound behemoth with hands the size of baseball mitts. His hair was long, his beard wild, and he had a silver-plated front tooth that gleamed when he smiled. And when Freight Train smiled, it meant someone was about to get hurt.

God's truth, I once saw that man-mountain flip a police cruiser on its top—with the cop still inside. Another time he took on a platoon's worth of shitfaced marines outside a bar in Winchester, California. Ol' Freight Train was outnumbered and surrounded, but then came that slow smile, out popped the silver tooth, and down went nine of those jarheads. It took a pool stick punched through his gut to finally derail him, but by then the damage was done. For his one-man assault on the United States Marine Corps the government charged Freight Train with—I shit you not—destruction of federal property . . . a charge they later dismissed.

I earned a few bucks mowing Gary's lawn back then, and watched as motorcycle outlaws from across the valley come thundering in on their Harley-Davidsons to raise a little hell. These were tough mothers—many of them Vietnam War vets searching for the same camaraderie they'd found in the service.

They wore patches on their backs with club names like Mescaleros, Hessians and Hangmen, and boasted of being "one percenters," the outlaw's badge of honor since 1947. That was the year a bunch of shit-faced bikers "rioted" at a motorcycle rally in Hollister, California—an event made famous by Marlon Brando in the 1953 biker flick *The Wild One*—then got slammed in the press as "the deviant one percent" of an otherwise law-abiding motorcycling public.

Over in San Bernardino, the Hells Angels took that as a backhanded compliment and began wearing a "1%" patch on their jackets, identifying themselves as outsiders who followed nobody's rules but their own. Many of the bikers who hung at my brother's place wore that diamond-shaped badge of honor, and it wasn't long before I was ditching the lawn mower and sneaking inside to be nearer those larger-than-life characters.

Sure, they sometimes got pissed off and ran my scrawny ass down the road, but I'd always worm my way back in. Eventually I was adopted as a kid brother and came to know their ironclad code of loyalty and commitment, which placed the brotherhood above all else: above jobs, above friends . . . even above their own families. To me those bikers were modern-day musketeers, saluting each other with bottles of beer while shouting, "Fuck with one, you fuck with all!"

FW1-UFWA: the universal battle cry of the motorcycle outlaw.

But by the late 1970s, the beer-guzzling, gang-brawling characters I'd grown up with were a vanishing breed in the San Jacinto Valley. Tired of the life and increasing pressure from law enforcement, outlaws like Freight Train had become more interested in raising families than raising hell. Of course, turf-pissing contests were still fought over the patches on their backs, but with the old dogs slowing down and the young pups lying low, the roar of straight pipes quieted in the valley, and a biker flying his colors became a rare sight on the streets of Hemet for almost two decades.

Then the century turned and a new, more aggressive generation of outlaw rolled into town, one pumped on steroids, fueled by testosterone and always looking for a brawl.

2

A Nation of Brutes

Johnny's Restaurant was a bar and steak joint fronting Florida Avenue, also known as California Highway 74, which cuts through the heart of downtown Hemet. To enter Johnny's you parked at the rear of the building and came in through the back door. There were no street-side windows, so it took a moment for your eyes to adjust to the dim interior.

Wasn't much to see, though. Once you squeezed past the narrow bar, the room widened into a dining area of worn carpet and ripped cushions. Sitting down was an adventure; you never knew when a spring might poke you in the ass. But despite its seedy appearance and musty smell, Johnny's was popular with the locals. Cheap beer and thick steaks had a lot to do with that.

A few weeks before he vanished forever, an old friend of mine was at the restaurant to celebrate. I'd known David back at Hemet High right up until my junior year, when I dropped out of school. Through the years we kept in touch, catching up on old news whenever we bumped into each other around town. He was a family man with two young kids and a pregnant wife, and that night at Johnny's the couple had gathered with friends and family for a baby shower.

It would be the last time many of them would see David alive.

After gifts were opened, the father-to-be headed for the empty pool table and grabbed a cue stick. And that's where he was, mucking around and minding his business, when four outlaw bikers entered through the restaurant's back door. They wore sleeveless denim vests called "cuts," with the devil-like image of Loki, the Norse god of mischief, sewn on the back. Beneath Loki was a bottom rocker that read CALIFORNIA, while above, in bold letters, was the name VAGOS. These full-patch outlaws were flying the colors of

Vagos logo.

the Vagos Motorcycle Club, a gang known throughout California as "Green Nation."

In the early 1960s, around the time I was still crapping my diapers, a group of biker misfits calling themselves the Psychos spread from Southern California's Temescal Canyon into the city of Riverside and beyond. With balls fit for a wheelbarrow, they even took root in San Bernardino, right in the Hells Angels' own backyard, sparking a turf feud that continues to this day.

As membership multiplied, the Psychos adopted a new name—Los Vagos, Spanish for "The Vagabonds" or "The Tramps"—and took green as their signature color. By the time Green Nation spread into Hemet, chapters had been established in Nevada, Arizona, Hawaii and Mexico, and the Vagos had become the largest and one of the most violent of California's biker gangs—a grab bag of weekend rebels, gearheads, ex-cons and violent sociopaths engaged in a whole laundry list of criminal activities, from gun and drug trafficking to assault and murder.

Leading his posse into Johnny's Restaurant that night was Big Roy Compton, a thirty-four-year-old tattoo artist with a muscular frame covered in ink, from the VAGOS MC on the back of his shaved and goateed head down to his steel-toed riding boots.

The president, or "P," of the Hemet chapter, was a convicted felon who once made his living transporting illegals, picking up Mexicans after they'd crossed the border and running them as far as Arizona. He and his old lady used some of those profits to bankroll a tattoo parlor in Hemet called the Lady Luck, which they opened right next door to a Baskin-Robbins. Little tykes would be licking ice cream cones on the sidewalk while large tattooed men stood nearby cutting farts and smoking weed.

Big Roy first hooked up with the Vagos in the nearby city of Corona, where the chapter was led by Mumbles, a wild man who could fling a knife into a knothole at fifty paces. But Roy had bigger ambitions. He wanted a Vagos franchise of his own. According to club bylaws, that required at least five warm bodies and the blessing of the Vagos international president, a potbellied gnome named Terry the Tramp, who, for sixteen years, had lorded over Green Nation from his home in Southern California's High Desert.

Johnny's Restaurant (since renamed) on Florida Avenue.

With Tramp's benediction, and using the Lady Luck as his base of operations, Big Roy got busy recruiting. First to come aboard as chapter vice president was Todd Brown, a man Roy had befriended during a stint in rehab. Big Todd was a juicer who'd slammed so many steroids in his thirty-six years that he looked like Captain Fuckin' America, all jacked up and cruising Hemet aboard a $30,000 Harley-Davidson— every nut and bolt of it stolen.

I never liked Big Roy and his amped-up bad-boy act, but I really detested his dirtbag sidekick Todd. Besides being one of the sneakiest sucker-punchers I've ever met, Big Todd was a backstabber who took pride in fucking a brother's old lady, then bragging about it. Hell, that sonofabitch would slip his dick in a rattlesnake if you held its head.

The other two Vagos in Big Roy's entourage that night were Todd's older brother, Doug, and a tough little Mexican from Northern California named Iron Mike. Big Doug was a loose cannon, usually spun out of his bald-headed gourd on crank. Even his closest buddies walked on eggshells whenever Doug was tweaking. You never knew what that scary fuck might do. Just as tough as Doug but nowhere near as crazy, Iron Mike had earned his cred with Chicano street gangs. That little hombre was a true outlaw, always down for the club. If Green Nation needed a volunteer to pop a bullet in someone's head, Mike would be first in line asking, "Which ear?"

From the moment Terry the Tramp granted Big Roy his club charter, the Hemet Vagos were off and pissing on their hometown like dogs marking turf. The way Roy had it figured, the city was Green Nation property now, and any objections would be overruled by brute force. Through fear and intimidation, the Hemet chapter demanded respect for that Loki patch on their backs, making life miserable for everyone in town. Young or old, male or female, didn't matter. When the Vagos appeared, the locals would lower their eyes and turn heads, afraid to make eye contact.

Just a few weeks before the baby shower, some of the Hemet boys were getting hammered at the bar when a mentally disabled young man with a hunched back accidentally bumped Big Todd on the way to the bathroom. Without waiting for an apology, the Vago spun and shoved the kid hard into the wall.

"Don't fuckin' touch me, freak!" Todd exploded at him.

Before the young man understood what was happening, Big Todd followed with one of his patented cheap shots, a roundhouse right that caught that dude flush in the head and dropped him like a sack of potatoes. And since Todd had his victim defenseless on the floor, he figured why not stomp him for good measure? So that's what he did. Over and over again.

It was ugly, man. Big Todd Brown was raging on steroids and completely out of his mind.

When the father saw what was happening, he rushed from the dining area to save his son. But the man didn't get far. Invoking the sacred outlaw motto, "You fuck with one, you fuck with all," the remaining Vagos intercepted that poor bastard and gave him a savage beat-down.

Their dirty work done, the gang scattered like cockroaches from the light, leaving father and son broken on the floor, covered in blood and boot prints.

And why?

Because Big Todd felt disrespected.

See, here's the thing about respect. In my experience, those who demand it most are usually the ones who deserve it least—like Hemet's jackbooted thugs. For motorcycle outlaws, giving and getting precious respect is probably the closest thing there is to a chiseled-in-stone commandment. Hell, it's almost a religious principle. In fact, every card-carrying member of the Vagos MC wears a patch on his cut that proclaims, We Give What We Get. In other words, give us respect and respect is returned. If not, you'll pay the price.

But the Vagos who were out to claim Hemet as their own had no fucking clue what "respect" meant. They figured it was something to be extracted with the heel of a boot and the twist of an arm. Hell, even a dumb bastard like me was smart enough to know that terrorizing civilians—anyone not part of the outlaw world—was a really bad idea. That kind of bullying does nothing to earn respect. What it earns are lifelong enemies . . . including one in particular who would come back to bite those bullies in the ass.

Of course, not every one percenter was a scumbag who behaved like an animal, raping and pillaging through life like Attila the Hun. That's way too simplistic. I met decent men who rode Harley-Davidsons and flew outlaw colors while recognizing the moral and social boundaries that should never be crossed.

The four Vagos who walked into Johnny's Restaurant that night were not those kind of men. These were the rotted apples spoiling the whole fuckin' bunch—low-life gangbangers in every sense of the word. Big Roy and company were bullies who got their kicks intimidating others, backed by the collective might of Green Nation.

As usual, the Hemet boys were looking for trouble the night they showed up in the middle of my buddy's baby shower. Far as Roy was concerned, a sign should have been hung over the bar announcing This Establishment Property of the Vagos. Of course, that ownership included the table where David was shooting pool, so Roy marched up to him and demanded it for the club.

Fact is, my friend had no idea who this arrogant prick was. David had never had a close encounter with the outlaw world before. He just knew he wasn't giving up the cue stick just because some bald-headed asshole with a patch on his back was commanding it.

So he respectfully declined.

Well, that was not the response the Hemet P was accustomed to hearing. So Big Roy gave Dave a shove.

Then Dave shoved back harder.

And that's right about where I walked in.

I'd noticed the row of Harleys parked on their kickstands behind

Johnny's and knew who they belonged to. I've got full-sleeve tattoos on both arms, many of them inked at Big Roy's Lady Luck. I'd worked on tree service crews with Big Todd. And since I rode Harleys and used to fight bareknuckle on the underground fight circuit, both those Vagos figured I'd make a kick-ass soldier for Green Nation and had tried recruiting me into the club.

"Freedom. That's what it's all about," Todd had once explained to me, pitching the outlaw life. "You've got all these guys behind you, George. We can do whatever the fuck we want. We're gonna sell dope and people will pay up because of who we are. You gotta come join us, man."

Fuck that shit. I could see prison sentences coming for every one of those punks. My buddy, Freight Train, who lived as an outlaw with the Hells Angels and understood the culture's downside, had experienced firsthand the brutality of turf warfare and the constant harassment from law enforcement. The road taken by the one percent was a bitch to travel, he'd warned me. Better to steer clear.

Ol' Freight Train had been preaching to the choir. At that point in life I was forty-two years old and had experienced my share of time behind bars. And that was never time well spent. No goddamn way was I getting busted again. I needed that Vagos patch like a fat kid needs another heaping helping of mashed potatoes.

As I stepped through the back door and entered Johnny's Restaurant, I fully expected to meet Big Roy and his jolly green men. What I never expected to see was my friend Dave knocking the Hemet chapter president flat on his ass.

And, man, it was beautiful.

It also sealed my buddy's fate.

Before Big Roy could climb off the deck, his three bodyguards sprang into action. While David's wife and guests watched in horror, the Vagos punched, kicked and stomped the shit out of my friend with bare knuckles and steel-toed boots. Almost before I could get between them, the bartender was calling for cops and an ambulance.

A week after paramedics hauled Dave's busted carcass from Johnny's, the man was out of the hospital but not out of danger. A few days later the father of two, with a third on the way, disappeared. I don't figure he'll turn up anytime soon, either . . . not without a solid lead, a good shovel and a whole lot of luck.

3

Midgets and Mayhem

Among the businesses scattered along Highway 74, the main thoroughfare that ran through the sprawling east Hemet neighborhood of Valle Vista, was a liquor store, two gas stations and, directly across from a trailer park, the broken-down apartment building that I once lived in and managed for a friend. There were three units in that single-story shitbox, each with a tiny kitchen, living room, bedroom and bath. The place was first built as a chicken coop, then converted into housing for Mexican laborers. Now it was just an eyesore begging to be torn down.

We called it "the chicken shack" or the "shack," or just "box of shit" on a bad day. A few weeks after David dropped off the planet, Detective Kevin Duffy of the Riverside County Sheriff's Department knocked on my apartment door. Duffy was the lead investigator on my friend's case and had heard I'd been inside Johnny's the night of the assault. Everyone knew the Vagos had something to do with David's disappearance, but no one was willing to talk to the cops. It was too dangerous.

Detective Duffy's investigation was dead in the water.

Duffy was a fair and honest cop, a decorated narcotics officer who had climbed the law enforcement ladder all the way to homicide. I'd known him since I was a young punk and he was just a kid deputy from the neighborhood. We had history, Duff and I. In fact, his was the first loaded gun ever pointed in my direction.

I don't know who was more scared that day, me or Kevin, but I can still picture that service revolver trembling in his hands, finger hard on the trigger and the barrel looking wider than a fuckin' drainpipe. I was

My friend Detective Kevin Duffy of the Riverside County Sheriff's Department.

eighteen and about to face charges that could put me behind walls for a long, long time.

Two years before facing the business end of Kevin Duffy's revolver—and just months after turning sixteen—I'd finally had enough of my adoptive father's bullshit. After Pat busted my arm, I vaulted the backyard fence for the last time and kept running.

It would be another twelve years before I returned to even the score. I can still picture the look on Dodi's face when I walked through the door as a grown man and asked to see her husband. She knew what I wanted by the look in my eyes.

I had inherited the same dark expression my father had when he was about to destroy someone. When I was ten years old and my uncle gave me a black eye, Dad checked himself out of a VA hospital and paid a visit. When he saw what his brother had done, I swear I saw that warrior's eyes go charcoal black. Dad stormed through the house, found my uncle and repaid him with a couple of shiners that lasted more than a month. I called that asshole "Raccoon" after that.

Now, twelve years after I'd vaulted the backyard fence to escape Pat's abuse, I was back as a twenty-eight-year-old man looking for some payback. And Dodi knew it too.

"Pat!" she finally called out. "George is here!"

"George?" came a puzzled voice from down the hall.

A moment later Pat appeared.

"We've got business," I told him straightaway. And he knew what I meant.

"Let's take it out back," he said.

I remember the grass was high. When I was a kid I used to mow the backyard and rake the leaves, but now everything was an overgrown mess.

"Well?" said Pat as he turned to me.

I didn't waste time. I hit the man hard. He fell to the ground, then tried to get back up. So I hit him again and he stayed down. And that was the end of it.

Fuck . . . is that all?

Me at sixteen years old, just before dropping out of high school.

Seeing my adoptive father bleeding in that tall grass might have given me a brief moment of satisfaction, but it was followed by a lifetime of regret. I wasn't proud of myself. I should never have done it. I should have let bygones be bygones.

As I reentered the house Dodi said to me, "I knew this had to happen someday."

I gave her a hug and walked out the door, never to return.

There's one thing I have to say in Pat's defense; the man might have been a hard-ass, but he provided for his family the only way he knew how. I took that work ethic with me—that and his knowledge of landscaping and tree trimming that I'd picked up while watching him work at Hemet's park and recreation department. These were skills I used for earning my livelihood after dropping out of high school at age sixteen, and I would return to them whenever my other ideas of turning a dollar turned to shit.

I started a landscaping business of my own, but my utter indifference to education and the five years I'd lost on my extended fishing trip to the Cascades soon caught up with me. It was a real wake-up call when I discovered that business accounts and contracts require reading and writing, never my strong suits. So I went out and hired me a midget with a high school education to handle the business end of things while I did the grunt labor.

This arrangement worked fine until I needed a new truck for my expanding operation. When I asked my partner to cut a business check, the little guy stalled and tap-danced around my request. Suspicious, I went to the bank and was told the entire business account balance had been wiped out.

The fucking midget had ripped me off for over sixteen grand.

Slightly ticked off, I grabbed my .30-30 Winchester and drove over to his house, a real nice place his father owned on a golf course. I announced my arrival by firing a rifle shot through the picture window while that thieving little bastard sat watching television. Then I informed his dad that the next bullet would go through his son's pint-sized head.

But that's not what got me arrested.

The midget's old man, a business executive in town, said he would keep the cops out of the matter and pay back half the sixteen grand his son had stolen if I'd call things even. I figured half was better than none, so we shook on the deal. That should have been the end of it, only I had this so-called friend who knew the whole story.

Pretending to be me, that asshole phoned the businessman, then threatened to rape his daughter and shoot more holes in his fancy house unless the remaining eight grand was dropped into a designated trash barrel outside the local Sambo's restaurant.

The midget's old man agreed to the blackmail, then called the cops.

The next day I'm hauling mulch in my pickup when I see a curious sight. My buddy is sprinting down San Jacinto Street with four sheriff's deputies in hot pursuit. Within minutes sirens are wailing, I'm surrounded by cruisers and a young deputy is ordering me out of the cab at gunpoint.

"Don't move!" shouted Deputy Duffy as I emerged with my hands up.

I found the kid deputy's tone decidedly unfriendly.

"Don't you fuckin' move!" he repeated.

So I didn't move. Kevin cuffed my wrists, read me my Miranda Rights, then hauled my ass to jail on felony charges of extortion, attempted rape and attempted murder.

Now my name was known across the San Jacinto Valley for all the wrong reasons. The district attorney, up for reelection, was determined to prosecute—apparently with the aid of my cock-sucking friend, who'd cut a deal with the D.A.'s office and agreed to testify against me in exchange for leniency. I was eighteen years old and looking at serious hard time: three consecutive fifteen-year prison terms.

But the superior court judge, who happened to be the same magistrate who'd handled my adoption, took both parties into chambers and pushed through a plea bargain. Afraid of going to trial, I pled to extortion and got ninety weekends in jail and 120 hours of community service, which was spent picking up discarded cigarette butts outside the county courthouse.

Now here I was twenty-four years later sitting in the shitshack across from Detective Duffy, who had become a good friend once he'd quit pointing his gun at me. After discussing the assault at Johnny's Restaurant, I asked Kevin point-blank, "When are your people gonna do something about the Vagos?"

"What do you mean?"

"They're causing chaos all over town, man. And I know those fuckers did David. We both know it."

"No, George, we don't. There's no proof they did it, and no one's talking. I haven't come up with a single lead."

"Well, you'd better find one quick. Because if someone doesn't stop these assholes, I guarantee more people will get hurt."

"And what do you expect me to do about it?"

"Your job," I said, snuffing out one cigarette and fishing for another.

"My job is homicide," Kevin said sharply. "If you're so concerned about the Vagos, maybe you should be doing something about it."

"I've told you what I know."

"Then find out more," Kevin said. "You know most of those guys. Why don't you talk to them?"

I paused from lighting the cigarette. Kevin saw the look of disbelief wash across my face.

"George, I'm spinning my tires here," he continued. "This investigation isn't going anywhere until I get a lead."

"What the hell are you saying, Duff?"

"I'm saying I could use a lead."

"What do you want me to do? Fuckin' stroll into the Lady Luck and ask Roy if he's killed anyone lately?"

Kevin smiled at the sarcasm and stood to leave.

"Just thought I'd put it out there."

He stopped at the door and turned before going out.

"Thanks for your time, George. Be a good boy."

Shooter's Food and Brew in Hemet was a bar that a friend of mine had named in honor of himself. Shooter came to the San Jacinto Valley after his wife passed away and his entire world went upside down. To take his mind off his loss, the man had sunk everything he'd owned into the bar, and that's where he'd first encountered the Vagos.

There was something about the outlaw mystique, of renegades refusing to be tied down, riding fast and free on the open road, that appealed to some men. Shooter was one of those men, and it wasn't long before he was badgering Big Roy to join the Hemet chapter. Instead Roy took advantage of Shooter's man-crush, stringing him along while his boys played free pool and drank booze on the house.

A few days after Detective Duffy's visit, I was sitting in Shooter's place and plying Big Todd with drinks at the bar. Guilt had gotten the best of me, and I'd decided the least I could do for my missing friend was ask a few questions that might jump-start Kevin's investigation. Unfortunately the questions I asked put the Vagos vice president in a foul mood, and it wasn't long before I ran that conversation straight into the ground.

Started out well, though, with Todd and me reminiscing about the good old days working for Hemet Tree Service, back when he was a seventeen-year-old ground man clearing the debris I chopped down. On the stool to the left of Todd sat a bearded Vago from the Norco chapter, who I didn't know by name.

"This motherfucker is crazy," Todd was telling the outlaw, jerking a thumb in my direction. "Climbs trees like a fuckin' monkey. It's unbelievable." Then he turned back to me. "Hey, remember that asshole who stole the chain saw?"

It was the same tired story Todd brought up every time we bumped into each other.

"Yeah, I remember," I told him. "I remember trying to warn you, but you had the chipper running."

Todd turned back to his buddy. "George is up in this fuckin' palm tree, like sixty feet off the ground, and he spots this prick lifting a chain saw off the company truck. So he pulls a gun and starts shooting at him."

Todd was laughing now. "Believe this guy? He climbs trees with a fuckin' Magnum strapped to his ankle."

"Three eighty," I corrected him.

"A three-fuckin'-eighty," said Todd. "So the prick is running with the chain saw and George is blasting away from up in the tree and that fuckin' kid is freaking out. He's like, ziggin' and zaggin' and shit."

Now Todd and his buddy were both laughing.

"He dropped the chain saw, though, didn't he?" I said.

"Fuck yeah, he dropped that chain saw," laughed Todd. "But you can't shoot for shit, guy."

"I wasn't trying to hit him, asshole."

"Well, you should have," countered Todd before taking a drink. "You should have popped that motherfucker."

I thought it was the height of fucking hypocrisy for Todd to bring that up. Hell, the man had been ripping off equipment from that company all the time to pay for his meth and cocaine habit long before I'd ever fired that .380 from the treetops.

Maybe I should have shot Todd instead.

Bullshit small talk followed until I finally steered the discussion toward my missing friend. I started trolling with some offhand remark like "Hey, whatever happened to that dude who gave you guys so much shit at Johnny's? What was that all about anyway?"

"Who we talking about?" Todd asked.

"About a month ago. The dude at the pool table. The one who knocked Roy on his ass."

Apparently that particular topic was a real buzz kill, because Todd immediately clammed up.

"Fuck that punk," he muttered.

"Hell, yeah," I said with a grin. "You messed him up pretty good." Then I threw in a casual "What the fuck happened to him anyway?"

It was a ham-fisted move that I immediately regretted. Big Todd took a long pull on his bottle, then turned with a smoldering look.

"Don't worry about it."

"Why would I?"

"That's right," he replied tersely. "Why would you? It's been handled."

I'd jerked the hook too hard, and let my fish get away. Big Todd was through talking. David had been handled, end of story. After that misplay there was nowhere to go but home, ending my brief and failed career as an inside man.

Or so I thought.

A week or two later Kevin Duffy called to ask for a private rendezvous out on Warren Road, an isolated two-lane stretch that hugs the western edge of the city. With the benefit of hindsight, I would have been better off leaving my truck keys on the counter and going to bed. Instead I headed out around 10:00 p.m., drove through town on Florida Avenue, then turned north on Warren.

There were no streetlamps along that straight stretch of worn-out asphalt, nothing but high-tension poles and open farmland. I continued through the dark landscape until the headlights found Kevin's unmarked SUV idling by the edge of a potato field.

I pulled beside him and spoke through the open window.

"So what are we doing, Duff?"

"Park your truck and climb in."

I squinted past him. There was a dark figure in plainclothes sitting in the front passenger's seat. I couldn't see him clearly, but I knew who he was. This was the lawman Kevin had asked me to meet, a young hard-charger who headed the newly formed special investigations unit with the Riverside County Sheriff's Department.

I climbed into the backseat of Kevin's SUV and he swung back onto Warren Road and continued heading north. Before long we'd left asphalt and started down a rutted dirt track that terminated at an old dump. Kevin killed the engine but left the dome light burning. The sheriff turned to look at me over his shoulder and introduced himself.

"Mr. Rowe, I asked for this meeting because Detective Duffy seems to think you'd be a good man to know."

I tapped out a cigarette and glanced at Kevin. "That right?"

"I understand you're friendly with Roy Compton."

"Well, you'd be wrong."

"I've seen you at the Lady Luck."

"I get tats there," I explained, displaying the ink on my forearm. "That doesn't mean we're buddies. I think Roy's a fuckin' prick if you want to know the truth."

Kevin and the lawman exchanged a look. I lit the cigarette and cracked the window.

"What's this about?" I said.

After a moment's hesitation, the lawman said, "Mind if I call you George?"

Before I could answer he called me George anyway.

"This is confidential, George. I need to know that what we discuss here stays between you, me and the detective. Can I have your word on that?"

I glanced at Kevin Duffy.

"Alright, fine."

"Okay, then," said the sheriff, pausing only briefly before launching his spiel. "For the past few months we've been running surveillance on the Lady Luck. We believe the Vagos have been violating state and federal laws in Hemet. Selling drugs. Maybe even firearms."

"How about murder?" I added.

"Maybe that too," said Kevin.

"We want to shut down the Vagos," the sheriff continued, "starting with Hemet. But to do that we need eyes and ears on the inside."

This took a few seconds to register, but once it clicked I looked at Kevin and said, "You gotta be shittin' me, Duff."

I'd been sandbagged.

"Just listen to the man, George," begged Kevin.

"Here's our problem," the sheriff quickly continued. "Any time we conduct surveillance on the Lady Luck, the Vagos behave like Boy Scouts. And every time we've raided the place it's been squeaky clean. No guns. No drugs. Nothing. We think someone's tipping them off. We're just not sure who."

I had a pretty good idea. Among the Lady Luck's clientele were a couple of Hemet cops who never seemed to pay for their tattoos. Free ink was Big Roy's way of saying thanks for the heads-up. That kind of relationship wasn't uncommon in the outlaw world. There were lots of biker wannabes posing as lawmen. One percenters tolerated this because a lawman in the pocket could be worthwhile. But truth was most outlaws would as soon spit on a cop as look at one.

"Just so I understand what you're asking," I said, trying to stay calm, "you want me to hang around Roy's shop and feed you information. That about right?"

"Close enough," said the sheriff.

"And can you explain just how the fuck I'm supposed to pull that off?"

The sheriff and Kevin exchanged a look. I knew what was coming, so I saved them the trouble.

"You're asking me to fucking join the Vagos, aren't you?" I said point-blank.

"We know it's asking a lot," said Kevin.

I shot him a hard look. "You think?"

"Let me ask you something, George," said the sheriff evenly. "If you had the ability to get rid of the Vagos in Hemet, would you do it?"

I looked him straight in the eye.

"You're asking me to snitch, pal."

"He's asking for your help," chimed in Kevin.

Tossing Big Todd a few leading questions was one thing, but this was the kind of help that could get a man killed. It was a known fact that the only thing an outlaw hated worse than cops was a snitch working for cops. Within the brotherhood, betrayal was considered the worst of sins, and the sentence for that ultimate sin was death. That was what these lawmen were asking that night; to raise my hand and volunteer for a possible death sentence. The more I tried to wrap my head around it, the more pissed off I got.

"Listen to me," I said, biting back anger, "nobody wants the Vagos gone more than I do. But that's your fuckin' job, not mine. I don't get paid for that."

"Would you like to get paid?" asked the sheriff. "Because I can arrange that. I could get you a motorcycle too. Anything you need."

He reached into his pocket and pulled out a cell phone.

"It's a throwaway," he said, extending it toward me. "The minutes are prepaid, won't cost you a dime. My number's already in it. You can call me directly any time, day or night."

I let the phone hang there. This slick sonofabitch was moving fast.

"I don't want your phone, Sheriff, and I don't want your money. I just want you people to stop all the fuckin' chaos."

"That's why we're talking to you," replied the sheriff. "Right now we're deaf and blind when it comes to the Vagos. If we're ever going to stop this, we need some inside help. Can you do that for us, George?" he said, proffering the phone again. "Will you help us get these guys?"

That question was still unanswered as we left the dump and headed back to Warren Road. I sat quietly in the backseat, smoking a cigarette and staring out the window at the dark outline of the San Jacinto Mountains. My friend's body was probably buried somewhere in the desert beyond those shadows. So who would speak for him?

Not me. Not yet, anyway. I trusted Kevin Duffy, but I wasn't so sure about his colleague. Something about that gung-ho lawman just didn't sit right with me—a nagging gut-sense that somehow, someway, he'd get my ass buried next to David.

No, I wasn't ready to answer that sheriff's call for help.

But I did take his phone.

The Devil's Trade

A much wiser man than me once said that every saint has a past and every sinner a future. Well, this sinner knows the exact moment his future began. It's scorched into my brain like a cattle brand. And it wasn't that night on Warren Road, nor was it David's disappearance. Nope. The game-changer came years before that, when an eight-year-old boy asked a question that shook me to the core.

"Daddy, are you a drug dealer?"

Was I a drug dealer?

Are you shittin' me? Is a frog's ass watertight?

I was twenty years old when I discovered drugs, a late bloomer, but once I got rolling there was no stopping me. A habit that started as recreation soon became a full-time occupation. I went from smoking pot and snorting cocaine to dealing it on the streets, then shifted into cooking methamphetamine in the desert.

Nasty stuff, crystal meth. Crazy addictive. Eats you alive. I was over six feet tall and weighed 148 pounds back then, a walking corpse that never slept, lit up and buzzing like a neon light. During one particularly brutal binge I was spun for a month straight before finally crashing out. After that I got myself a tattoo on my left arm of a grotesquely distorted face: the face of crystal meth.

That was the monster that lived inside me.

On crank my ego was out of control. I thought I was God Almighty, and to the customers I serviced maybe I was. After all, Ol' George had the big bag—everything those tweakers needed. I was making a ton of money off their addiction and spending even more. My pockets would be stuffed with twenty grand one day and empty the next. I'd blow it all on toys or loan it out to friends and customers. Sometimes the money came back, sometimes not. And when it didn't there was hell to pay.

I became a feared man around town. An amped-up beast with a chip on his shoulder and a .380 strapped to his ankle. A friend once told me that he loved to see me coming but couldn't wait for me to leave. Yup. I was a real badass motherfucker. Couldn't pay me? Fine. I'd screw your old lady. And believe me, I screwed plenty. Methamphetamine will turn a righteous woman into a whore. She'll trade what's between her legs in a heartbeat if it means a dealer in her pocket.

Sex for drugs. Don't mind if I do.

And if I didn't want the pussy, I'd haul everything you owned until I got paid. Around the valley they had a name for me; the U-Haul Bandit. If a customer stiffed me, I'd back a U-Haul truck to his front door and strip the house right to the walls.

Hell, I'd even take the cat.

There was a time when I had close to seventy U-Haul storage units jammed with the personal belongings of customers who owed me money. Imagine the cost to rent those units every month and you'll get some idea of the cash I was banking as a drug dealer.

Over in neighboring San Jacinto stood a little nondenominational church called the Pottery House. During my years selling dope, the preacher there was bound and determined to salvage my soul, railing against the evil of my drug-dealing ways. Well, that preacher might have been a man of God, but he was also a man with a serious heroin addiction. Doctors were pulling veins from his legs to rewire his neck, because all his main cables had collapsed and he had only that one place left to slam the junk. This Bible-thumping hypocrite knew all about the U-Haul Bandit, knew about those storage units packed with property I'd confiscated. He called it "Satan's stuff" and warned I'd suffer eternal damnation unless I purged myself of those ill-gotten gains.

I wasn't concerned about eternal damnation at the time, but I do know my life as a dealer was hell on earth. All I have to do is stand naked in front of a mirror to be reminded of those dark days. There's a bullet scar on my left shin, put there by a nervous tweaker who shot me through his car door, and old knife wounds on my bicep, hand and left forearm, which is where a blade got stuck in bone and had to be surgically removed. Turn me around and there's even a scar on my ass where a buck knife went through my buttock and into the scrotum, tearing my testicle in half.

I was never afraid of knives. Any man who showed a big knife on his belt was usually a coward. I kept mine hidden on my backside, a 120 buck in a custom sheath that went crossways across the belt and pulled from the side. I seldom used it. Whenever someone came at me with a blade, I got inside of him quick, grabbed the wrist and broke his fuckin' arm.

In the drug world I stood out because I knew how to make money. But there were people just as ruthless as me who wanted to take away what I had. It was a stressful way to live, constantly watching your back, and after a while I started thinking that maybe the better play was to turn to manufacturing and leave the slinging to others. Cooking was where the real money was, anyway. Hell, I was already snorting the shit, why not profit on that nasty habit?

It was a Hells Angel who first taught me the Devil's trade. He was a friend of my buddy Freight Train, and I badgered that Angel for two years until he finally agreed to take me under his wing and teach me how to cook meth.

Our first classes were held in a garage, where the dude had his equipment set up like a small laboratory. There was a large glass globe with nipplelike cooling towers used to cook and separate ephedrine, the prime ingredient in the manufacture of meth. Nowadays meth-heads are forced to boil down Sudafed to extract the same shit, but in those days I could get my hands on big drums of it. Breeders actually mixed ephedrine with chicken feed to make their birds crank out the eggs faster. The nation's henhouses were clucking with hopped-up chickens.

After seventy-two hours of cooking, when the brew had finally boiled down and separated, the garbage was skimmed off the top and the choice stuff harvested from the bottom. That's where the money was. That's what I was after.

Following my graduation from the Hells Angels Cooking Academy, I took my little operation into the Mojave Desert, where I set up shop in a rat-infested shed near the Marine Corps base at Twentynine Palms. Out there in the blast-furnace heat of the Mojave, where inside temperatures exceeded one hundred degrees, I truly felt like I was plying the Devil's trade in Hell.

Every batch of meth I cooked yielded twelve pounds of high-grade dope, which I sold to a Mexican drug dealer I trusted. To every pound of pure meth, that Chicano added four pounds of cut, which meant that forty-eight pounds of product went into the San Jacinto Valley and beyond. God only knows how many lives I helped destroy with that toxic shit.

It was around this time that I was introduced to a woman named Darlene, a single mom, twelve years my senior, with a house and three sweet kids. Darlene would teach me more about love and life than any other woman I've known before or since. But back then, in the midst of my drug phase, I wasn't exactly writing sonnets and looking for soul mates. Up to that point in my life I'd managed to torpedo just about every relationship I'd ever been involved in, including a long-suffering girlfriend who supported my addictions while I ruined her credit, and two brides in short-lived marriages—the first, doomed from "I do," when I was a dumb kid with a cocaine problem, and a second, which I have absolutely no fuckin' memory of . . . the whole blessed event lost forever in a haze of cheap bourbon, fake tits and psychedelic mushrooms.

Now there's a horror story.

My mother and little sister, Lin Ann, had moved from Hemet out to Laughlin, Nevada, where the heat really cranked in the middle of the Mojave Desert. The Colorado River cut right through town, and during the baking summer months Laughlin turned into a rolling party of racing boats, getting laid and getting wasted.

I was fresh off a stint in county jail for grand theft auto—which, in the interest of accuracy, was really grand theft motorcycle. One of my meth customers owed me a shitload of money, which, of course, she didn't have. I was ready to bring in the U-Haul when she bought me a Yamaha 900 crotch rocket with a bad check. When the authorities came to collect the bike I basically told them, "Fuck you, that's on her, not me."

The judge didn't agree. One year in county, three years probation.

I was still under that probationary cloud as I headed for Laughlin for a weekend party on the Colorado River. I was dealing meth and blowing a ton of money on expensive toys back then, and that day I was hauling a real beauty. Two beauties, actually, both exceptionally fast: a flat-bottom racing boat with a 660-horsepower motor and a twenty-year-old hottie with synthetic tits.

On our way through Laughlin to the Colorado River, I stopped to visit my mother and little sister for the first and last time. As much as I detested Mommy Dearest, that's how much Lin Ann loved that woman. She loved Mother's bawdy sense of humor, how she would drop her shorts on the highway and moon passing cars or rip a loud fart in a crowded restaurant. Noble traits to be sure, but our perceptions of that hateful bitch were far apart. On Mother we would never agree.

The two of them were living with Mom's recently retired husband,

Bob, who must have heard stories about me, because I caught attitude the moment I walked in the door. My first offense was sweating on the man's furniture. My second was raiding the fridge and stealing his baloney—which, in my defense, my sister later copped to.

Anyway, by the time I'd allegedly eaten Bob's baloney I was already plastered on Wild Turkey and, unbeknownst to me, my date had lifted a MasterCard from his wallet as a honeymoon present. I don't remember that. I don't remember the wedding that must have preceded the honeymoon. Hell, I don't even remember the weekend. All I know is, when I finally sobered up Monday morning I'd run up the credit card and married the brick shithouse.

My mother and younger sister, Lin Ann.

When she informed me we were husband and wife, I thought it was a joke—until I saw our wedding photo. There I was, alright, me and bazooka tits getting hitched in a Nevada chapel. One look at my face and you knew the wheel was turning but the hamster was dead. I had this foolish half-cocked grin and eyeballs the size of silver dollars, like I'd just sat on a red-hot poker. A friend of mine later explained I'd eaten psilocybin mushrooms that day, which explained a lot. Apparently mushrooms, chased by mass quantities of Kentucky bourbon, can make a guy do funny things.

Like get married.

I had the charade annulled a

few weeks later, but making MasterCard go away was not quite as simple. Bob pressed charges, and Mother testified against me—testified in court against her own son. And when the trial was over, the judge nailed me good.

Grand larceny. Probation violation. Sixteen months.

I was back in the slammer again.

Most of that stretch was served in Riverside County Jail, but near the end I shared a cell with a Mexican behind the walls at Chino—a California state prison that's louder than a fucking kennel at dinnertime.

Chino was primarily a receiving center where cons are held before getting shipped to long-term destinations. I never got shipped, and I wasn't there long, but during my stay I was forced to listen to the Chicanos barking at each other and singing their songs from sundown to sunrise, which made for some very long and sleepless nights.

It took years after my prison release to forgive my mother for all the misery she'd put me through, but by then she was gone. The woman died in 1999 after decades of drug and alcohol addiction. Her death devastated Lin Ann.

I skipped the funeral.

My new girlfriend, Darlene, had heard plenty of horror stories about the U-Haul Bandit. She knew all about my less-than-stellar reputation in the valley. But instead of running the other way, she was intrigued. Believing there was good in George Rowe even if I couldn't find it in myself, that woman took me into her home and shared her family and affections.

Unfortunately, instead of returning that love and trust, I abused the hell out of it in my usual fashion. Unbeknownst to Darlene, I was storing the meth I manufactured in her garage. And if that wasn't underhanded enough, I was sneaking around behind her back and screwing anything with a pulse and a legal pair of tits. It took a birth announcement in the local paper to finally expose my cheating ass. There it was, spelled out in black and white for Darlene and all of Hemet to see.

Guess who the father was?

Darlene was devastated.

"You don't know what love is," she told me that night. "You think love is fucking? Two dogs can fuck. That's not love."

Darlene was right. That woman was always right. But I was so messed up and out of control I didn't know what I was doing or what I had. I'd done hard drugs and hard time, fucked up bad men and fucked over good women. Deep down, I knew the madness was destroying me and just about anyone within reach, but I didn't know how to stop it.

It took an eight-year-old to hit the brakes for me.

Darlene's youngest was like a son. I'd helped raise that child since he was in kindergarten. Hell, he even called me Daddy. But the boy had heard some schoolyard talk and wanted a straight answer to his not-so-simple question.

"Daddy, are you a drug dealer?"

Fuck, yeah, I was a drug dealer. One of the biggest in the valley. But that's not what I told him. Looking that child straight in the eyes, I flat-out lied.

"No, buddy," I answered. "Daddy's not a drug dealer."

It was exactly what that kid wanted to hear, and he skipped away happy. But I was left feeling like a worthless sack of shit.

What a gutless coward I was. What a miserable human being. And it wasn't just the drugs and the dealing, it was all the other fucked-up things I'd done in my lifetime, most of which I've yet to confess. At that moment I couldn't stomach the man in the mirror. Not for another second. Like a puss-filled boil, my past had to be lanced.

I stood from the chair, walked straight into the garage and returned with twelve pounds of high-grade methamphetamine. Darlene's jaw nearly hit the floor as I flushed every last gram of it down the shitter.

"I'm done," I told her.

That woman had prayed to see me clean. But now that the moment had come, she couldn't believe it.

"You won't last," she said.

For once Darlene was wrong. I never touched drugs again.

Not long after the big flush, I took the Pottery House preacher's advice. I removed the padlocks from my storage units, threw open the doors and walked away. As word got around, the meth-heads came swarming like flies to the mother of all yard sales. They carted off thousands of dollars' worth of "Satan's stuff," but I didn't care. That preacher man was right. Unloading the past felt pretty damn good.

Months later the Pottery House threw a rummage sale, and a bunch of my old U-Haul property ended up tagged in the church parking lot. Caught with his hand in the cookie jar, the hypocrite preacher hung his head and explained to me why he was selling all the shit he'd grabbed from my old storage units.

Turns out Satan's stuff had brought nothing but hard luck to God's chosen junkie.

Shortly thereafter, I left Darlene and her family—including the little guy who got me started on the road to clean and sober. Darlene never asked me to go, but once I was clearheaded enough to understand what I'd put her through, I walked anyway. Maybe it was guilt. I don't know. I'd like to think I did the right thing. That for love's sake, I finally set that good woman free.

She'd suffered enough.

Taking my first baby steps on the road toward redemption, I felt like a man awakened from a drug-induced coma: suddenly twenty-seven years old without a clue how I got there or where I was going. I wanted to rejoin the world, become one of the "normal" people, but it was hard breaking from the past when you were defined by it. "Drug dealer" was a damn hard reputation to shed. I no longer wanted to be that person, but the world wasn't letting me be anything else. If I wanted a second chance, I had to earn it. So I pulled up my boots and began walking the walk.

My first steps led me down into the church basement where Narcotics Anonymous held weekly meetings. I'd always heard a junkie needed group support to avoid temptation. Well, that was some fucked-up group, let me tell you. I knew most of those addicts. Hell, at one time or another I'd probably sold drugs to half of them. The majority were in that basement not because they had a burning desire to get clean but because they were under court mandate. More than once I saw those tweakers duck into their connect's house to get high before a meeting.

Six weeks later I walked out of Narcotics Anonymous for good.

I was never a religious man, but religion was where I turned next. My father, a tribal Indian, had raised me an atheist—reverential of nature, not some anonymous supreme being with a bushy white beard. Dad used to preach that the roads we take in life are the ones we pave ourselves. But shortly before he died, a VA hospital chaplain turned the old man's thinking around and convinced him to join the Jesus team. I guess Dad was no different than many of us in that respect. When he felt he'd lost control over his life, he surrendered to The Man. And because my father embraced a higher power, he believed all his sins would be forgiven.

That sounded pretty good to me.

I found myself standing outside Catholic churches, looking for the courage to step inside and embrace the mystery of faith. I was a sinner desperate for forgiveness, but I felt unworthy to sit among the righteous. I finally grew some gonads and made it through the door, only to conclude that maybe faith and forgiveness don't require a priest or a church—that maybe it's something personal between you and the Almighty. So I bought myself a jailhouse Bible, written so any ten-year-old could understand it, and began to study.

Seek and ye shall find, sayeth the good book. And that's just what I did. Much like that first trip to Hemet in mother's Oldsmobile, I was again looking for signs. A way back to God's good graces. A return to sanity after all the madness and chaos of my life.

I just had to keep my eyes open.

When the Vagos came to town and began harassing the locals, that was the first sign. I saw it but never stopped. When David vanished, it was as if someone had taken that sign and slammed my face with it. And now that meeting with the sheriff had me thinking . . .

Was this the time? Time to get right with The Man?

Through a long and sleepless night I paced the floor of my shack in Valle Vista, chain-smoking cigarettes while praying hard on what to do. By sunrise those prayers had been answered. This wasn't just about payback for the Vagos, it was about paying back a community that I'd dumped on for years. Here was an opportunity to honor the vow I'd made to God and myself when the sins of my past, along with twelve pounds of high-grade crystal meth, went flushing down the shitter.

You had to live where I lived, see what I saw, to understand the way I felt. I could have moved on and lived life like any other cleaned-up drug addict and been alright, but the Vagos were behaving like animals and had to be stopped.

Only who would cage them?

I already knew the answer.

No one would. No one could.

No one but me.

5

Bagging the Golden Goose

There are hundreds of motorcycle clubs throughout the country with members who follow the rules of the road and society, like all good citizens should. But in the playground of life, there will always be the misfits, loners and bullies who choose not to play well with others. And when those bad boys band together and begin picking on the rest of us—or even each other—they fall under the state of California's definition of "criminal street gang," which is, to wit, a *group of three or more persons whose activities include the commission of violent criminal acts; have a common name or identifying symbol; and whose members have engaged in a pattern of criminal gang activity."

This description originally targeted the Hispanic and African-American street gangs, like the Crips and Bloods, that were causing havoc throughout Southern California in the 1980s. Of the more than 120,000 gang members reported in cities across the United States during that time, over half were residing in Los Angeles County. By the midnineties there were over a thousand gang factions in the Los Angeles County area alone, and gang-related homicides accounted for nearly 40 percent of murders countywide.

The California Street Terrorism Enforcement and Prevention Act (S.T.E.P.) passed by the state legislature in response to that growing menace was eventually broadened to include one percenter clubs like the Vagos. Every outlaw biker in California can probably recite the salient section of California Penal Code Section 186.21, which reads, *". . . the State of California is in a state of crisis which has been caused by violent street gangs whose members threaten, terrorize, and commit a multitude of crimes against the peaceful citizens of their neighborhoods. These activities, both individually and collectively, present a clear and present danger to public order and safety and are not constitutionally protected."*

The S.T.E.P. Act particularly resonated with one percenters because it allowed judges to slap gang enhancement penalties on those found guilty of crimes committed while a gang member. A felony conviction, for instance, might add from two to ten years to a sentence depending on the crime's severity. In other words, if you were in a gang, five could get you ten.

So was the Vagos MC a criminal street gang?

According to the state of California, the answer was yes as defined by the S.T.E.P. Act.

A group of three or more persons whose activities included the commission of violent criminal acts?

Check.

Had a common name or identifying symbol?

Check.

Members engaged in a pattern of criminal gang activity.

Check, check, check.

Every California outlaw fears the S.T.E.P. Act even more than the dreaded RICO. RICO is a federal statute originally used to prosecute organized crime. RICO is the most potent weapon in the federal arsenal, and the statute that all one percenter gangs fear most. A successful RICO prosecution could potentially bring down an entire outlaw motorcycle club and lock away its key members for a long, long time. But the legacy of S.T.E.P. is evident everywhere within the California penal system. Thousands of gang members serve extended prison terms thanks to S.T.E.P., and a good number of them once rode outlaw.

Of course, the one percenters will claim they're just a bunch of rough-and-tumble bike enthusiasts who love the freedom of the open road and the camaraderie of like-minded men. They'll bitch that S.T.E.P. is just another example of how law enforcement tramples the constitutional rights of law-abiding citizens.

Bullshit.

I was practically raised by one percenters, some I still consider family, and I can tell you there was only one reason they wore that 1% patch and declared themselves outlaws. Those boys took real pride in straddling the hairy edge of what society considered civilized behavior. And too often they stumbled and fell on the wrong side of the law because of it. It was a dangerous line to walk, but it came with the territory.

It's what they signed up for.

Of course, when an outlaw finds himself in court wearing ankle bracelets, he'll piss and moan about being picked on. He'll gripe that he was singled out and unfairly persecuted by "The Man" because of the patch on his back. It's hard to believe these people actually buy into their own hype. Law enforcement wouldn't waste time and resources on a bunch of Harley-riding free spirits if they hadn't been committing crimes. Otherwise every motorcycle club in America would be under siege by the government. No, law enforcement comes down hard on the patch because laws are being broken by the men who proudly wear it.

With some of the most violent one percenter gangs in the country based on the West Coast—including the Vagos, Mongols and Hells Angels—Southern California has always been ground zero in law enforcement's battle with America's outlaw culture. And the lawmen most experienced at targeting OMGs (outlaw motorcycle gangs) in that corner of the world are those working at the Los Angeles Field Division of the

Bureau of Alcohol, Tobacco, Firearms and Explosives, a federal agency under the jurisdiction of the United States Department of Justice.

For two decades now, a handful of ATF undercover specialists have been a constant thorn in the side of California's outlaw bikers. Fact is, most of the largest OMG takedowns in United States history came as a direct result of that group's expertise.

Every outlaw in the state is aware of those ATF boys, and every outlaw club works constantly to keep those special agents and their hated CIs (confidential informants) from infiltrating the ranks of the brotherhood. This tug-of-war between the one percent who refuse to compromise their lifestyle and the lawmen determined to hold them accountable has been waged since the end of World War Two. That was when returning GIs, who learned to ride and repair motorcycles in the service, banded together on war-surplus V-Twins and rode off to have some fun.

Over time those bikers' reckless definition of fun had them butting heads with law enforcement, but then things got territorial and clubs began turning on each other like children fighting over the same sand-box. This roughhousing was tolerated to a point, but when the bullies stepped outside the box to brawl with the rest of us, law enforcement began smacking them down. For the ATF, this evolved into a marathon game of Whac-a-Mole. Every time the feds clobbered an outlaw on the head, another popped up. They simply wouldn't go away.

The Los Angeles Field Division of the ATF has been whacking away at Green Nation and its international president, Terry the Tramp, since the late 1990s. In 1997, Darrin "Koz" Kozlowski, one of the ATF undercover specialists out of Los Angeles, managed to infiltrate the Vagos Hollywood chapter posing as an outlaw. The agent's cover was soon blown and the operation folded, but two years later the ATF went after the Vagos once again, this time using a confidential informant named Hammer.

Hammer was a full-patch Vagos and known narcotics trafficker doing time on a parole violation. With only a handful of months to go before his release, he was ordered to do an inside hit for the Nazi Low Riders, a white supremacist prison gang. Hammer declined the job, which pissed off the Low Riders and put his life in jeopardy.

Hammer was desperate to get out from behind the walls, and his parole officer put him in touch with ATF. In exchange for a "get out of jail free" card, Hammer agreed to inform on the Vagos, going under with his old chapter in Pasadena. Operation Green Nation folded prematurely but resulted in the arrests of a dozen Vagos members on firearms and narcotics charges. Mission accomplished, ATF relocated Hammer to Utah, where he was later found drowned in a Jacuzzi, done in by a drug overdose.

Since that time, no special agent or CI had been able to penetrate the Vagos membership. And for good reason. Tired of cops and rats sneaking in the back door, Terry the Tramp and his nervous minions squeezed their butt cheeks tight.

Hammer (right) while undercover with the Vagos in 1999.

The sheriff from Riverside understood this, which was why he was dangling money and motorcycles before me like carrots on a stick. That lawman knew damn well that any stranger who tried buddying up to the Vagos now would make those assholes pucker up. But George Rowe was a different story. I was no stranger. Both the chapter president and his second-in-command had tried recruiting me into the club. The Hemet Vagos wanted

me on their team; all I had to do was walk through the door and an-
nounce, "Here I am, boys, I'm all yours!"

But that wasn't going to happen—at least not with the sheriff as my
partner. I'd survived forty-two years on pure instinct, and there was just
something about that lawman that set five-alarm bells ringing. So when
I called Detective Duffy the next morning and told him I might be willing to hook up with the Vagos, the offer came with a caveat: I'd put my
ass on the line, but not for his task force buddy.

At first Kevin tried changing my tune; the special investigations
unit had the experience . . . his man could be trusted. But my mind
wouldn't be changed, and when the detective realized that, he stopped
trying.

"Alright, you go with your gut," Kevin said at last, "and I'll see what
I can do."

I'd be lying if I said there were no second thoughts as I waited for
Kevin Duffy's return call. Matters weren't helped by the sheriff, who
kept hounding me on that throwaway phone. He was hot for an inside
man. I just wanted him out of my life. So I blew up the call minutes
and tossed that phone in a nightstand drawer.

Within a few days Kevin called back with news. He'd found someone he thought I could work with, an ATF agent working out of the Bureau's Los Angeles field office. Because Kevin didn't trust his brothers
in blue, he suggested another meeting at the dump off Warren Road.
As an alternative I suggested a daylight rendezvous in Bee Canyon, a remote area of dirt trails and scrub brush ten minutes from the apartment,
which I knew like the back of my hand.

Heading into the parched foothills east of Valle Vista, where nothing much
lived but snakes and buzzards, I passed the ranger station and turned
up Bee Canyon Truck Trail. Not long after I pulled off the road and
parked in that empty place, a silver Ford Expedition came lurching up
the dirt track and pulled in behind me.

I stepped from the cab and started toward it cowboy style, cigarette dangling from my lips and a .380 revolver tucked into an open shoulder holster. I wasn't supposed to be carrying a firearm—I was a convicted felon—but I figured I was one of the boys now and could get away with it.

Kevin Duffy popped from the passenger's seat, snapping, "Hide that thing!"

Guess I figured wrong.

He gestured for me to take his place up front, and I did as ordered while he climbed in back. I slipped into the seat and nodded to the man behind the wheel.

My first impression of Special Agent John Carr was that he looked like he belonged on a surfboard off Redondo Beach. Carr was in his late thirties, with a muscular build, slightly Asian features and jet-black, shoulder-length hair. During his time undercover with the Mongols MC, the members gave him the road name "Hollywood."

The ATF agent who would become a partner and confidant through my three grueling years as a federal informant was a former athlete who loved the camaraderie of the team and the thrill of eighties crime dramas like *Miami Vice*. He found both in law enforcement, where he'd discovered an affinity for undercover work. Only a week after graduating the academy, Carr was out in the field buying illicit machine guns. It would have been a short-lived career, except the weapons dealer, sniffing a mole, executed the wrong man.

Back in the day, I'd get high on coke and meth. John Carr got high on the action. By the time we met in the wilds of Bee Canyon, he'd worked over two hundred drug and weapons cases, infiltrated the Mongols, handled scores of undercover agents and informants (including Koz and Hammer) and been involved with some of the biggest motorcycle gang takedowns in United States history.

Within law enforcement circles, Special Agent Carr was one of the true rock stars.

Kevin Duffy had heard of John Carr through a sheriff's deputy working with the One Percenter Task Force, a group Carr had formed with the Los Angeles County Sheriff's Department two years earlier. Now here was the ATF special agent sitting next to me, sizing me up—curious to know if I'd make a legitimate candidate for undercover work.

Right away Kevin wanted assurances I'd be safe in government hands. To his credit, Carr didn't bullshit him.

"Detective, if we go forward with this," said the agent, "my only guarantee is that I'll have your man's back for as long as he's under." Then he turned to me and said, "Fair enough?"

"Fair enough," I answered.

Agent Carr was a straight shooter. I hadn't known what to expect, but I liked the man immediately.

He asked about my background, my experience with one percenters and whether I'd ridden with any biker gangs—which I hadn't.

"But you do ride?" he asked.

"Pretty much all my life," I told him. "My old man bought me a scrambler when I was a kid. But I couldn't reach the brake pedal, so the only way to stop was by jumping off the fuckin' thing."

Carr grinned. "What are you riding now?"

I sheepishly glanced at Kevin, who answered for me.

"George doesn't own a motorcycle at the moment," he said.

Sad, but unfortunately true. And I was still kicking myself for selling that beautiful machine. I'd custom built a Harley shovelhead old-school. She had a big 106-inch motor, drag bars, raked frame, suicide shifter and, oh yeah, fuck the turn signals. Man, I loved that chopper, but I'd needed quick cash to finance a new and expensive hobby . . . gambling. That's right, ol' George had swapped one addiction for another. With a personality like mine, walking the straight and narrow was a never-ending struggle. For every two steps forward there was that inevitable step back. And gambling was a monster one.

A few months before our meeting in Bee Canyon, I'd sold that shovelhead for chump change to a dentist who rode with another motor-cycle club in Hemet called the Bros. That Harley was worth twice what "Doc" paid for it. But, hey, at least I could play the slots.

I just couldn't ride with the Vagos.

"No bike, huh? I can see how that might be a problem," said Carr, straight-faced. "Funny thing about bikers. They ride bikes."

The fucker had a sense of humor too.

"Tell you what, though," he continued. "If we go forward and if you get in—and that's a pretty big *if*—we'll find you a bike."

"I'll get in," I assured him.

"It's possible," replied Carr. "You seem like a likable guy. You're outgoing. You've got a look that fits. And Detective Duffy tells me you know the Vagos in Hemet. That's no small thing. But the chapters are being cautious right now. The Vagos got burned not too long ago. I know because I was one of the guys that burned them."

Carr was talking about Operation Green Nation. Even before Hammer OD'd in that Utah Jacuzzi, Green Nation's border had been on lockdown. Joining the Vagos now was like being screened through cheesecloth. Fortunately for me, that wasn't the case in Hemet. Big Roy wanted to lead the biggest, baddest outlaw chapter in all the land—one that would grab the attention of Terry the Tramp up in Hesperia—and he was on an aggressive recruiting drive to make it happen. Like the English press gangs of old, they'd even muscled members away from the Bros MC, including Doc, who owned my old chopper.

"I'll get in," I repeated confidently.

"Let me ask you something," said Carr. "What exactly are you look-ing to get out of this, George?"

There was no hesitation.

"I want to catch whoever did David and get those assholes off the street."

"And that's all?"

"Isn't that enough?" I said. "People in Hemet are afraid, okay? I'm just trying to do what's right."

Carr swallowed a smile. I knew how I sounded—like an idealistic Eagle Scout taking a break from escorting little old ladies across the street. Thing is, I meant every word.

Carr was understandably skeptical.

"George, people always want something."

"Look, this isn't about money if that's what you're thinking," I said heatedly. "You just asked me what I wanted, and I told you. That's it. End of story."

But Carr still couldn't wrap his head around it. An agent drew a paycheck while undercover, an informant worked off his case and stayed out of prison. Me, the man with nothing to gain and everything to lose, was asking for nothing and risking everything.

In his twelve years with the Bureau, Special Agent Carr had pretty much seen and heard it all. But this was a new one for both an agent and an agency with a storied history of busting motorcycle outlaws. No private citizen had ever volunteered for such an assignment, let alone risked their neck without reward. Sometime later, while recalling our first meeting, John Carr said he thought I had to be naive, full of shit or just plain crazy . . . maybe all three.

There would be times when I thought so myself.

"Alright, George," he said at last. "You start hanging around with the Vagos, and we'll see where it takes us. If it looks like you can get in, and if you're still willing to do this thing, I'll pull the paperwork together and we'll make it official. That work for you?"

"Works for me."

He extended his hand and I clasped it firmly.

"You know, there is one thing," I said quickly.

Carr's jaw tightened. I knew he had to be thinking, *Here it comes.*

"When this is all over," I said, "I want five minutes alone in the cell with Todd and Roy. That's all I ask. Five minutes to teach those bitches a lesson."

"I can't promise that," said Carr matter-of-factly. "But if we get to that point, I'll see what I can do."

Good enough, I thought. I pumped the agent's hand and sealed the deal.

In hindsight I realize John Carr must have known the shitstorm I was headed for. He'd sailed that way countless times with others. Of course, blaming anyone but myself for what followed would be like suing Marlboro for shoving those coffin nails in my mouth. Truth was, it was my decision—and mine alone—to go under. Special Agent Carr was never anything but straight with me.

Moreover, the man was doing his job. The day I fell into Carr's lap was the day the feds bagged their Golden Goose. Someone with the right connections and no suspicious background or agenda. Someone who could slip easily into the brotherhood of tight-knit one percenters and bust them from the inside. The ATF would have been fools not to cash in.

On the drive home from Bee Canyon the enormity of the task ahead started tap-tap-tapping at my mind. I held a brief conversation with the man in the rearview mirror. It went something like, *What the fuck, George? What kind of crazy shit are you getting yourself into?*

It's true I hadn't yet signed on the dotted line, but paperwork was just a formality. I'd pushed my chips all-in, a commitment that had my guts twisted into a double clove hitch. Had I another half ounce of brains, I would have kept driving to the I-215, made a run to LAX and caught the next flight to Peru. But bailing on the vow I'd made to God, myself and the people of Hemet was unthinkable now. I'd been many things in my life; a quitter had never been one of them.

Anyway, if I was going to do this thing, the timing would never be as good. I had no wife, girlfriend or family to place in harm's way. My old man was long gone, my mother had died a few years earlier and both sisters had moved on. My adoptive family had washed their hands of me following the infamous "midget affair." Yes, I'd had a son out of wedlock, but he was with his mom and I seldom saw him. I was free and clear to infiltrate the Vagos.

The only sticking point was Old Joe.

Old Joe was my best buddy and trusted partner in Family Tree Service, my Hemet landscaping and tree-trimming business. If I was headed somewhere, chances were Old Joe was riding shotgun in the truck. During the fifteen years I'd known the man, we'd formed a kinship tight as blood. Didn't start out that way, though. When I first laid eyes on Joe, I thought he had to be the dumbest sonofabitch I ever saw, with a long, gangling body, a slow way of talking and a nose so big it arrived before he did.

Only my friend wasn't stupid. Far from it. Old Joe had once been a supervisor for a big medical equipment firm up in Orange County, where he'd shared a white-collar home with his wife and two kids. Hell, the man even coached Pop Warner football. But then his wife divorced him and took their youngest with her. And when the older boy moved in with his girlfriend, my buddy was left all by his lonesome in that big empty house.

Joe's father was a Methodist minister who'd married the church organist and retired to Hemet in the early eighties. After the preacher died and his wife suffered a paralyzing stroke a few weeks later, Joe played the dutiful son and moved down to Hemet to care for her. Unfortunately his mom was gone within a year.

Alone again, with his career over and too much time and money on his hands, Old Joe started abusing methamphetamine. I know this for a fact because I was his supplier back in the bad old days.

Meth beat Joe up pretty good. In his gentle, soft-spoken way, my friend would be the first to tell you he wasn't the most handsome sonofabitch on the planet, but tweaking—that's what meth-heads call the high—didn't help his looks any. Meth rotted the teeth, sucked up his cheeks and wilted that man's face like a baked apple. It took a little time, but my buddy managed to kick that nasty habit, only to fall hard into alcohol. When the IRS came calling a few months later and seized his family home for taxes, Old Joe threw up his hands and hit rock bottom.

Now he was living in a fifteen-foot travel trailer, bought from a dude named Pooch, that I'd parked under a tree at the far end of the chicken coop. When I returned to Valle Vista from Bee Canyon, Joe heard my truck arrive and emerged from his trailer. I was in no mood to talk, so I went straight into the apartment, grabbed a glass and poured myself a stiff jolt of Turkey.

My buddy knocked once and stepped through the door as I was pouring another.

"Where you been," he said in his lazy drawl.

"Had some business."

"That right? Something I should know about?"

"Nothing that concerns you," I said.

Joe fidgeted uncomfortably. "Everything alright, George?"

"Everything's fine," I said before draining the bourbon.

He lingered a moment, then drifted back outside, quietly shutting the door behind him. I never kept secrets from Joe and I hated to start now, but this was a big one, and I didn't want to open my mouth until I'd finalized things with Special Agent Carr. Besides, there was no telling how Old Joe would react to the news. Yes, he saw the Vagos as a bunch of misbehaved children who needed a good belt whipping, but there was no love for the United States government either. Just a few years earlier the IRS had snatched his family home and booted him into the street. Now here I was, sleeping with the enemy.

6

God of the High Desert

There were three steps on the road to becoming a full-patch biker—the same any recruit had to follow when joining a club like the Vagos. First was the hang-around phase, when you and the membership sized each other up. As a hang-around you were like a wallflower at the school dance, hoping for an invitation to strut your stuff. Until then you were expected to back the club in a brawl and wear their colors as a sign of loyalty. With the Vagos, this might mean a green bandana tied around the head or hanging from a back pocket.

If the members liked what they saw, you were invited to prospect, a courtship that often took months. A prospect with the Hemet Vagos wore a single rocker sewn on the lower back of his cut that said "California," identifying the chapter's home state. Back then there were over three hundred greenies riding outlaw up and down the West Coast, with more chapters in Arizona, Utah, Nevada, Oregon and over in Hawaii.

Without a doubt the most difficult part of becoming a patch holder was the humiliation that came with prospecting. In effect, a prospect became the club's personal bitch. If a full-patched member dropped his pants and commanded you to wipe his ass, you'd damn well better do it. Trust me, it took real willpower to survive this—especially when you were a forty-two-year-old man like I was. But if you could stick it out through months of bullshit tasks and degradation and the members voted you in, you were awarded full-patched status in the club. This 'til-death-do-us-part marriage meant you'd earned the right to wear the Loki center patch framed by the top and bottom rockers, pay your weekly dues and attend church meetings—those weekly sessions when patches in each chapter gathered to discuss club business.

For me, one of the most emotionally draining aspects of gang infiltration was buddying up to the people I was working to send to prison. By

Big Roy Compton, president of the Hemet Vagos.

necessity I was forced into long-term relationships with human beings I wouldn't wish on my own worst enemy. Of course, there was no way around this dilemma. For the sake of the mission I had to hold my nose and take the plunge. So around the holidays in late 2002, I walked into Big Roy's Lady Luck tattoo parlor and hinted I might be interested in joining Green Nation.

Roy, Todd and most of those Hemet boys welcomed me with open arms. I say most because there was one Vago who seemed suspicious of me right from the get-go. He was the chapter's sergeant at arms, responsible for club discipline and security, a three-hundred-pound blob named North, who hit like a sixty-pound schoolgirl. North was one of a handful of Vagos who'd recently come over to the Hemet chapter from another motorcycle club in town called the Bros.

Bro's Toy Box was a motorcycle repair shop with an interior decorated in red and white, the same colors found on the club's patches. Red and white were Hells Angels colors, and the Bros had some far-fetched notion of someday joining that select company. Their president was the shop's owner, a union boilermaker named Bro, who could carry a car engine in his hands just like my buddy Freight Train.

Despite the red and white décor, the Bros were theoretically a support club for the Hemet Vagos. That all changed when Big Todd started feuding with Bro over a transmission part he thought he deserved for free. When Bro told him to fuck off, Todd convinced Big Roy they should forcibly shut down the Bros and take the club's members for themselves, doubling the size of the Hemet Vagos in one fell swoop.

So on a night when the Bros were holding church inside the Toy Box, Big Roy's crew came calling, and some were packing guns. They were backed by another Vagos chapter from the city of Corona, one led by an outlaw named Mumbles, who weighed one hundred pounds dripping wet but fought like the Tasmanian devil. Mumbles's forte was knives, which the man could fling with precision from long distances, like some kind of freaky circus act.

At one Green Nation campout, some Northern California Vagos bet three thousand bucks their knife-throwing champion could best Mumbles. With total confidence we upped the bet to five and turned our boy loose. Well, Mumbles started dealing steel from sheaths hidden all over his body. They came from his back, his belt, his ankles, his boots, hell, maybe even his ass, I don't know, but one after another those blades nailed a tree trunk about sixty feet away—THUNK, THUNK, THUNK, THUNK, THUNK! When that little fucker was done his knives were grouped tighter than a virgin's cha-cha. It was an impressive performance and an easy five grand.

Mumbles was carrying those blades the night that he, Big Roy and the rest of the Vagos stormed Bro's Toy Box. Once inside, they demanded the Bros turn over their colors—which was a big no-no in the outlaw world. Few sins trumped a man giving up his patch. In most cases, try taking the colors off an outlaw's back and you'd best be prepared to fight and die.

I say most cases, because apparently the Bros weren't so keen on self-sacrifice. Instead, confronted by superior numbers, loaded weapons and Mumbles's sharp steel, they peed their panties and gave up their colors like a bunch of playground pussies. Only Bro himself manned up and stood tall.

"Fuck the Vagos. You want this patch, come and take it," were his defiant last words.

I admired Bro for his stand. Of course, after the Vagos finished

Big Todd Brown.

whipping him with a tire chain they ripped the patch off his back anyway. But at least the man kept his dignity.

Oh, and Big Todd walked out of the Toy Box with that transmission part he coveted . . . free of charge.

As for Bro's chickenshit brothers, a handful opted to join the Hemet Vagos—including North and Doc, the dentist who'd bought my Harley shovelhead, and the only two chapter members older than I was at the time, an ex-con named Sparks and another the Vagos christened Buckshot.

Road names, bestowed by the club when a prospect reached patched status, were sometimes real head-scratchers, but that wasn't the case with Sparks and Buckshot. Sparks got his name simply because he was a certified electrician. And Buckshot—well, Buckshot had barely escaped the business end of a shotgun down in Mexico. His brand-new Harley, on the other hand, hadn't been so lucky.

In addition to those turncoats, Big Roy had scraped together a handful of other recruits for his chapter, including Ready, who worked as a tattoo artist at the Lady Luck, Jack Fite, a notoriously violent human being, and Jimbo, a muscle-bound juicer who supplied the Vagos with anabolic steroids. I never touched that shit myself. I'd heard too many horror stories about shriveled dicks and wooden balls.

And then there was Crash.

If ever there was an appropriate road name for a motorcycle outlaw, Crash was it. That big bastard crashed his stock Harley just about anywhere and any way humanly possible. And because we came into the club around the same time, I found myself traveling many nervous miles beside that spun fool, worrying whether he would dump his bike and take me down with him. With the exception of my mother, I think that crazy Vago gave me more migraines than any other human being on the planet.

First time I laid eyes on Crash he was standing outside the Lady Luck wearing a skintight tank top and a green bandana, eyeballing me over his ratty moustache like he

Crash, my fellow prospect and one crazy-ass sonofabitch.

was king shit. I had no idea where that dude had come from, but prison would have been the obvious choice. The man had that behind-the-walls mentality, a way of talking and behaving that was hard to define but easy to recognize when you'd hung around that type as long as I had.

Crash had fathered a crew of kids with a woman so skinny she'd almost disappear when she turned sideways. Wasn't long before I discovered he had another love in his life: crystal meth. Methamphetamine has been the one percenters' drug of choice for many years now; its use is so prevalent that in the summer of 2001 the feds pulled the trigger on Operation Silent Thunder, sweeping up a large meth ring in the California High Desert that included several Vagos.

From the late sixties into the seventies, "Reds" were the outlaw world's preferred drug. Sold in red capsules under the brand name Seconal, the pharmaceutical was prescribed as a sedative. But that drug was anything but sedating for the bikers who abused it. Reds amped a man up and made him fearless enough to commit murder, which was not uncommon in that particularly violent era. For their own survival, outlaw clubs began banning the use of Reds. After a brief fling with PCP, they hitched their wagon to methamphetamine. Man, outlaws just loved their crank. Gave them that little extra giddy-up they needed to keep riding and partying straight through 'til morning.

In Crash's case, meth just made his incredibly inept riding even worse. The man would continue to be a terror in the saddle for as long as I knew him, but when I first hung with the Vagos, the bigger concern was the chapter's sergeant at arms. Right out of the gate, North was telling Big Roy I couldn't be trusted—that I just might be a snitch.

As true as that might have been, there wasn't a chance in hell that fuck could have known what I was up to. That closely kept secret was between me, John Carr and Kevin Duffy. Every precaution had been taken to safeguard my identity. Regardless, the word was out there now. North had started the rumor mill grinding. And once that snitch jacket gets hung on a man, it's damn hard to remove. This was the worst possible start for someone in my situation, and my only defense was calling North out as a "fat, lying bastard" and demanding proof of my infidelity. The sergeant at arms promised he had a reliable source and would show his hand soon enough.

"If I find out this is true," Big Roy warned me, "if it turns out you're a rat, I will personally fuck you up, George."

Yup. North was going to be a problem.

I'd been hanging around the Vagos about a week when I finally told my buddy Old Joe that I was thinking about joining the Hemet chapter. The conversation came up during one of our early-morning chats on the drive out to a tree-trimming job.

"I don't get it," said Joe. "You've been doing nothing but bitchin' and complaining about those people."

"Just gonna try it. See where it goes," I said.

"But why? Why would you do that? They're like a bunch of kids who never grew up. Why the devil would you want to hang out in bars and get into fights and all that other childish stuff?"

Fact was, there was no rational explanation. Nothing I could say would make a damn bit of sense, so I shut my buddy off with, "Don't worry about it."

End of conversation.

Freight Train, who I'd stayed in contact with over the years, was even more upset—and that big Hells Angel didn't mince words telling me so. Both he and his brother Donny, who was a full-patch Vagos one generation ahead of Big Roy and the Hemet boys, unanimously agreed I was a "dumb motherfucker."

Of course, they didn't know my true motive for hooking up with the Vagos. Nor would I have shared it with them. Regardless of our past history, there was zero tolerance for snitches among outlaws of any generation. Had the brothers known I was working on behalf of the feds, they would have tag-teamed my ass and kicked it from one end of Riverside County to the other.

•   •   •

Not long after I first started hanging with the Hemet Vagos, I went on my first official "run" with Green Nation—the annual New Year's Run to Buffalo Bill's casino on the California-Nevada state line. Club runs— always a good excuse to gather members in one location—were usually organized at the chapter level, but the largest, like the New Year's Run, were handled by national and its top dog, Terry the Tramp.

Tramp was best known for plotting runs to a biker bar north of San Bernardino called The Screaming Chicken or farther south to Mexican border towns for cerveza and señoritas. But because the Vagos' international president had a hard-on for the slots, the largest runs were usually reserved for the Nevada casinos.

By New Year's 2003, the year of my first Vagos run, Tramp had reigned over Green Nation for seventeen years, governing his minions from his ranch-style home in Hesperia, a High Desert city in the Mojave. As testament to the devotion their international P inspired, many a Vago would have taken a bullet for Tramp. In fact, in their own way, many already had. Men had gone to jail on their leader's behalf. It was telling that the rank and file had a pet name of their own for the man.

They called Tramp "God."

The fact that their supreme being had clung to power for nearly two decades was no small feat and certainly no accident. Terry Lee Orendorff was a survivor, bred with street smarts, a criminal's cunning and a gift for manipulation. Born in 1947, he was raised in El Monte, California, by his alcoholic stepfather, kept in a one-car garage like a caged dog. When Dad let little Terry out for some fresh air, the budding mechanic built himself a motorcycle, took off to raise hell and never looked back. He followed his stepbrother, Parts, into the Vagos and became the San Gabriel chapter president in the early 1970s.

While Tramp inspired a good deal of fear and awe among his subjects, those he terrified most were chapter presidents like Big Roy

Compton. Green Nation thrived on the weekly dues that members forked over at the chapter level, a percentage of which went to Tramp at national. But whenever a larger injection of cash was needed, Tramp found reasons to fine the chapters for every conceivable offense—fines that could run into thousands of dollars. For this reason, Big Roy was constantly on guard against pissing the international P off. Not only did he fear those hefty fines but Tramp had the power to confiscate a man's motorcycle and convert it into quick cash.

Not coincidentally, the largest fines seemed to hit the membership around the holiday season—right after Thanksgiving and during the weeks leading up to the New Year's Run. There was good reason for this. Tramp had a big gambler's itch, and to scratch it that high roller needed lots of cash. God's ignorant flock didn't have a clue back then, but their shepherd was pocketing tens of thousands of dollars and blowing it on slots and blackjack.

The New Year's Run to Buffalo Bill's offered even greater opportunity for Tramp to line his pockets. As members arrived after a long day of riding through the Mojave Desert, they'd find stands set up with all kinds of Vagos merchandise for sale—from Green Nation T-shirts to Vagos-branded jewelry. And every member was encouraged to spend freely. After all, it was for the good of the club . . . and what was good for the club was even better for Terry the Tramp.

Buffalo Bill's casino stands on the California-Nevada border in a town identified on maps as Primm but which we called "State Line." Buffalo Bill's and two other casinos had been erected in that desert wasteland for a singular purpose—to snag Southern California gamblers before they could spend all their money in Las Vegas, forty miles to the north.

Nevada's dens of iniquity were always popular destinations for motorcycle gangs like the Vagos, and huge magnets for trouble. Only eight months earlier, members of the Mongols and Hells Angels found themselves rubbing elbows at Harrah's Laughlin. Wasn't long before that elbow-rubbing led to brawling, which led to killing. When the chips stopped flying, two Angels and a Mongol lay dead. Just to even the score, a third Hell's Angel was murdered on his way back to California. Meanwhile at Harrah's the cops doing cleanup recovered nine guns, sixty-five knives, and assorted bats, hammers and wrenches.

On Tramp's orders, the Vagos descended on Buffalo Bill's from all directions: Northern California, Oregon, Nevada, Arizona, Mexico—even Hawaii. I knew for a fact a lot of those boys hated making that New Year's Run, especially the poor bastards from the Northwest, who froze their nuts off, forced to ride their Harleys through snow and ice.

Terry the Tramp wasn't about to suffer that kind of discomfort. No fuckin' way, man. Braving the elements was strictly for the peons. Instead the international P came motoring into State Line behind the wheel of his big ol' Cadillac. And when Tramp wasn't driving that boat, chances were you'd find him cruising along in a brand-new Corvette the suckers of Green Nation had bought him for his birthday.

Without a motorcycle to call my own, I was also four-wheeling it to Buffalo Bill's that afternoon, same as Tramp. And that was just fine with the Hemet chapter. Whenever one of their bikes broke down they knew George would be there to roll it into his truck bed and haul it home. Besides, no fuckin' way did I want to ride a bike through the Mojave in late December. The desert was cold as a penguin's cooch that time of year. So I piled into my pickup, cranked up the heat until the cab was nice and toasty, then followed the Hemet Vagos as they rode out of town and started north on the I-15, bundled against the cold with their cuts worn over leather jackets.

A few more chapters joined the pack as it rumbled through Victorville and roared toward Barstow in the High Desert. From there it was a frosty two-hour grind through the empty Mojave all the way to State Line.

The Primm casinos came into view miles before you arrived, rising like mirages above the desert landscape. And you couldn't miss Buffalo

Bill's. The place had this crazy amusement park vibe going, with a giant roller coaster twisting around the hotel and a Ferris wheel off to one side. Walk through the hotel and head out back and you'd even find a giant buffalo-shaped swimming pool.

As I stepped onto the casino floor, I could feel the fever coming over me again. In those days I had a gambling addiction that could have gone toe-to-toe with Terry the Tramp's. Entering a casino was goddamn intoxicating: the cheers from the craps tables, the flashing lights, those ringing bells.

Ding. Ding. Ding. Ding. Ding.

Man, it was like the Sirens calling Ulysses to the rocks.

The place where I'd blown most of my money was an Indian-owned casino that sat a few hundred yards from the banks of a cement river channel north of Hemet. To reach Soboba Casino, I used to drive off-road, charging eight miles up that channel when the water ran low just so I could spend my money faster.

Ding. Ding. Ding. Ding. Ding.

I have no idea how much wampum I donated to that tribal den, but it was a shitload. There were Fridays I couldn't meet the Family Tree Service payroll because I'd blown it all on slots. I'd have to tell my six-man crew, "Sorry fellas, I'm flat busted this week . . . see you on Monday." All those poor bastards could do was shrug their shoulders and pray I wouldn't blow their paychecks again the following week. Sure, I'd occasionally hit the jackpot, but more often than not I'd walk out of Soboba like a whipped dog with my tail between my legs.

The situation wasn't much better at home. I was with Darlene when the gambling bug first bit, and that poor woman did everything but chain me to the bedpost to keep me from donating her life's savings to the Indians. I remember one day when I was supposed to be at work but snuck over to Soboba with Old Joe instead. When we finally left the casino, the sun was down and I was in deep shit.

I needed a good excuse to hand Darlene, but the best I could come up with was some lame-ass tale about my truck getting stuck in the mud. To sell that ridiculous lie—and despite Joe's angry protests—I had us both rolling around in the river muck like a couple of moon-touched fools. At one point the current caught my shitfaced partner and swept him half the length of a football field, which really messed with his vodka buzz. In the end it was all wasted time because Darlene had already come out to the casino's parking lot and found Joe passed out in the truck.

As I wandered through Buffalo Bill's, I noticed a Vagos entourage surging across the casino floor. This was the first time I laid eyes on Terry the Tramp, the big man himself. The club's international president was being escorted through the warren of slot machines by six patched bodyguards. I remember thinking the man looked nothing like I'd pictured him—nothing like a commander in chief.

Tramp was short and rotund, with an ample beer gut and shoulder-length white hair sprouting from either side of his bald noggin. To me the head Vago looked more like a circus clown than the leader of California's largest outlaw motorcycle gang. But Tramp was not a man you laughed at. Who knows how many badass hombres underestimated Terry the Tramp in his time and learned the hard way that looks could be deceiving.

I stood and observed the man they called God, watching as he paused to feed coins into a slot machine while his security team stood dutifully at their posts, ever vigilant for would-be assassins.

It was goddamn ridiculous.

When Tramp ran short of coins, he would tap the shoulder of the monstrous, mullet-headed human being that headed security. This was a signal for Rhino, the Vagos international sergeant at arms, to start gathering donations from the various chapters so his boss could continue feeding the slots.

But Rhino was more than Tramp's faithful change chimp. The forty-year-old was a feared ex-con who'd earned his road name for an obvious reason. The man was constructed like one of those four-legged African tanks, with a powerful body and a neck as thick as his head. As chief enforcer for all of Green Nation, Rhino was the baddest motherfucker in the neighborhood. Nobody was safe from that brute, not even those closest to him. Rhino had shot and killed his first wife "accidentally." I'm sure wife number two was understandably nervous.

As I watched Rhino hurry through the casino collecting tribute for his boss, Big Roy appeared and kicked me off the casino floor. Because I was a hang-around I wasn't supposed to be having fun like the big boys. My job was a supporting role, and for the rest of my time at Buffalo Bill's that meant I would be babysitting one of the patched members who was bedridden in his hotel room.

R&D Steve was an Army vet who worked as a designer for R&D Motorcycles in Hemet. He was close to fifty years old when I met him but looked twice that age—that's how bad cancer had beat the man up. So there we were, me and Steve in that hotel room with the heat cranking full bore. My ass was sweating, but that poor bastard was shivering like we were in Nome, coughing up chunks of mucus the size of golf balls.

I swear you could smell death in that room.

Poor R&D. I could almost relate to what that man was going through. I had experienced my own personal hell with the big C. Almost ten years earlier, after I was diagnosed with colon cancer, the surgeons snipped out thirteen feet of my intestines. Then they ran me through that particularly brutal brand of medieval torture called chemotherapy and radiation.

My skin was so fried I could peel it off. My guts were boiling, my eyebrows were burning, my throat was on fire. I couldn't keep food down. My waist-length ponytail disappeared, and my hair fell out in clumps until I was bald. For three years I couldn't take a decent shit . . . it was diarrhea every goddamn day.

Five different times, for three months a stretch, I endured that hell. And each time the cancer returned. Finally I'd had enough. I told the doctors I was through. There was nothing left to give. If cancer was going to end me, so be it. I figured I could deal with the pain of dying, I just couldn't handle the torture it took to survive. The doctors sent me on my way with pain prescriptions for Vicodin and morphine—but those pharmaceuticals just made me fuzzy-headed and depressed, so I stockpiled the pain meds instead and put my life in God's hands.

Is the cancer gone? I don't know . . . and I don't want to know. I'm still here, and that's good enough for me. But R&D Steve wasn't so fortunate. Three months after our long night together at Buffalo Bill's, that Vago was dead and buried.

7

Happy Trails, Motherfucker

In the weeks following the New Year's Run I began spending more time with the Vagos, hanging around the Lady Luck or drinking at bars the Hemet boys frequented. By all appearances George Rowe was "down" for the club. With the exception of North, who was still sniffing around me like a fat hound, I was considered one of the boys. I was in. As Special Agent John Carr put it, it was time to make things "official."

In March of 2003 I drove out to the ATF's field office in Van Nuys, California, gripping the steering wheel with my left hand because my right was in a plaster cast up to the elbow, busted on a trimming job. The process of becoming a confidential informant actually kicked off a few days before when I met Carr in a Burger King parking lot several blocks from his office.

"How'd you get that busted wing?" he asked as I climbed into his car.

"Fell out of a fuckin' tree."

"That'd be a bitch riding a bike like that. Thank God you don't own one, huh?"

"Hey, bust my balls all you want," I told him, "I can still brake with my foot . . . and you ain't gettin' out of your promise. I want that bike."

Carr took my photograph, rolled my prints, had me sign some papers, then sent me on my way. Now I was meeting up with him again in Van Nuys to make everything official. I was about to be signed, sealed and delivered to the federal government. We met in the building lobby and I trailed the special agent up the stairs to the main offices.

"There's a sheriff down in Riverside who met with you not long ago, an associate of your pal Kevin Duffy," said Carr. "Know who I'm talking about?"

"Yeah, I know who you mean," I said. "That guy's been pressuring me like a motherfucker."

"Yeah? Well, he flew up here a few days ago in a helicopter to talk about you."

A helicopter! Holy shit. I had myself a stalker with a badge.

"He was pretty upset," Carr continued. "He thinks I'm trying to steal you away from him."

"What the fuck am I? His girlfriend?"

Carr half-smiled at this. "Something like that."

We entered a mostly empty office area. Only a few agents were at their desks talking on the phone or doing paperwork.

"What'd you say to him?" I asked.

"I said call George right now. If you're going to be the guy on this case, knock yourself out. If George is good with that and he wants to work with you, I'll walk away." Carr motioned me into his office. "That's when he offered to share you. Kind of like a joint custody arrangement."

The agent parked himself on the edge of his desk. "Listen, George, here's the deal. I'm not about to get into a pissing contest with another agency over you. That's not gonna happen. The biggest mistake we could make would be allowing two handlers. Only one guy controls an informant, and that's just the way it works, understand?"

"Yeah, man. Absolutely."

"Well, then, you've got a decision to make. You've already been shopped to this guy in Riverside. And if that's the direction you want to go, I won't stand in your way."

"Hell, no."

"You sure about that? Because once you sign those papers, you're with ATF."

"Just hand me the pen."

The agent smiled at this. "I'll call the sheriff and tell him you're not going through with it. That you got spooked. We'll keep your pal Duffy in the loop but no one else. The fewer people know what we're doing the better."

I shook my head and grinned. "A helicopter? No shit."

We left the office and walked down the hall to a conference room where I met Special Agent Jeff Ryan, the man who would serve as Carr's right-hand man during my time undercover. Ryan had started with the Border Patrol down at the Brown Field Station in San Diego before transferring into ATF as a special agent at the Los Angeles Field Division. Next to him a folder was laid out on a polished conference table. I took a seat opposite John. He opened the folder, then glanced up at me.

"You ready for this?"

"Hell, yeah, man. Let's do it."

"Before we get into it," said Carr, "let's be clear about something." He leaned forward on his elbows and studied me intently for a moment. "I understand why you're doing this thing, George. I know how badly you want to get rid of those guys in Hemet. And I admire you for it. I really do. Nobody's ever come out and volunteered for something like this before. But you need to understand something too. This thing isn't going to happen overnight. It won't be game over in two weeks or even two months. An operation like this takes time to find out exactly what these guys are doing and gather enough evidence to make a case. There's a lot of hard work involved. Having said that, if you're willing to put in the hours, so am I. For as long as it takes."

To be honest, when I made the decision to go under, I had no fuckin' clue what I was doing. I really did think my involvement would be just a matter of months. I'd help get those sons of bitches off the street, slap the dirt from my hands and get back to living again. But I was here now. I was committed. And I'd be goddamned if I was going to quit before I even got started.

I nodded at the folder. "What you got?"

"Okay," said Carr.

He began sliding documents in front of me to read, a skill I'd managed to improve upon since the days when I was a high school illiterate. Most of the papers concerned my conduct as an ATF confidential informant—basically the dos and don'ts of working undercover. Once each document was read and explained, I initialed and signed on the dotted line.

After the folder was closed I was fingerprinted, thumbprinted, photographed and numbered—the whole nine yards. In the process, I was made virtually invisible to almost everyone, including those within the federal system. For instance, any receipts I signed while working undercover would be tagged to an ID number, and only John Carr, my handler, and a few of his superiors knew which number pointed to George Rowe. In this way I was protected from any leaks—accidental or otherwise—that could endanger my life.

Carr introduced me to several of his ATF colleagues that day, including Special Agent Darrin Kozlowski, the agent who had infiltrated Green Nation only to have things blown apart when the Vagos had sniffed a rat. Koz had been introduced into the Vagos by an informant back in 1997, but the ATF hadn't had the kinks worked out of their undercover program yet and had lacked the ability to completely backstop the fictitious identity of their UC guys. That situation had changed in the years since. Now agents could roll under a false identity with everything in place; name, past history, a place to live, a workplace. It was all there and practically foolproof. In the years since Koz had barely escaped the Vagos with his skin, he'd climbed right back in the saddle again, successfully infiltrating both the Mongols and Warlocks motorcycle clubs.

Also introduced that day was John Ciccone, the ATF agent widely considered the most productive case agent expert in the country. Ciccone had set a high bar for making outlaw motorcycle gang cases that few could match. The man was case agent for one of ATF's more high-profile busts, when special agent Billy Queen went under with the Mongols MC starting in 1998. Posing as outlaw Billy St. John, Queen spent two years gathering evidence on the Mongols. On the day of the takedown, forty-one of them were busted.

Ciccone shook my hand but didn't sound overly confident about my chances of breaking in with the Vagos. After all, his man Koz was one of the top undercover specialists in the country, and he hadn't succeeded. Not only that, but as Ciccone was quick to point out, I didn't own a motorcycle. I think in his mind I'd already failed. Maybe he had a bug up his ass that morning, but I got the impression Ciccone wasn't a fan.

Once Ciccone moved on, Carr handed me a Dr Pepper and sat me down in his office for a private conversation.

"Listen, here's how this works," he explained. "You just keep getting tight with the Hemet chapter. See what they're up to. Find out who's really running the show down there. We'll start local and see where it takes us."

"What do you mean?"

"I mean in these types of cases, one thing often leads to another. We follow the evidence, and if that takes us outside of Hemet, so be it."

That made me a little uncomfortable. The Hemet boys were the ones I was after. If ATF wanted to clean up the Vagos' messes elsewhere, that was their business. Already I didn't like the way this was going, but I kept my mouth shut.

"And another thing," continued Carr. "We're out to gather criminal evidence on weapons and drugs and anything else that constitutes a felony, but don't try to come off as something you're not—like some kind of big dope dealer. If you get outlandish with made-up stories, I guarantee that three days later you won't remember what you said and someone will call you out on it. Don't bullshit these guys, George, understand? You don't want to trip yourself up."

"Todd and Roy know I'm a fuckin' gun nut, so that works," I told him. "But I don't use drugs anymore."

"Then we won't go that way. We'll stick with guns. You've got a felony conviction, and it's illegal to sell weapons to a felon. But when the time comes, ATF will front you the money and you'll make the buys."

"Alright, I'm ready," I said, rubbing my hands together in anticipation. "Let's go."

"We're not going to push things just yet. I want you to keep a low profile and show the chapter you're committed. And remember what I said. Be yourself. You're just an average Joe Blow."

I nodded. "Gonna put a wire on me?"

"We'll get to that soon enough."

"What about a bike?"

"Soon enough," John repeated.

He pulled out a pad of paper, scribbled on it. "I'll be in touch in the next few days. Here's my direct number."

He ripped off the page and handed it to me. "I don't have to tell you to be careful with that, right?" He smiled and proffered a hand across the desk. "Let's take these guys down, George."

I lifted my cast. John switched up and offered his left. We shook and it was done.

"Oh, one thing," I said to him before leaving the office. "I'd like to include my friend Joe on this."

"Bad idea," said John without hesitation.

"Joe knows how to keep his mouth shut."

"Oh, yeah? Does Joe drink?"

I hesitated.

"Listen," said John before I could answer. "If the Bureau is going to invest time, money and resources in George Rowe, they're going to want their investment protected. Right now it's just you, me and Detective Duffy in the inner circle. You don't want it getting much wider than that, okay? Because the wider that circle gets, the more dangerous it is for you. Doesn't take much to compromise operational security. Man gets a few drinks in him, talks to the wrong person . . ." He shrugged. "Believe me, it's happened before. Now, I can't stop you from talking to this friend of yours. That's your call. But, dude, I'd strongly advise against it."

I considered this a moment, then replied, "Joe's like a brother. I'd trust him with my life."

"I hope you're right," said John, "because it's your life we're talking about."

I was telling Special Agent Carr the ironclad truth when I said there was no one on the planet I trusted more than Old Joe. That man always stuck with me through thick and thin. He was my best friend.

Years before, when the IRS seized Joe's home for unpaid taxes, I'd pulled him off the floor and invited him to live with me in Hemet. Darlene and I were still together at the time, and Joe took a spare room in back, sharing space with Ollie, the family dog. It was a long, hard fall from business executive to rooming with a Labrador retriever, and Old Joe's self-worth was officially shot to pieces. In a desk drawer I came across a stack of letters he'd written to his boys but hadn't been able to bring himself to mail. In my opinion, what that wrecked soul needed was a new focus and direction. Just like me.

At the time I was the Hobo Kelly of landscapers, crossing the valley in a rusted pickup with a ladder strapped to the bed and an old wood chipper hitched to the back. My business was gradually being rebuilt— no small feat given the hit my reputation took after I went to jail—and I figured it might be a good time to take on a full-time employee. And since Joe looked nothing like a midget, I hired him to drag and stack brush for room, board and fifty bucks a week.

The man hated the work. "This isn't for me, George," he'd gripe whenever I was within earshot. But that shitty job gave Joe a reason to haul his depressed carcass out of bed each morning, and that was a start.

With Old Joe at my side, business took off. We began adding new clients and making money. I bought a new pickup and replaced the wood chipper, leased a bucket truck and hired more full-time employees. None of them midgets.

Of course, Joe wasn't always employee-of-the-month material. I showed up at a job site one day and found him drunk on his feet, trying to move leaves with the wrong end of a rake. Even so, I liked and trusted the guy. And despite the drinking (or maybe because of it) we bonded as brothers . . . just a couple of screwed-up kindred spirits.

I banged on the door of Old Joe's trailer. When he opened it, I hoisted a half pint of vodka I'd bought on the way back from Van Nuys.

"Can I come in? Got something important to talk about." I followed Joe into the trailer, and he tucked himself in behind the small dining table. I set the bottle on top, then grabbed two plastic cups from beside a stainless-steel sink.

"These clean?"

"Clean as they're gonna get," said Joe.

I set the cups on the table and poured them half full of vodka.

"You know how pissed off I've been about the Vagos," I remarked as I finished pouring.

"No, not really," said Joe. "Lately I don't know what to think."

"I'm gonna explain that, partner. I just want you to know I've decided to do something about those bastards."

Joe lifted his glass. "That right? Like what?"

"Like work with the feds to take 'em down."

Joe lowered his glass without drinking.

"I'm going undercover, buddy," I told him. "Gonna work for the

ATF. That's where I was this afternoon, over in Van Nuys signing papers."

Joe's eyes remained fixed on the table. I could almost read the man's thoughts. My buddy was certainly no fan of the Vagos, but he absolutely despised the federal government that had taken his family home.

"This is a big fuckin' deal," I continued as I parked myself on the fold-out bed. "You can't tell anyone, understand?"

Joe refused to look at me.

"Well, c'mon, man. What do you think?" I finally asked.

My friend lifted his head. "What do I think?" He raised his glass in mock tribute. "Happy trails, motherfucker. Have a good life."

He tilted the cup and drained the booze.

I wasn't sure what response I expected from my friend, but in hindsight I suppose "Happy trails, motherfucker" made the most sense. Joe was smarter than I was—smart enough to realize that sooner or later he'd be putting his life in harm's way by sticking with his old pal George.

"Do you know what you'd be getting me into?" he asked, leaning forward with an intensity I'd never seen before. "Do you even know what you're getting yourself into? Don't be stupid, George. You've got a good life, brother. A nice business. Why would you risk it?"

I understood the man's point. Yes, there was a lot to lose, but I had no intention of letting my life slip away. Despite John Carr's warning, I still held some deluded notion that it would be "mission accomplished" after three to six months undercover. I'd just slip out the back and nobody would ever know it was ol' George Rowe who took the Vagos down.

"Partner, with or without you I'm gonna do this thing," I told him. "You can go your own way if that's what you really want. No hard feelings. I just wanted you to know what's going on, that's all. I figure I owe you that much."

Joe grabbed the bottle and poured himself another. He was done talking, so I left him in the trailer to think things through, then I climbed into my truck. I had to get over to Johnny's Restaurant, where Christie, my girlfriend at the time, was waiting. She was the daughter of a notorious motorcycle outlaw named Blind Buck, a man who was dealing drugs in Hemet back when I was known as the U-Haul Bandit. Blind Buck was the P of the Mescaleros, one of the oldest biker clubs in town. A big bruiser, over six feet tall and north of three hundred pounds, who viewed life through thick, Coke bottle lenses.

Christie's old man might have been half blind, but he was also a vicious, drug-dealing sonofabitch who would stick a knife in you if you so much as looked at him cross-eyed. People in town were scared of Buck, and I was warned, more than once, to watch my back, because the big bastard was out to nail me for dealing on his home turf.

Funny thing was, for a dude with a tough-guy reputation, that big Mescalero was just a big ol' momma's boy. Bucky's mommy even paid his rent. If not for her, I don't think that outlaw would have had a friend in the world. He hadn't done a lick of jail time because everyone else had done it for him, earning Blind Buck a long list of enemies through the years. The man lived in a constant state of paranoia, seldom leaving his house because he felt certain someone out there in the big bad world was just itching to get even.

I had no sympathy for that brutal bastard, though. Buck ruined lives. It must have pissed him off to no end when I showed up years later to date his little girl.

As I turned onto Highway 74 and pulled up to a stoplight, a horn honked from behind. I recognized the face in the rearview. It was Billy, a punk I'd known since he was in diapers. I used to sell methamphetamine to his parents before his dad transitioned into heroin and died when his heart quit. Now Billy was following in his old man's footsteps.

I pulled over, hopped from the truck and walked back to say hello. When I got to the car, I recognized the girl sitting in the passenger's seat. She was the Hemet fire chief's daughter, a twenty-year-old beauty on her way to an early grave. I'd seen her around town from time to time; we had mutual friends, and I knew she was the mother of Billy's year-old baby girl. I also knew another poorly kept secret: the girl was a hard-core heroin addict. In fact, with the exception of a few timeouts for detox, she'd been slamming the shit since age sixteen—every single day, four years straight.

"How you doing, Jenna?" I asked her.

"I'm okay, George," she said cheerlessly. But that pretty young thing didn't look okay—and she wasn't looking so pretty that day either. You can tell an addict by their pinpoint pupils and those dark circles under the eyes from dehydration. The sucked-up cheeks told me Jenna was also a heavy meth user. Scabs on her skin and the faded, yellowish bruises told me something else.

That girl was being abused.

We soon parted company, and I was on my way to the Lady Luck again. A few days later Billy would be locked behind bars at the South-west Detention Center in Temecula, charged with assault and battery. I wouldn't bother mentioning any of this if not for the fact that the young lady who put him there—that beautiful young heroin addict—was about to impact my life in ways I could never imagine . . . and for years to come.

That night at Johnny's Restaurant I was drinking with Christie when some long-haired dude with a shitty disposition began making noise at the same pool table where my friend David had made his fatal mistake months before. This gum-flapping twenty-something was drinking hard and running his mouth harder, boasting loudly that no one should mess with him because his uncle was vice president of Green Nation's Norco chapter.

The Norco Vagos, based an hour's drive northwest in the territory known as Horsetown USA, billed themselves as the clean and sober chapter. Members were expected to say no to drugs and alcohol at all times, which was a joke, because Quickie John, the P of that group, later got nailed with a pound of dope.

I was familiar with Quickie and his reputation as a man who could move forty bucks out of your wallet faster than you could blink, but I'd never met his second-in-command, the Norco vice president and uncle of this asshole who was talking trash that night at Johnny's. I decided to ignore the kid and let him run his mouth, but when my girlfriend got fed up and told him to shut the fuck up, things got heated in a hurry.

"Fuck you, cunt," he snapped at her from the pool table.

Well, that's all that woman needed to hear. Christie was a biker's child, wilder than I was, and had a hair-trigger temper to boot. That girl didn't take shit from anyone.

The two of them started blasting verbal broadsides at each other across the restaurant, each one nastier than the last. As a hang-around I wasn't supposed to throw down with anyone unless I was given the go-ahead from a patched member. There were a handful of patches in Johnny's that night, but not one of those boys had the least bit of interest in defending my girlfriend, so I took it upon myself to silence that loud-mouthed punk.

Here's something you should know about me. The only time I remember crying tears of sorrow was the day my old man keeled over and died on my lap. I was ten years old. From that day on, if there were tears in my eyes it meant just one thing: somebody was about to get hurt. Guess you might say it was the equivalent of Freight Train's silver tooth.

I was blinking back tears as I crossed to the pool table and stood watching that long-haired sonofabitch line up his next pool shot. Just before he struck the cue ball, I snatched it away.

"What the fuck?" he growled, bolting upright.

"What'd you call my old lady?" I said to him.

"You mean the cunt?" he spat, gesturing toward Christie.

POW! I hit him in the head with my arm cast. The kid staggered but didn't fall.

"Motherfucker!" he screamed. "Do you know who I am?!"

BAM! I plastered him again, and this one finally shut him up. Whoever the fuck he was.

To the casual observer, hitting an opponent upside the head with hard plaster might have seemed a bit unsportsmanlike, but when you were confronting an angry drunk wielding a cue stick and you only had one good hand, you used what you had.

It was a lesson learned through years of hard and painful experience. This was not my first rodeo. I fought near a hundred men as both a street brawler and underground bareknuckle fighter—and I was in all kinds of battles against all kinds of opponents. When I wasn't wearing an arm cast, I was an open-handed fighter, quicker than most. Striking open-handed kept the muscles loose and covered more area on a headshot than a clenched fist did. This was a technique used by Freight Train to great effect, but I'd learned the principles much earlier from a gentleman my dad had befriended during the Korean War then brought over to the States fourteen years later.

His name was Mr. Lee, and after my old man divorced Mother, that Korean followed us up to the California Cascades to teach me what he described as "kung fu"—sort of a Karate Kid, Mr. Miyagi wax on–wax off kind of deal.

From age five to nine, I studied with the master right up until he got booted out of the country for a long-expired visa. Every day I walked over to his house or he came over to mine, and we'd practice for two hours. Those four years of instruction, financed by my terminally ill father, were just one more way the old man prepared me for a future without him.

Mr. Lee drilled me relentlessly in the martial arts, and, man, I really hated it. And who could have blamed me? I was a kid living in paradise with a dirt bike to ride, woods to hunt and lakes to fish, and I was being forced to endure endless pushups and repetitive moves with some middle-aged Korean dude. What I failed to understand at the time was how much all that instruction would later come into play as I fought my way through life.

And believe me, I fought plenty.

Over the following days word spread through the Vagos that I was in serious shit with the Norco chapter for bashing their VP's nephew with my cast. And it wasn't like I could avoid those fuckers either. Big Roy was throwing a coming-out party that very same weekend—Hemet's first sponsored club run in the town of Winchester. Norco was planning to be there, as was the uncle of the punk I'd knocked senseless.

I don't mind saying I was concerned. I figured there was a better-than-even chance the Norco boys were planning to jump my ass, especially since I was still a Vagos hang-around waiting for an invitation to prospect. My gut instincts were shouting "Run, motherfucka, run!" and my instincts were seldom wrong. They'd served me pretty well through the years, warning me away from some pretty hairy situations. But this time I was ignoring those urgent whispers . . . mainly because I felt I had no choice.

"I've got some bad vibes about this, partner," I told Old Joe as we worked a tree-trimming job the day before the run. "Just feels like something's coming."

"What do you want me to tell you?" said Joe, who'd been giving me the silent treatment ever since I'd shared the big secret. "This is what you wanted, isn't it?"

I could see Joe's cold shoulder wasn't the one to cry on, so I shut up and began strapping the climbing gaffs to my calves.

"Alright, you want my advice?" blurted Joe just as I was about to start up the tree. "It's pretty simple. Get out while you can. You don't have to do this."

He was right, of course. I could have walked away and saved myself a lifetime of headaches, but that wasn't who I was—it wasn't how I was wired. I was raised never to quit a fight, and I didn't intend to start now. It's like my adoptive father, Pat, used to say; "Boy, if you come home from school with your ass whipped, I'm gonna whip yours."

That was the kind of sage advice that made me a little hellion as a kid and kept me fighting through high school and beyond. It didn't help that I was a scrawny little bastard either. Before a late growth spurt, I was the smallest kid at Hemet High. Combine my height insecurities with the fact I could barely read or write and you had yourself an illiterate punk with a me-against-the-world mentality, a little-man Napoleon complex and four years of instruction from a Korean kung fu master.

Bottom line was, little Georgie didn't play well with others, and if you didn't like it, fuck you.

I was already volatile anyway, constantly picking fights with my classmates, but my anger kicked up another notch when I was separated from the rest of the student body and thrown into something called Opportunity Class, widely considered a classroom for "retards."

In those days the principal of Hemet High School hated my guts—understandable, given my antisocial behavior—and it seemed Mr. Vanderwater was hauling me into his office to suspend my ass every other week.

I was suspended for blowing up a lavatory toilet with a cherry bomb (not guilty, Your Honor), for screwing a senior girl in a second-floor stairwell (guilty as charged) and twice for smoking pot on school grounds (which never happened). It was true I hung out with the potheads—I preferred hanging with those laid-back dudes—but toking weed made me sick to my stomach, so I stuck with cigarettes and screwed my lungs instead.

Principal Vanderwater couldn't have cared less. The man wanted me expelled and was willing to do just about anything to make it happen, even if it meant bending the truth for the greater good. Twice he lied to Pat and Dodi, telling them I was smoking pot during school hours, and twice Pat punished me for those lies with a beating. To make sure I stayed out of trouble, he'd drop by the school during lunch period to keep an eye on me.

One afternoon while doing his usual lunchtime surveillance, Pat's pager went off. When he dialed back the number he found himself talking to Principal Vanderwater, who told him I'd just been caught smoking weed again.

It was more bullshit from the principal, and now Pat knew he was being lied to.

Furious, he stormed into the school yard, grabbed me by the scruff of the neck and headed straight for the school office with a bunch of my classmates in tow. They'd heard Pat's marching orders; "Either you kick that bastard's lying ass or I'll kick yours."

I couldn't believe my ears. I'd been given the green light to waylay Principal Vanderwater. We turned into the office, leaving my classmates outside in the hall gawking through the glass, then waited at the counter for Vanderwater to appear. When he finally did, he got the surprise of the school year when I hit him with every bit of strength I could muster.

As you can imagine, that was the punch heard round the halls of Hemet High for a long time. The police were called and Principal Vanderwater threatened to have me prosecuted. Must have changed his mind, though, because he took the matter to the school board and got me thrown out of Hemet High instead. A year later, sometime during junior year, I dropped out of school for good. That had to be a glorious day for Vanderwater. Man must've thrown himself one helluva party.

There would be many anxious moments during my time undercover, moments when I honestly wondered if I'd ever come home again. Countless times I thought of walking away, or bent the ear of the Man upstairs, asking Him to keep me safe. But heading for Winchester that day for the Hemet chapter's first annual run was the first time I'd felt a real sense of danger and self-doubt.

Despite those feelings, I wasn't about to bail on my commitment to Hemet, the ATF and myself . . . I wasn't going home with my ass whipped. Because the hard truth was, I was a forty-two-year-old sinner who'd never done a damn thing he was particularly proud of in life. And I saw that mission as my once-in-a-lifetime chance to finally succeed at something worthwhile . . . something I actually believed in.

I had to keep going no matter what.

So there I was in the parking lot of a Winchester biker bar, helping set up folding chairs for the big Vagos bash, when the Norco chapter came rumbling in on their Harley-Davidsons. You could always spot those Norco boys, man. The patches sewn on their cuts, awarded in recognition of services rendered to the club, always looked brand-new and ready to wear. That's because Quickie John, the Norco P, handed them out for practically any occasion. He thought they made his chapter look cool.

Perfect church attendance? Get a patch.

Eat all your vegetables? Get a patch.

Wipe your ass properly? Sure, here's a patch for that too.

As soon as those Vagos dismounted they approached Big Todd, who pointed in my direction. I kept unfolding chairs but watched them coming from the corner of my eye—maybe six or seven of them, trailed by that smart-mouthed punk I'd popped at Johnny's. I figured this was it. I was about to get gang jumped.

"You George Rowe?" said the patched Vagos leading the group.

"That's me."

"I heard what you did to my nephew."

So this was Uncle Mike, Norco's vice president.

"Your nephew called my old lady a cunt," I told him. "What would you have done?"

Mike glanced briefly over his shoulder at the long-haired douche before pointing at my arm cast.

"So you hit him with that?"

"That's right."

"You hit my nephew with a fuckin' cast?" said Mike, heating up.

"Yup."

Like I've said, I fought a lot of men over the years, and experience tells you when an opponent is preparing to unload. The body coils and there's a look in the eyes that's primal—almost wolflike. You can recognize it when you know what to look for.

That day, facing Uncle Mike, I was definitely seeing it.

I felt my senses sharpen and my mind snap into focus. My body was tuned in now, primed and ready for the assault to come. Usually I let the other guy take the first swing; it always put me in the mood to rumble. Once Uncle Mike took his best shot, I was pretty sure what would be coming next. The rest of the Norco boys would immediately pile on and turn a fair fight into a lopsided rout . . . it was the outlaw way. I planned on using my arm cast to block some of those blows— with luck maybe even break a few hands—but I also knew I had an ace in the hole. There was a buck knife sheathed on the back of my belt. If I had to pull that blade to save my skin, I'd do it without a moment's hesitation.

"Hold up!"

Just as we were about to dance, Big Roy was cutting in.

"I know all about what happened, and I'm gonna handle it," he told Uncle Mike. Then he turned to the nephew and announced loud enough for everyone to hear, "There's at least four other guys here who saw what happened at Johnny's. You were out of line, and you know it."

The punk kept his mouth shut.

"George is a Hemet hang-around," Big Roy told Uncle Mike. "If anyone's gonna punish him, it'll be us."

I felt like the naughty schoolboy again, caught between my adoptive father and Principal Vanderwater.

Mike thought it over a moment then told Roy, "Alright, P. But if you don't take care of this, we will."

That said, he walked away with his nephew and the rest of the Norco Vagos in tow. As soon as they'd cleared earshot Big Roy turned on me and hissed, "You owe me, motherfucker."

"I appreciate it, Roy, but—"

"Shut the fuck up and listen," he snapped. "Don't ever make this chapter look bad again, do you understand me?" Then he pointed at the ground. "When you're done setting up the chairs, I want you to find a fuckin' broom and sweep."

I looked around.

"You want me to sweep the parking lot?"

"Are you fucking deaf? I said clean up this mess."

Man, I was pissed. Here I was, a grown man being ordered around by a punk-ass bitch. Any other time I would have grabbed that prick by the throat and bitch-slapped him six ways to Sunday. But for the sake of the mission I swallowed that asshole's shit and swept the parking lot, daydreaming of the day John Carr would throw open Big Roy's cell door and I'd step inside for a little payback. I'd beat that bastard bloody, then walk right out again with a parting "Now clean up this mess."

Man, I couldn't wait.

8

The Fire Chief's Daughter

George, it's Billy. Listen, I really need you to do me that favor."

"Huh? Who the fuck is this?"

The phone call had slapped me from a sound sleep, and it took a few seconds to clear the cobwebs and realize who I was talking to. Billy was on the line again, that crazy kid who'd been tossed in the can for beating up his even crazier girlfriend. He was calling from the jail in Temecula for a third time, and each plea was growing more desperate than the last.

"You gotta help me, man. I don't know what else to do."

"Neither do I," I said. "Already told you there's nothing—"

"You can tell that bitch to drop the charges," he jumped in. "She'll listen to you."

"Billy—"

"George, if Jenna testifies against me, I'm fucked. I am totally fucked. Please. There's no one else. You gotta talk to her, George. Please."

This was one more aggravation I didn't need, but the kid was facing serious jail time for assault and battery, and he was freaking out. I knew Billy wouldn't quit calling until I did as he asked.

I rubbed my eyes and sighed, "Where is she?"

I drove out to the place where Billy figured his old lady might be shacking up—a house belonging to one of her longtime tweaker pals. Jenna was supposedly there trying to get clean ahead of a drug test with Child Protective Services. If she failed it, there was a strong possibility she would permanently lose the child she and Billy had made together.

My knock went unanswered, but the door was unlocked, so I let myself in.

The place was a shithole. I moved through the living room into the kitchen, where I found the counters littered with rotting food and fat flies. I headed into the hall, then turned into the first bedroom. And that's where I found Jenna.

The girl was on the downside of a high, laying half naked on the bed and curled on her side. She seemed to recognize me standing in the doorway but barely moved.

"What are you doing here?" she mumbled.

"Billy asked me to check on you."

"Fuck Billy," she said, closing her eyes. "Fuck that asshole."

I walked to the edge of the bed and noticed the rubber tubing and an empty syringe on the nightstand.

Jenna always had a sweet tooth for heroin. In high school she'd spread that shit on tinfoil, put a match to it and chase the dragon, sucking the smoke through a straw. Then she took it a step further when a girlfriend got hold of her diabetic aunt's syringes. At her peak Jenna was shooting up every four hours like clockwork. By the time I walked into that room, the twenty-two-year-old had slammed so much junk that the veins in her hands and wrists had died and the crooks of her elbows were plastered in scar tissue. Lately she'd taken to injecting that shit into her neck's main cable. That way it went straight to the dome.

"Are you just gonna lay there feeling sorry for yourself?" I said to her.

"Maybe," she murmured.

"The hell you are. Take a shower and get dressed. You're coming with me."

I took her by the arm and hauled her to a sitting position.

"What the fuck?" she snapped at me.

"C'mon, get up."

"Where are we going?"

"Out."

She looked at me thoughtfully a moment then down at her bare feet.

"I don't have shoes."

"Where are they?"

"I told you. I don't have any."

I walked around the bedroom, checking the floor for shoes, then headed into the hall telling her, "I'll find some shoes. You take a shower."

Jenna as a teenager, a few years before we met.

I think it might have been one of the few times Jenna ever listened to me. She cleaned herself up and threw on some clothes while I scrounged a pair of shoes from her friend's closet, which were too big but walkable. Then we piled into my truck and headed for the OK Corral, a bar Jenna had been sneaking into since she was fifteen. We pulled up stools at the bar and I ordered her a Zombie, the strongest drink I could think of.

With all she'd been through, I figured the girl could use it.

• • •

Jenna was originally from Big Bear, a mountain community in the San Bernardino National Forest, but she and her little sister didn't stay rooted for long. Her folks had a messy split when the girls were young, then her mother got heavy into drink. By age thirteen, Jenna was following in Momma's footsteps, sneaking Gentleman Jack from the cupboard and smoking marijuana behind her school.

One year later, tired of life with Mother and an abusive stepfather, Jenna called her old man, who was then Hemet's fire chief, and begged him to come rescue her. He did as his daughter asked and eventually gained custody. It's a sad irony that the chief was also one of Hemet's drug and alcohol counselors at the time—the man other parents would send their kids to for help. But not even he could control his wild child. Despite all his training and best efforts, the man lost his own daughter to heroin.

Of course, Jenna wasn't born an addict, but once she got a taste for the lifestyle she jumped into it like a teenager cannonballing into a swimming pool. By the age of sixteen the girl was slumming in flophouses, slamming heroin, smoking meth and fucking a different partner every other night.

One of those partners was Billy, and once that tweaker and Jenna hooked up it was like putting a lit match to gasoline. Ever the romantics, the couple began spending nights together making crank for resale. Law enforcement eventually caught wind of their little enterprise, and the two fled to Arizona, where Billy had family.

But there would be no happily-ever-after for these two young lovers.

They moved into a twenty-foot travel trailer off a dirt road in the Golden Valley, where Billy began beating her on a near-daily basis, the physical violence escalating until the day he crushed her nose. Jenna checked in at the emergency room to have the nose repaired, but doctors refused to give her pain medication. When she asked why they told her she was pregnant.

After throwing a tantrum, cursing at doctors and slapping the walls, Jenna returned to the trailer to plan for her abortion. Seemed like the thing to do. After all, junkies are a self-serving breed, and babies only get in the way of that me-first lifestyle. Jenna wasn't in the best of health at the time either. After three years of slamming heroin and taking every other drug imaginable, she was justifiably afraid her kid would pop out looking like something from a carnival freak show.

Because Arizona frowned on abortion, she and Billy scraped together all the cash they had and headed for Nevada. Only a funny thing happened on the way to the doctor. The idiots detoured into a casino and gambled away all their abortion money.

Now it was back to Arizona, where Jenna resumed the high life. So high, in fact, that before she knew it six months had passed and now, by law, it was too late to abort. Meanwhile Billy started injecting speed, and that sent Daddy into a whole 'nother level of violent. He and Jenna were driving the back roads in his Impala, arguing as usual, when Billy pulled a gun and tried shooting his girlfriend's foot off. The bullet missed its target, went through the floorboard and shot out the tire instead. Billy regained control of the car but lost control of himself. After pulling the Impala off the road, he dragged Jenna into the street by her hair and beat the snot out of her. When he was finished he shoved her back into the car and drove on three tires going one hundred miles per hour back to the trailer, where, out of his mind, he kicked Jenna until she fell unconscious.

As Jenna's due date approached, her mom drove out to Arizona and took her daughter back to California. A few weeks later Jenna delivered a daughter one month premature. Miracle of miracles, the kid wasn't born with a craving for heroin-in-a-bottle.

Now a young mother, Jenna tried to do the right thing and clean up her life. She started by going back to school while her mom watched the baby. The girl might have been a drug addict, but she was a damn smart one. Although she'd spent most of her high school years high on dope, she still graduated one year early. Despite her best intentions, however, the old cravings soon returned and Jenna tumbled back into drugs. To survive, she turned to welfare and sold dirt weed to finance her heroin addiction. The state stepped in, took the baby away and handed temporary custody to Jenna's mom, passing the child from one addict to another.

Then, just when it seemed things couldn't get any worse, Billy came back into her life. He assured Jenna he was a changed man, ready to be a faithful husband and loving father. Hell, the new-and-improved Billy even came bearing gifts, a passenger van with a kiddie seat strapped in back. But their kumbaya moment didn't last. As soon as the couple climbed into the van they were right back to arguing again. You can pretty much guess what happened next—and if you guessed Billy plunging a screwdriver into Jenna's back, you would be correct.

He shoved her out of the van and hit the gas as Jenna was punching him through the open window, causing the van to veer headlong into an olive tree. Jenna didn't bother checking on his condition. Instead she ran off and called the police. Billy ended up behind bars on an assault and battery charge.

Ah, young love.

So that was the young woman sitting beside me at the OK Corral bar; the fire chief's daughter who had already packed a lifetime into twenty-two years of hard drugs and violent abuse.

As the drink arrived in front of her, Jenna said to me, "The first time I ever saw you, you were on your bike in the parking lot at Mickey's Liquor Trade. Do you remember?"

I shook my head.

"Well, I remember you. You looked so confident. The way you held yourself with your head so high. I asked Billy who you were and he said, 'That's George Rowe. Why? Do you want to fuck him?' Then he hit me."

She said this as a matter of course and took a sip of the Zombie— a drink guaranteed to kick anyone's ass.

"You know, I've heard things about you," she said after a moment.

"Oh, yeah? What have you heard?"

"Well, it's not good," she said coyly. "Whenever I've asked people about George Rowe it's never like, 'Yeah, I know that guy.' It's more like, 'I hate that fucking guy,' or 'That dude used to sell me dope.'"

She took another sip and looked at me hopefully. "Do you still sell dope?"

"Not anymore," I answered, taking a pull on my bottle. "I got clean about ten years ago."

"And now what?"

"I own a tree service."

Jenna played with her drink then said offhandedly, "Do you have a girlfriend?"

"Not really," I answered. Which was a lie. I was seeing Christie at the time.

Jenna set her half-empty glass on the bar and studied it a moment.

"What are we doing here, George?"

"You mean in this bar?"

She turned with a level gaze. "You know what I mean."

"I already told you. Billy wanted me to check on you."

"That's all?"

I thought for a moment, then said, "And he doesn't want you pressing charges."

Anger flashed in her eyes—a look that, unfortunately, would become all too familiar.

"He can go fuck himself," she hissed. She drained her glass and ordered another Zombie. "You know we've got a kid, right?"

"I heard you have a little girl."

"Did you know Billy tried to kill her?"

"When was this?"

"Last year in Arizona, before the baby was born. He was cheating on me. I saw him go inside this tweaker pad with this chick, so I grabbed a pickax from the shed and started hitting his fuckin' Impala with it. I put holes all over that thing."

Jenna paused as the bartender showed up with her drink.

"People tell me I have a temper," she said, lifting the glass.

"No shit," said I.

"I get it from my mom. I remember she used to say to me, 'We don't need no stinkin' men because we are badass babes."

She smiled at the memory and took a drink. "Where was I?"

"With a pickax."

"Right. So Billy comes running out of the house and chases me across the yard with a broom handle. I tried to climb a fence, but I was seven months pregnant and couldn't make it, so I just sat on the ground and let him beat me. But then he started kicking me, so I decided I'd better run. When he caught me again he started hitting me in the stomach with that broom handle, and the whole time he's screaming, 'You're not going to have that baby, bitch. You're not gonna have my kid.' "

Jenna lifted her glass in triumph. "But guess what? I had his fucking kid."

She took a healthy swallow, then paused to reflect.

"That asshole was always doing shit like that. Like this one time he had me pinned to the floor of our trailer with one hand and he's got a gun pointed at my face with the other. And then he started shooting. The bullets are hitting all around my head and ricocheting off the concrete slab under the trailer. I could smell my hair burning, that's how fuckin' close those bullets were. When he let me up there were holes in the floor the shape of my head."

"That's messed up," was all I could think to say.

"So the next morning I grabbed my pink lady—that was this little gun I owned with a pink mother-of-pearl grip—and I straddled Billy while he was sleeping, pointed the barrel at his nose and said, 'Good morning, motherfucker.' "

I grinned at this. "Should've pulled the trigger."

"I never got the chance. He grabbed the gun out of my hand and hit me in the head with it. Then he starts yelling at me, 'Run, bitch, you got six seconds' and started counting. And I ran too, because I knew that sick fuck would kill me. I ran into the desert and hid behind a Joshua tree until I knew he was gone."

I shook my head. It was just too crazy. Jenna drained her Zombie and set the empty glass on the bar. Man, that girl could drink.

"Thank you, sir," she said to me, "may I have another?"

After we left the OK Corral I took Jenna back to the shack in Valle Vista. Old Joe came out of his trailer to introduce himself, but my date was shitfaced and made a lousy first impression.

"She's younger than Christie," Joe scolded when Jenna was out of earshot. "What are you doing with a kid?"

I wasn't sure myself, but I had a pretty good idea—and it wasn't exactly a noble one. I'd really like to say I was a gentleman, that I did the right thing and tucked that poor girl into bed to sleep off her drunk. I'd like to say that, but I'd be lying. Truth is I wanted to fuck her brains out.

But when Jenna shed her clothes, my stomach nearly turned. Jesus Christ, if you could have seen the shape that girl was in. Never mind that her body was emaciated, it was also covered with ugly welts and bruises. Swear to God, she had black and blues that literally ran from her head to her toes. Never in my life had I seen a human being that looked like that. Here was the poster child for battered women, and, man, it really pissed me off.

Of course, that didn't stop me from screwing her. Hell, no. I downed another glass of Wild Turkey, then Jenna and I did the nasty all night long. The next morning, after I'd driven her back to her girl-friend's place, Billy called from the detention center, anxious to know if I'd talked to Jenna about dropping the charges.

"Check this out, Billy," I said, swallowing my anger. "I fucked her instead."

"Wait? What's that?"

"Yeah, I did your old lady last night. Not only that, but I'm not gonna ask her to drop the charges. How's that sound?"

The phone went silent a moment before Billy spoke again.

"Well, that sounds fucked up, George," he said bitterly.

"Not as fucked up as you. What kind of man are you anyway? Christ, I've never seen a woman beat up so bad. And she doesn't even own a decent pair of shoes."

Figured I'd throw that one in for good measure.

There was another long pause before Billy said, "Know what? I'm okay with it, George. I probably would have done the same thing."

I didn't know if the kid was serious, stupid or just angling for another shot at getting those charges dropped. Didn't matter, though. Whatever the reason, I was done with that asshole and hung up the phone. Over the course of the next few days Billy tried calling back, but I refused to talk to him. Eventually he took the hint, and that was the last I heard from that sonofabitch . . . at least for a couple of years anyway.

Now that I was through with her old boyfriend, I had Jenna all to myself. In the following weeks I was drawn to that girl like the slots at Soboba. I just couldn't get enough. And before I realized enough was too much, it was too late. I'd invited her to share my home.

Old Joe thought I'd made another mistake of Godzilla-like proportions. He still hadn't gotten over the fact I was working with the feds; now I was bringing a heroin addict into the apartment. Not only did he think my timing was incredibly bad, but according to him, Jenna was an out-of-control bitch.

"I don't get it," he said to me one day. "What's the attraction?"

"Well, the pussy's pretty good," I answered with a stupid grin.

But Joe wasn't laughing. My friend thought I was a goddamn fool, being led by my dick instead of my brain—not the first time he'd seen that behavior. "You've gotta learn to separate your wants from your needs, brother," he lectured me. "You might want that girl, but you don't need her. Especially not now."

Once again the man had a valid point, but Old Joe didn't know the whole truth. With Jenna it wasn't just about getting into her pants. No question the girl was an all-pro in the sack, but like my decision to go under for ATF, taking that damaged soul under my wing had less to do with her pussy than my past.

Truth was I understood the fire chief's daughter. We were birds of a feather. I'd fallen into drug abuse about the same age and remember wishing someone would intervene and save me from my own self-destruction. Not only that, but Jenna had been evicted from the tweaker pad where she'd been crashing and had nowhere else to turn. She'd torched every bridge.

When you're using and abusing you really don't care how your addiction impacts others—even those you love most. Every person that touched that girl's life had been put through hell. Her mom didn't want her, her dad didn't want her. Nobody on God's earth wanted that addict around—except maybe her misery-loves-company junkie friends. If I didn't help that drowning soul, who would?

So I tossed her a lifeline and dragged a crazy woman into my home.

Right out of the gate it was nothing but drama. I quickly learned that trying to contain Jenna was like trying to wrangle a wild horse. You couldn't get a rope on her. And just when you thought you had that bitch corralled, she'd jump the fence and off she'd gallop, looking for her next high. Of course, there wasn't far to go at first. I kept that untapped supply of cancer pain meds stockpiled in the medicine cabinet, and from day one that girl was into them like a kid run amok. All that candy was at her fingertips now, and Jenna couldn't swallow it fast enough. Within a few months the whole stash was wiped out.

I guess in that way she was a lot like her mother, whose pill addiction began when Jenna was thirteen. One day her mom was drunk and tried to move a pot of hot chicken soup from the stovetop to the fridge.

The lid came off, and the broth splashed over her legs and feet, scalding them so badly she was checked into a burn unit for two weeks of skin grafts. The woman came out the other side with scars on her legs and a taste for painkillers, spending her days at home popping Fentanyl and pounding whiskey.

Once Jenna had swallowed my stock of cancer meds, the girl went looking for her next high. She didn't have far to travel. The hooker who lived in the apartment next door was also a speed and heroin freak. One heroin addict could tell another from a mile away, and Jenna identified that kindred spirit immediately. Not only were the pupils pinpoint day and night, but there was a smell that oozed from the body's pores, the smell of coffee grounds and chili powder, which was what the dope was cut with.

Christ Almighty, it was beyond ridiculous living with that woman. I could almost understand why Billy beat her.

Okay, maybe that's a stretch . . .

. . . or maybe not.

9

Point of No Return

You've got to be willing to die for your brothers, George. Could you do that? Could you die for the club?"

After two months as a hang-around with the Vagos, I was beginning to wonder if I'd ever take the next step toward becoming a full-patched member. You can hang around forever, but you have to be invited to prospect. Well, the day Big Todd knocked on my door to deliver the rah-rah speech about the importance of commitment and loyalty, I knew I was on my way.

"Absolutely," I said with as much false sincerity as I could muster.

"Loyalty to the club. That's what it's all about."

"I'm with you, Big Todd."

Six years earlier Terry the Tramp had the same talk with ATF undercover agent Darrin Kozlowski. Koz was on the threshold of becoming a Vagos prospect when Tramp summoned him for a test of loyalty. He wanted to know if Koz had the right stuff to be a Vagos.

"Would you die for the Vagos?" asked Tramp.

"Yes, I would," answered Koz.

"And do you have what it takes to kill for the Vagos?" Tramp asked.

"Could you kill someone even if you were doing it for a brother you didn't like?"

"Yes, I could," answered Koz.

And just like that, the ATF agent became a prospect.

Now Big Todd was regurgitating the same bullshit.

Even with all the right answers, though, my path to prospecting would not be as smooth as it had been for Special Agent Kozlowski. That's because three hundred pounds of lard still stood in my way.

North, the Hemet chapter's sergeant at arms, continued to question my trustworthiness, and his accusations were putting Big Roy in a tight spot. Roy wanted me in the club because I was a good brawler and he wanted more bodies in the chapter, but he was smart enough to realize the danger of taking a man with a big question mark slapped on his forehead. Green Nation was still reeling after Hammer flipped for the feds, and if Big Roy allowed another rat into Tramp's green house, the Hemet P would almost certainly have his charter yanked and his motorcycle confiscated.

And me? I would almost certainly end up dead.

That's exactly what happened to another Vagos hang-around over in San Bernardino just a few weeks later. Nobody outside the Berdoo chapter knew the whole story, but a Vagos wannabe named Dennis Daoussis, whom the club called Shorty, was ambushed during a church meeting and beaten near death by the members. Leading that assault was Rhino, the mullet-headed beast who served as Green Nation's international sergeant at arms and Tramp's chief enforcer.

As Shorty lay semiconscious, the patches zip-tied his wrists and ankles, wrapped his head and mouth with electrical tape, rolled him in a carpet and tossed his body into the bed of a Dodge pickup owned by Kilo, the chapter's sergeant at arms.

Rhino and Kilo drove east through the San Gorgonio Pass, then north on Highway 62 toward Landers. On a dusty back road in that High Desert town, Shorty was executed. Rhino pressed a gun to the hang-around's left temple and blew his brains out.

When the body was discovered two days later, evidence led police back to the house where the assault had taken place. All the bloody carpeting had been pulled up, and a couch and love seat were in the backyard waiting to be power-washed. The Vago who lived there was arrested as an accessory to murder, but, ever loyal to his brothers, Hulk kept his mouth shut and refused to implicate Rhino and Kilo. Guess he figured the law wouldn't kill him but the Vagos certainly could.

Which is why I was a little nervous as I filled out forms for a background check that would be run by an actual cop friendly with the crew, a process required of all prospective Vagos. I didn't figure there was anything in my past that could get me rolled in carpet and hauled off for execution like poor Shorty, but when you were operating undercover and the stakes were life and death, there was always that sliver of doubt pricking at your brain.

The completed forms would be handed to a police sergeant we called "Crusher," who worked out of Cathedral City, a community just south of Palm Springs. Through law enforcement channels, Crusher would screen prospect applicants for red flags. With the law's help, Terry the Tramp hoped to sniff out informants before they could burrow too deep, and Sergeant Crusher was his most valuable bloodhound.

Thanks to Todd's big mouth, I learned the Vagos had several lawmen in their back pocket: a U.S. Border Patrol agent living somewhere near Temecula, a San Bernardino deputy who was selling the Vagos guns he should have been destroying, and their background checker in Cathedral City, Sergeant Crusher.

According to Todd, Crusher made himself a pretty good living playing both sides of the fence. He knew the locations of Mexican drug houses and when their shipments came in, so it was just a matter of kicking down doors, taking their drugs and money and splitting the proceeds with the Vagos. The setup was almost foolproof. After all, what Mexican drug dealer—probably an illegal to begin with—would call 9-1-1 to report getting ripped off by a cop?

Crusher had lobbied hard to ride outlaw with Green Nation, but national had no intention of allowing law enforcement into their ranks—especially Rhino, who detested anyone with a badge. As a compromise, Terry the Tramp put Crusher at the helm of a newly formed support group called The Green Machine. Green Machine members, like my buddy who owned Shooter's Food and Brew, were servants for the parent club much like the Sons of Hell were dick-suckers for the Hells Angels. Whenever the Vagos required strength in numbers, The Green Machine would roll with them. These outlaw wannabes paid dues, sported patches and rode Harleys just like the big boys, but even a lowly Vagos prospect had more clout than Crusher, the newly ordained president of The Green Machine.

Regardless of whether everything panned out satisfactorily with the sergeant's background check, Big Roy made it clear I'd never be welcomed as a Vagos prospect until North had his day in court. The chapter's sergeant at arms was handed a deadline to make his case that I was a snitch, and when the time came for him to shit or get off the pot, I finally got to meet North's mysterious man behind the curtain.

The source for the snitch rumors was a Hemet businessman I'd known since I was a kid. We used to attend Alateen meetings together—basically group therapy for the children of alcoholic parents. My accuser's name was Howard, once a chubby, smart-as-hell student who eventually opened a rubbish removal service in town—not exactly the line of work you'd expect from a man with an Ivy League future.

I met the dude face-to-face at Johnny's Restaurant on a night when most of the Hemet chapter was in attendance. Big Todd suggested we conduct business away from the prying eyes and ears of customers, so I followed him, North and Howard out the back door and into the parking lot behind Johnny's.

Todd wasted no time getting to the point.

"So what's the deal?" he said to Howard. "You accuse Big George here of being a rat. Where's the proof?"

"I don't need to show you a thing," Howard retorted. "I know what I know."

"You know what you know?" Todd said incredulously. He turned to North. "What kind of bullshit is this? Where's the paperwork you promised?"

"Turns out there is none," said North sheepishly. "I'm going on what he told me."

"That's all you fuckin' got? This asshole's word over a brother?"

"You calling me a liar?" snapped Howard.

Todd gave him a brusque shove, and North quickly stepped between them.

"Alright, alright," said North. "We're here to talk, so everyone just relax."

Todd stabbed his finger at Howard over North's shoulder and barked, "Don't you fuckin' raise your voice to me, motherfucker!" Then he spun toward me. "You'd better beat the shit out of this fat fuck, George."

Surrounded by two patched Vagos and the hang-around he'd accused of being a rat, my old Alateen buddy looked understandably nervous.

"Alright, Howard," I said as calmly as I could. "Why are you spreadin' shit about me?"

"I'm just saying what I heard," he replied with false bravado.

"Who'd you hear it from?" I said. "Give me a name."

Howard wouldn't say. Either that or there never was a name.

Todd growled at North, "Your guy's got nothing. This is all bullshit."

North didn't disagree. With his key witness crumbling under cross-examination, the sergeant at arms had lost his stomach for argument.

"Like I said, it's what he told me," North muttered defensively.

And then, straight out of left field, Howard looked at me and blurted, "Where's the money you owe me?"

"What? What the fuck are you talking about?" I said.

"You never paid me for that eight ball."

So that's what this was about. An unpaid debt that I had no memory of.

An eight ball was three and a half grams of methamphetamine, which Howard claimed I'd taken years before without paying for it. North had been running with these snitch rumors for weeks, making my life miserable and endangering the mission, all because one fat bastard believed another. I realize how crazy that sounds, given the fact I really was trying to infiltrate the Vagos, but the truth had nothing to do with the fiction.

"You accuse me of being a goddamn snitch because this asshole thinks I owe him money?" I said to North, biting back my anger.

"You owe me for that eight ball," insisted Howard.

"Whip his ass, Big George," Todd goaded.

"So I owe you money, huh?" I said to Howard. "Well, guess it's my bad then. Here, let me pay you back."

I struck a sudden, snapping blow to Howard's face that bloodied his lip.

"How's that, motherfucker? We square now?"

Now I spun on North again. The sergeant at arms took a defensive step back, expecting another swing.

"This shit is over, man," I barked at him instead. "It's fuckin' over."

Vindicated at last, I made a triumphant march back into Johnny's. When I told the Vagos what had happened, Iron Mike gave me a big hug. A few minutes later, North approached, looking contrite.

"Sorry, brother," he said. "You know I was just doing my job looking out for the club."

Once the snitch tag came off and my background checked out, the path was clear for me to become a Vagos prospect, phase two on the road to becoming a full-patched member of Green Nation.

In Hemet, Vagos church meetings were held every Wednesday night at 7:30. While patch holders huddled in living rooms and garages discussing club business, their hang-arounds and prospects remained in the street, standing guard over the motorcycles . . . sometimes even squatting over a bucket of suds, washing them down. On the Wednesday following that inquisition at Johnny's, Crash and I were called into North's garage and officially made prospects of Green Nation.

In a small ceremony before the patches, we were given the bottom CALIFORNIA rocker for our cuts and told to sew them on in five minutes or lose them. And the rule was you had to sew that patch on tight, too, because if a member could get his fingers under it he could rip it off your back and take it, sending you right back to hang-around.

Crash and I were now officially chapter slaves, bound to hang, drink and ride together until one or both of us became a patched member. That was just how it worked in an outlaw club, for better or worse. And with crazy Crash at my side, I had a hunch things would get worse before they got better.

"Alright, you two," said Roy once the patches had been sewn. "Sing us the prospect song."

Man, a shudder still goes through me whenever I think of that goddamn song. Every Vagos prospect was expected to memorize it and belt out the lyrics whenever a patch holder demanded it.

The song begins "I am a Vagos prospect, as you can clearly see . . ."

And that's as far as I can go. During my time prospecting I must've sung that fucking song a thousand times, but almost every word of it has been mercifully bleached from my brain.

"I am a Vagos prospect, as you can clearly see . . ."

No. Forget it, man. It's too painful to even *try* to remember.

So now I had my California rocker and a foot in the church door where the patches would congregate on Wednesday nights. But it was the 22 tattoo, etched into the side of my head by Ready at the Lady Luck, that really stamped me as Vagos property. For all you elementary school grads, the twenty-second letter of the alphabet is V . . . and V stands for Vagos. As the green ink was applied just behind the ear, I thought of the day in Bee Canyon when John Carr and I first met. That ATF special agent and some of his colleagues had doubted I'd ever make prospect. Yet here I was, being branded like a heifer—George Rowe, property of Green Nation.

At that point I figured why not go all the way and really sell it for ATF. I'd show the world I was down for the club and eliminate any doubts about my commitment to the Vagos. So I pointed Ready to a new canvas on the back of my bald head and asked for one more tattoo.

I was now a giant step closer to getting my hands on that prized patch in the middle, the god of mischief himself . . . Loki. Only to get there I needed a Harley-Davidson under my ass. Hauling broken-down bikes in a pickup was fine for a hang-around, but to ride as a member of an outlaw motorcycle gang a Harley was required—the only machine any self-respecting one percenter would ever mount.

John Carr had promised he'd replace the shovelhead chopper I'd sold to Doc the previous year, so I entered his name in my Nextel as "Uncle John," a relative who bought motorcycles at government auction and flipped them for profit. It should go without saying that the first call I made after leaving the Lady Luck was to Uncle Johnny Law.

"We're in business," I told him, almost giddy with the news.

"You're prospecting?"

"Fuck yeah," I boasted. "Got me a twenty-two tattoo and everything."

"Big step, George. Congratulations."

"Never mind that. Time for Uncle John to deliver on that Harley he promised."

I drove home to Valle Vista high on success and anxious to share the news with Jenna. In the few months she'd been living with me, the girl had tried her best to make our little chicken coop a home. She'd spent a fair amount of time slapping lipstick on that pig, including a picket fence around the dirt yard out front and curtains on the windows. Inside the shack beads had been strung to create privacy between the living room and bedroom, paintings were mounted on the walls, flowers were tucked in vases and butterflies were spread all over the fucking place. That girl was a nut for butterflies; butterfly paintings, butterfly pictures, butterfly plaques, ceramic butterflies, plastic butterflies . . . it was like *Silence of the Lambs* in that apartment, except with butterflies instead of moths.

As I entered the shack, Jenna stepped through the beads.

"What would you think about me prospecting with the Vagos?" I asked her right off, setting her up nicely for the big reveal.

"I think that would be a really stupid thing to do."

Talk about a buzz kill. But I guess I should have expected it. Jenna was already familiar with the Vagos when she came into my world. Ready had tattooed her at the Lady Luck. She was friendly with some of the Hemet VOLs (Vagos Old Ladies) from high school, and she'd known Big Roy and Big Todd before I ever entered the picture. Knew them well enough, in fact, to decide they were idiots.

"Well, it's too late now," I told her, turning my head and tapping the freshly minted 22 tattoo behind my ear.

"Oh, my God. You actually did it," said Jenna, unable to hide her disappointment. "I never thought you'd actually do it."

"And check this out."

I turned around to reveal the California rocker on my cut and the bigger surprise on the back of my head; tattooed in two-inch green letters the words GREEN NATION.

"What'd you do that for?" she groaned.

"It's mandatory," I said . . . which was horseshit.

The girl looked at me like a turd that needed flushing.

"Having a brain in your head is mandatory too," she snapped, then turned around and disappeared through the beads.

Jenna must have figured her boyfriend had officially joined idiot nation, but there was nothing I could do about it. I wasn't about to share my double life with a drug addict. How the hell could I? The girl was a loose cannon. If I confided over breakfast that I was working with the feds, I'd end up buried by lunch.

My "Green Nation" tattoo, inked at the Lady Luck.

That's what happened to Hammer, the federal informant who overdosed in a Jacuzzi. That CI made the golden mistake of telling his girlfriend he was working with the feds. Turns out she was related to someone who knew someone, and when she and Hammer split up, well, hell hath no fury. That scorned woman went sideways and single-handedly destroyed both her boyfriend and his mission. ATF's Operation Green Nation folded like a limp tortilla.

No, I wasn't telling that crazy bitch a goddamn thing. Best to keep my two lives separate. There would be the George Rowe who ran a business and rode with the Vagos motorcycle club and the George Rowe no one but a handful of people knew, the George who was headed down the rabbit hole as a confidential informant for the federal government.

Two parallel lives and never the twain should meet. At least not until the plug was pulled and the whole shithouse came crashing down.

•   •   •

"Come to L.A., prospect, I've got your bike."

Baby, it was Christmas in July when I got that call from Uncle Johnny Law. I headed to the federal building with visions of beautiful Harley-Davidsons dancing in my head. John Carr led me to the underground garage to present my new toy . . . and my jaw nearly dropped.

There it was, propped on its kickstand—the ugliest hunk of shit I'd ever seen. The bike was a Harley Touring Classic, a cop motorcycle with a massive dash. I had this gut feeling the feds never expected me to graduate past the hang-around stage, and once I made prospect they had to scramble around for something, anything, that might qualify as a motorcycle.

So this rat bike was it.

I lowered myself into the saddle, managed to get that pig running, then tried gunning it up a plank and into the bed of my truck. But the ramp fell and I plowed right into the bumper, busting the Harley's headlight.

Should've taken that as a sign.

"Helluva start," said John, straight-faced.

I ignored the smartass, set up the plank and nailed it on my second try.

Before I pulled out of the garage, John had a warning for me. Outlaw clubs confiscated a member's bike for any number of infractions, and opposing gang members didn't hesitate to steal one from a rival.

"Whatever you do," cautioned John, "do not lose that bike."

"Who the fuck would want it?" I fired back as I drove out of the garage.

As soon as I got back to Valle Vista, I wheeled that ugly beast off the truck before anyone could see it and pushed it through the front door of the shack—leaking oil all the way. Right there in the living room, I stripped it down, then built it back up again. I gave that Touring Classic new tires, new brakes and a new clutch, then rebuilt the motor and cut off the handle bars to move them closer . . . hell, I gave that turd a complete makeover. Only thing I left in place were the side bars where the saddle bags used to be—they were the only thing holding that rat bike together. In the end I did everything I could to make that Harley look outlaw, but ultimately no matter how much sugar you sprinkle on shit . . . it's still shit.

Even Jenna was embarrassed by that ugly duckling. The only cool thing about it, she pointed out, was that the pipes spit blue flames. Sad but true, my machine would take home the trophy for the ugliest bike in Green Nation two years in a row. And I never even entered the contest. The pig just got pushed up there for judging by a bunch of smart-asses. It was damn embarrassing, but at least I had a bike under my ass, and that meant I could finally ride with the Vagos and start some serious intelligence gathering for the ATF.

My first opportunity came a few weeks later when Big Roy announced that Terry the Tramp had decreed another national run—this time to a biker bar out near Yucca Valley, a community between Twentynine Palms and Palm Springs. The Vagos were going to gather in the desert with several other motorcycle clubs in support of some charitable cause like Save the Whales or Save the Tits. The Vietnam Vets would be there, so would several of the law enforcement clubs like the Blue Knights and the Choir Boys.

Law enforcement motorcycle clubs had chapters located all over the country. In California you had the Choir Boys in the High Desert and Los Angeles, the Blue Knights in Big Bear and San Bernardino, the Lords of Loyalty, started by the California Highway Patrol, in San Diego and the San Fernando Valley . . . the list went on and on.

On appearances alone, the only thing that separated a club cop from a motorcycle outlaw was the hair and the badge. In just about every other aspect they were the same animal. Both had chapters, bylaws, prospecting requirements and club patches. Hell, they even had similar mottos. The Vagos wore a patch on their cuts with the initials VFFV, which stood for "Vagos Forever, Forever Vagos." The Choir Boys have "Choir Boys Forever, Forever Choir Boys." And the Blue Knights? You guessed it: "Blue Knights Forever, Forever Blue Knights." More than one defense attorney, in support of an outlaw charged as a gang member, pointed out these similarities to a jury.

Not unlike one percenters, many cops growing up as social misfits find their identity as part of a brotherhood. And, make no mistake, law enforcement was most definitely a brotherhood. Sometimes the line between cops and outlaws gets so blurred that it's hard to identify one from the other. When a California motorcycle officer was killed on duty a few years ago, the Choir Boys showed up at his funeral wearing sleeveless shirts, denim vests and bandanas. Lot of those boys were closer to the outlaws they were trying to bust than they'd like to admit.

Cops and criminals. The blue line was very thin, indeed.

When I called Uncle Johnny Law to let him know about the upcoming desert run, he thought it was a great opportunity to gather intelligence. My handler was especially interested in learning more about the recent murder of Dennis "Shorty" Daoussis up in Landers. So we made plans to meet the following afternoon at the Little Luau Hawaiian BBQ in Beaumont, a restaurant fourteen miles north of Hemet, where John would set me up with some state-of-the-art recording gear and offer some pointers on how to avoid getting my ass killed.

This would be my first real test in a long process of collecting criminal evidence against the Vagos, but not the first time I'd gone out wired. That had happened two weeks earlier when John sent me into the Lady Luck just to get "the feel" of what it was like to wear a recording device. My handler hadn't been after information. He'd just wanted me to hang out for a few minutes and shoot the shit with Big Roy and the boys.

We sat in the front seat of John's Expedition in a secluded location while he hooked me up. And my first thought was, *Man, if this is what I've got to wear, I'm done.* There was a recorder, maybe the length and width of two cigarette packs, held to my chest by a Velcro strap that went around my body. A wire microphone that came off the recorder was taped to my skin. I swear it felt like a scene from *The Godfather*. John was outfitting me old-school—not the way they do it nowadays—and it was terrifying.

And it wasn't just the size of that chunk of metal on my body that had me spooked. Unlike trained government agents, informants are rarely comfortable when they first wear a recording device. There's that initial, almost paralyzing fear of being found out. Even the tiniest device hidden on the body can seem gigantic to an untrained CI. You feel the thing, you know where it's at and the only thing you want to do is hide that recorder where no one can find it—and if that means shoving it up your ass, well, so be it. I swear you can stand and have a conversation with someone a thousand times and it all flows smooth and natural, but strap on a recording device and suddenly you're acting a little strange and the person you're talking to wonders why you're sweating and talking gibberish.

Or at least that's the way it seemed to me.

"You sure that's a good spot?" I said as John finished placing the microphone.

"It's a good spot."

"But how do you know?"

"I know because I've done this a few times in my life. This spot is good. I know it works here. Just relax, George. You're going in there for a low-key conversation, that's all. There's no pressure."

"Easy for you to say. What if they search me?"

"Why would they search you?"

"How the fuck should I know? You're the expert."

"They're not gonna search you, dude." John paused to study me a moment. "Look, I know you're nervous. And that's understandable. Everybody gets nervous at first. But, trust me, the more you do this, the easier it gets."

He went back to taping.

"You ever get caught with one of these on you?" I wanted to know.

"Nope. Never have. There was this one time when I was wearing a shirt that was too tight and you could see the wire under it. And I'm sweating, so the tape keeps coming loose and I have to keep patting my chest to keep it from slipping. The dude I'm talking to is looking at me like I've lost my mind."

"What happened?" I asked.

"Nothing. The mic finally came off and slipped down my pant leg." He finished taping the wire. "In the old days I used to strap the recorder right to my balls. I figured those guys weren't keen on searching my nuts."

"That sounds pretty good to me," I said through a tight smile.

John grinned and handed me my flannel shirt. "This will work just fine."

"Yeah, sure. Remind me again why we're doing it this way?"

"Because this is about interacting with the people you're recording. Getting comfortable with that feeling. If you can pop your cherry with this device, the other shit we've got for you will be a piece of cake." John paused a moment, then added, "Trust me, George, I wouldn't let you go in there if I thought it was dangerous."

"Oh, no?" I said, voice dripping with sarcasm.

"Not unless you freak out and rip your shirt off or something. You're not gonna do that, are you?"

"Rip my shirt off? No. But I might piss in my pants."

I opened the passenger's door.

"Remember," he said as I left the car, "no pressure. Just act natural."

Natural my ass. I climbed into my truck and drove to the Lady Luck. Before entering I lit a cigarette, took a deep breath, then stepped through the front door.

Swear to Christ, the instant I arrived it felt like every eyeball was on me. I just knew those boys could see and smell that big hunk of metal under my flannel shirt—the flannel shirt I was wearing on a hot day in Hemet. With a denim cut over it no less.

Within seconds I was sweating like a whore in church.

Big Roy and Iron Mike were in the shop that day, so was Jimbo, the muscle-head who supplied steroids to the chapter, and Ready, the tattoo artist who had recently been patched into the club. I fell into conversation with Iron Mike but don't remember a word we said. I just kept thinking that Vago knew what I was up to, that any second he would push me against the wall and pat me down. Of course, in hindsight, my fears were unfounded. At that point I was still a hang-around, and no club business was being discussed at Big Roy's place. Still, at that moment and in that context, the experience was incredibly nerve-wracking.

After what seemed an eternity, I walked out of the Lady Luck like a man who'd just finished a marathon. Man, you could have taken that flannel shirt and wrung it out right there on the sidewalk. But at least I'd done it. I'd passed my first test going wired.

Now it was time for the real deal.

The morning before the Vagos run to Yucca Valley, Old Joe and I piled into the company truck and headed off to do a job estimate. Along the way I told him about the meeting I was about to have with John Carr at the Hawaiian BBQ in Beaumont.

My friend went quiet, as was usual when this topic came up, and turned his gaze out the window. From the moment he'd found out I was working with the feds, Joe had kept his distance from me. And I understood that. I respected the man's position. But that didn't change the fact that I still wanted him on board. So I asked Joe to come meet Special Agent Carr at the Little Luau.

It was a long moment before he answered me in that easy drawl, slow and thick as molasses.

"You know I'm a nonviolent guy, George," he began. "I'm no rabble-rouser, and I've got no criminal record. I don't go looking for trouble, but it seems like that's where you're taking me."

"Hey, man, you know I'd never—"

"Hold on, brother," Joe interrupted. "Let me finish. I've been thinking about this for a while now. To be honest, I really didn't know whether I was going to stick around. I mean, somebody throws something like that at you, and you're thinking, *Wait a minute. I didn't sign up for this.* Understand what I'm saying?"

"Sure I do."

Joe's gaze wandered back to the window now. "But you've been more of a brother to me than my own flesh and blood. Every time I've needed help you've been there for me." He turned back to me. "You're my only true friend, George. You've always stuck by me, so I'm sticking by you. From here on out, whatever happens, happens to the two of us. Okay?"

And that's where we left it. Old Joe and I never spoke of the matter again. From that day forward, my buddy was on board.

Around noon we drove up to Beaumont and found a table in the Little Luau. John Carr wasn't there yet. An hour later he still hadn't shown up.

One thing I quickly learned about working with Special Agent Carr—the man was chronically late. John finally arrived without apology, ordered the beef teriyaki combo, and got down to business. And because Old Joe was at the table, he was the first topic up for discussion.

"George didn't give me much of an option with you," John said to him. "The cat's out of the bag and there's no putting it back in again, is there?"

"No, sir, I guess not," Joe replied. "And I understand your concern, Agent Carr. But George knows I'm a man of my word. My father was a minister. He raised me honest. And if I tell you I'll keep your secret, you can count on it."

That was good enough for my handler. After some meaningless talk, the two shook hands, and Old Joe grabbed the truck keys and headed out to the parking lot to give us some privacy.

"He's a good man. You stick with him," John said the moment Joe was through the door. "My dad always told me women will come and go in your life, but your true friends will be the ones who are there with you in the end. I think that fits your buddy to a tee."

My stint as a working CI was about to begin, and John wanted to give me a crash course on how to survive in a very dangerous business. As the handler, John would be keeping tabs from a distance. But fact of the matter was, as an informant, I was pretty much on my own. When things go wrong for a CI, they can go wrong fast. By the time the cavalry arrives, there's little to do but clean up the mess.

Informants die. That's the nature of the beast. And that's the risk Special Agent Carr wanted me to understand. We left the restaurant and piled into his Ford Expedition. I shouted out the window to Old Joe that we'd be back in a half hour, and off we drove.

"We need hard information, George," John explained as we headed in the direction of San Bernardino. "And there's no detail too small. I can't stress how important that is. Details are what can make or break a case. Some actionable intelligence we learn tomorrow may connect up to something we get two or three months down the road. It's like a puzzle, and if enough of that puzzle comes together, we've got a chance to get these guys on a RICO."

The Racketeer Influenced and Corrupt Organizations Act was orig-inally intended to prosecute the Mafia, but the government expanded its use in the late 1970s to include outlaw motorcycle gangs. The Vagos were already classified as a criminal gang thanks to California's S.T.E.P. Act, which also slapped convicted outlaws with gang enhancement penalties, effectively doubling a man's sentence.

But under RICO, all of Green Nation could be brought to its knees. If I could gather enough indictable evidence to show a pattern of orga-nized criminal behavior on the part of the Vagos, the leadership could very well be prosecuted and the entire club dismantled.

Problem was, proving a racketeering case in court against an outlaw motorcycle gang was no cinch.

The feds had already tried that gambit in 1979, when they indicted Sonny Barger and members of the Oakland chapter of the Hells Angels. But the prosecution was unable to prove that the Angels had conspired on an organizational level to break the law of the land. More recently, the Los Angeles field division of the ATF had gathered enough evidence against the Mongols Motorcycle Club to shut it down under RICO and have all the club's trademarks confiscated.

But that case was overturned on appeal.

No question RICO was a powerful hammer against organized crime. But it was also powerfully hard to prosecute outlaw motorcycle clubs using that federal statute.

"Here's what I want you to remember, George," John explained. "It's okay to ask questions, but stay in your comfort zone. Let it come natural. Don't press these guys to talk. If it doesn't feel right, it probably isn't. So just take it slow."

"Got it," I said.

We arrived back at the Little Luau to find Joe snoozing in the truck on the other side of the lot. John threw his car into park and turned off the ignition.

"I want you to know I've brought in a task force deputy with the L.A. County Sheriff's Department to work this case with us. An undercover guy. One of the best in the business. He'll be out there with you."

"How will I know him?"

"You won't. He'll look just like any other outlaw. But he knows who you are, and he'll be watching your back."

Later I'd meet a few of these undercover lawmen. And John was right. You'd never know they were cops to look at them. They looked like outlaws, rode like outlaws and drank like outlaws . . . and no outlaw was ever the wiser. They were the intel boys. They never came out, they were always under. They'd shake your hand, hop on their Harleys and ride back to the office to type their reports.

"And I'll be there too," John continued. "I'm sure you'll see me around. Whatever you do, don't fucking wave to me."

"How 'bout this?"

I flipped him the middle finger.

John smiled, then quickly grew serious again. "Just remember what we've talked about. Keep things casual. And don't forget about this guy, Daoussis. Somebody with the San Bernardino chapter knows who killed him."

"I'll do what I can."

John reached into the backseat and came forward with a wooden box.

"I know how much you were looking forward to that microphone I had you wearing at the Lady Luck." He smiled. "But I think you'll like this even better."

It was the recording device that would become my trusted partner for the duration of my time undercover. This wasn't some hunk of metal from those old Mafia movies, with the recorder strapped to the chest. No, sir. This was real high-tech, science-fiction-type stuff. I had audio. I had video. George was beaming to the satellites, baby! I can't get more specific than that; too many agents and informants are still using it in the field. Let's just say that even if the Vagos had known what to look for, they wouldn't have found it.

You know, on second thought—and this is for the Warlocks, Pagans, Outlaws, Mongols, Angels and all you other one percenters out there— we hide that gear up our ass, fellas.

Go fish.

I hopped out of the Expedition and headed for the truck. John called before I'd gone too far.

"Oh, hey, George. One more thing."

I came back and leaned through the open window.

"I've named the operation. I'm calling it Twenty-Two Green. What do you think?"

I thought that sounded pretty cool. Look out, motherfuckers. I've got your color and I've got your number.

Operation 22 Green. Oh, yeah . . . that's my baby.

10

Wired

The Vagos rumbled east on the I-10 through the San Gorgonio Pass, then turned north on the Twentynine Palms highway, passing beyond the mountains and into the brick-red hills of the Mojave. Although I didn't realize it at the time, this was the same track Kilo and Rhino had followed as they'd hauled Dennis "Shorty" Daoussis in the bed of Kilo's pickup, rolled in a carpet and headed for execution.

Hanging with the Vagos was not my idea of keeping good company, but I must admit I enjoyed running with the herd during my time undercover. Man, if you love riding motorcycles like I do, there's nothing like screaming down a highway with a pack of Harleys rolling in tight formation, front tire a foot off the wheel of the man in front, hands high on the bars and the straight pipes clapping like thunder. It's one hell of a head rush.

I would have enjoyed the ride even more had I not been aboard that shit-ass Touring Classic the feds stuck me with. As I shook, rattled and rolled down that desert highway, my machine was throwing off parts like a mutt shedding fleas. There goes the muffler, bye-bye taillight, off went the peg beneath my foot. The poor bastards cruising behind me were zigging, zagging and cursing as they dodged my flying debris.

But losing that rat bike one piece at a time was not my primary concern as we thundered toward Yucca Valley. Nope. I had much bigger problems—because ol' Crash was running right beside me.

Thing is, when you were barrel-assin' along the open road at ninety miles per hour you really wanted to trust the rider in the saddle next to you. Unfortunately, because we were both prospects, that man was usually Crash . . . and that crazy sonofabitch scared the hell out of me. The entire trip I'd been cheating my wheels ahead of his, because no way did I want to get caught running behind that uncoordinated fuck.

I was just beginning to think I was home free when, sure enough, there went Crash. I veered away sharply as he bounced off the blacktop and his Harley went somersaulting down the road, throwing off pieces of chrome and steel. It was a miracle no one else went down, because I'd witnessed that ugly scene before. I'd watched packs with over two hundred riders suddenly fly all to pieces, men and machines tumbled and tossed like jacks across the freeway. And when something like that happened and the dust settled, it was like bloody carnage across a battlefield.

As we hauled Crash's busted carcass off the pavement, the first word out of his mouth was "pothole."

Bullshit. There was no fuckin' pothole. That was just Crash doing what Crash always did best.

After the pack dusted itself off, we started north again on the highway. Just as we were approaching Yucca Valley, a shitbox sedan with missing hubcaps appeared ahead, steering close to the road's apron to allow the horde to pass. When it came my turn, I was surprised to see John Carr behind the wheel.

His hand was raised against his chest and he was flipping me the finger.

The pack veered off the highway and started down a long dirt road that plugged straight into our destination—a biker bar out in the middle of the desert. Several Vagos chapters were there when we arrived, along with riders from the Vietnam Vets and some of the law enforcement clubs. Can't remember for sure which ones, but I believe the Blue Knights were there.

I dismounted the Harley and was about to rest my saddle-sore ass when I heard the words I would come to dread.

"Hey, prospect!"

Some bearded asshole with Loki on his back was pointing toward a Porta Potty standing out among the rocks.

"Climb up on that shit-shed over there and sing us the prospect song!"

The Prospect Song.

Fuck.

Like I've said, when a patched member gives a prospect an order, you follow it—no matter how humiliating. I climbed onto a boulder, then pulled myself onto the roof of one of the portable toilets scattered throughout the property. And there, atop my magnificent Porta Potty stage, I faced an audience of two to three hundred bikers and began to sing . . .

"I am a Vagos prospect, as you can clearly see . . ."

As I sang atop that portable toilet I recall thinking that Old Joe had been right: signing up with ATF had been a really dumbass move.

That's about when the shed began to tip.

I shifted my weight quickly, but it was already too late. Gravity had me. All of a sudden I was going one way, the shit-shed was headed the other, and what had been dumped from hundreds of bowels and bladders went splashing across the desert. The audience must've loved it, though, judging by the cheers and applause that followed my big finish.

I needed a fucking drink.

As the bikers cleared a wide path to the bar, I spotted a familiar face among them. It was that young sheriff from Riverside, my stalker with a badge who'd flown a helicopter all the way to Los Angeles to win me over. The lawman was trying to blend in with the crowd, but the scowl aimed my way was pretty obvious. John Carr had told the sheriff I'd decided against becoming an informant. Yet here I was riding with the Vagos, and the bloom was off the rose. I ignored my spurned lover, wiped shit from my shoes and entered the bar.

The interior was crammed shoulder to shoulder with Vagos, vets, biker cops and women—and by women I mean Vagos old ladies and chicks wearing low-cut shirts and high-cut shorts. Oh, those groupies. Guess the patch and the Harley must have been some kind of aphrodisiac that made good girls want the bad boys. I swear you could take the ugliest motherfucker on the planet, stick a patch on his back and a motorcycle under his ass, and he'd have the hottest chicks in the bar hanging off his arm. Unfortunately in the outlaw world it wasn't uncommon for some of those young ladies to get pimped by the club. Females were little more than property to most of these guys, and they'd pass 'em around like puff pastries and chicken wings.

Over near the bar, Big Todd was engaged in conversation with a barrel-chested dude sporting thick, tattooed arms. This was Crusher, the sergeant detective from Cathedral City and president of the Vagos support club, The Green Machine. Todd waved me over, but I wasn't prepared to mingle just yet. My recording device had yet to be activated.

Besides, Sergeant Crusher made me nervous.

My prospect application had sailed through when that crooked cop had run it for red flags—the ATF had plenty of safeguards in place—but that didn't make me any more comfortable being around him. I was fine with Crusher busting his Mexican drug dealers and taking their money, but that fucker was part of the law enforcement fraternity, and cops talk to cops. There was always that chance—however slim—that somehow, someway, something might slip.

When I'd first mentioned Crusher to John Carr, he was surprised the sergeant and the other lawmen holding hands with the Vagos hadn't shown up on ATF's radar. John wanted to nail those dirty bastards in the worst way, especially Crusher. But the situation was tricky. If word got out that the sergeant was being internally investigated, the Vagos might get suspicious and start hunting for another snitch like Hammer. It was a serious operational security issue that John had yet to fully resolve.

I waved Todd off, then pushed through the packed house to the bathroom, where I waited in line for a toilet to open. Once inside the stall I activated the recording device, flushed the toilet and headed out again.

Slipping back into the crowd, I was having flashbacks to that nerve-wracking day I walked into the Lady Luck wearing that big-ass recorder strapped to my chest. But the nervousness evaporated as confidence grew. The recording device was practically undetectable, I realized, and no one was paying attention to me anyway. They couldn't care less about George Rowe. I was just another bald-headed, tattooed son-ofabitch in a room crawling with them. Before long I found myself pleasantly relaxed . . . maybe even a little bit cocky.

I headed with newfound confidence toward the bar. Crusher must have grown tired of buying Todd drinks and moved on, because Todd was looking around for his next victim. I swear, I don't think that son-ofabitch ever bought a round in his life. He couldn't hold a job, so his hands were always in someone else's pocket. Especially mine. I was Todd's personal ATM, constantly spitting cash. And it was all withdraw-als, man, never a deposit. For every buck that went out, not a damn cent came back. In the old days I would have backed a U-Haul to Big Todd's front door and cleaned house.

"Hey, Big George. Got twenty bucks I can borrow?"

"Make mine a Corona," I told him, handing over the Jackson.

I scanned the crowded bar as I waited on my beer and spotted Terry the Tramp sitting at a table in the far corner with some of the national officers. Sitting next to the international P was his secretary-treasurer, a burly Chicano with the name Ta Ta stitched over the right pocket of his cut. Ta Ta was a tough thirty-nine-year-old hombre who wouldn't hesitate to beat down another patch if he had it coming—even one of his own. But as far as I could tell, the man also had respect for the civilian world. At one of the big national runs, some no-class Vago had ripped off a vendor selling custom knives. Ta Ta ordered every patch to buy a knife from that civilian and apologize on behalf of the brother who'd ripped him off. I think if Ta Ta had been the man in charge, and known how Big Roy and his thugs were harassing the people of Hemet, he might have pulled their patches.

"Here you go, prospect."

Big Todd handed the bottle across to me—without change—and I wandered off toward Tramp's table for a closer look at "God." Standing guard over the club officers was Rhino. I felt that giant's gaze boring into me as I approached, but I avoided eye contact and found a wall to lean on. I was just close enough to overhear conversation at the table and figured the recording device would pick it up. John Carr told me the thing could snatch a whisper from across the room.

As I sipped beer and pretended not to listen, a burst of laughter from the table announced the arrival of a massive biker wearing a greasy T-shirt that read I SUPPORT THE VAGOS. This man-giant who strode from the crowd was probably late fifties, well over six feet tall and three hundred pounds, with a fat, bushy beard and hair flowing to the middle of his back.

Tramp shouted at him, "Hey, Bubba!" and stood to greet the big biker.

"How you been, Tramp?" boomed Bubba as the two clasped hands and hugged.

"When you comin' into the green?" Tramp chided him.

"Yeah, brother, you need to take a full patch," added Ta Ta from his seat.

"No disrespect, you know I love you guys, but that's not my bag," said the big biker, who then threw out his arms and said, "I want to ride the way I want to ride, when I want to ride."

"Fuckin' A," laughed Ta Ta as he clasped Bubba's meaty hand, adding, "no disrespect."

By asking around I learned Bubba was well known and well liked among the one percenters, just a friendly ol' bastard who loved to ride motorcycles. The big biker was tight with practically every stripe of Southern California outlaw: Vagos, Hells Angels, Mongols, Devil's Disciples—completely color blind when it came to the patch.

As Bubba bullshitted with Tramp I noticed Rhino watching me more closely, so I stopped holding up the wall and pushed my way back toward the bar. Big Todd was gone when I arrived, no doubt chasing his next free drink, but there was someone sitting at the far end that interested me: a Vago named Sammy who rode with the San Bernardino crew. Sammy was good buddies with North, the Hemet chapter's sergeant at arms, who was fencing stolen property for his brother from Berdoo.

I greeted him with a friendly "Hey, Sammy, how you doing, man?"

He was already half in the bag and didn't seem to recognize me at first. I squeezed in beside his stool and slapped a fraternal hand on his shoulder.

"It's George Rowe from Hemet, man."

"Oh, sure," said Sammy. "How you doin', brother?"

"I'm good. Heard you guys had some excitement in Berdoo, huh?"

"That right?"

"Yeah, I heard Hulk got busted."

Sammy turned away and resumed drinking.

"Don't know much about that."

I'd learn later that in fact Sammy knew everything about that. He'd paid three grand to Shorty for a stolen motorcycle that was never delivered, and ultimately that's what got that hang-around executed. Turned out Sammy was also in the truck with Rhino and Kilo as they drove toward Landers with poor Shorty rolled in a carpet like a bloody burrito. Sammy never made it, though. On the way to the execution he got cold feet and asked to be dropped off at a biker bar called The Crossroads.

Now here he sat as an unindicted accessory to murder.

Of course, I didn't know any of that at the time, but Sammy sure was fidgeting on his stool like he'd been a naughty boy.

"Yeah, man," I said after taking another swig of beer. "Think the cops busted Hulk for killing that hang-around in Landers."

I swear Sammy went white when he heard that.

"Don't know anything about it," he answered abruptly. Then he knocked back the rest of his drink and cleared the stool. As I watched Sammy disappear into the packed room, a muffled *pop* came from somewhere outside the bar.

Apparently everyone else heard it too, because heads snapped to attention like a herd of nervous antelope. All those outlaws, cops and vets knew exactly what that sound was.

A gunshot.

I fell in with the crowd as they funneled through the front door and emerged in the brilliant desert sunlight. I was drawn with the others

Rhino, Green Nation's international sergeant at arms.

toward a commotion in the parking lot but found myself blocked by a knot of pissed-off bikers. As I squeezed past them, I saw the reason for their anger—a wounded Vietnam vet lying bloody on the ground, cradled by one of his buddies. Some of the biker cops were surrounding the pair with guns drawn, and a bunch of revenge-minded vets were edging closer.

I asked the Vago next to me what happened.

"Fuckin' pig shot him."

"Why? What'd he do?"

"Not a goddamn thing," said a vet standing to my left. "The cop was disrespecting our brother, so he went after him. That's when the cop pulled his fuckin' gun."

"Pig gets a gun and a badge and thinks he's above the law," groused the Vago.

This was nervous time, man. There were a lot of angry bikers concealing weapons in that parking lot, and those cops were on the verge of reenacting Custer's Last Stand.

Within minutes there were sirens wailing over the desert. A line of cruisers soon appeared, roaring up the dirt road toward the bar, a cloud of dust boiling in their wake.

These were local police, and when they arrived on the tense scene their instincts were to give their fraternal brothers the benefit of the doubt. They had the biker cops put away their weapons, then cuffed the wounded vet on the ground.

An angry murmur spread through the crowd.

"You cocksuckers!" one outlaw shouted.

"They shit on our Constitution and wipe their friggin' asses with the Bill of Rights," grumbled another.

I'd heard that outlaw's lament before, but now I had it recorded. Special Agent Carr might appreciate that one.

A few days after the desert run, in what would become our weekly Friday ritual, John and I met at the Little Luau Hawaiian BBQ in Beaumont. I asked about the vet who got shot, but John hadn't heard any news. When lunch was over we headed out to his Expedition to download the recordings and switch out to a fresh device.

"I don't think there's much you can use there," I warned him as we piled into the car.

"You'd be surprised," said John.

Kilo, the San Bernardino chapter officer who assisted in the murder of "Shorty" Daoussis.

"It's like I told you before, sometimes what you think is meaningless turns out to be the most important thing."

"Yeah, well, I'm just saying."

John began setting up the device for download.

"So this guy Sammy was the only Berdoo member you spoke with?"

"There was one other patch, but he didn't say shit. I got the feeling Sammy knew something but not this other guy."

"What's this other guy's name?"

"Umm . . . don't remember. Don't think he ever told me."

John shot me a look of reproach.

"He's recorded?"

"Far as I know."

"Listen, George. It's critical when you're undercover to ID the voice. If you're talking to someone, say the name out loud. Same thing with a license plate. Say it so you've got it. If the recorder's not on, go somewhere and turn it on, then speak the name or the number or whatever. And don't try to keep it in your head, either. If you wait more than a day, forget it, you'll never remember."

"Fuck," I said, exasperated.

John smiled at this. "Don't worry, dude. You'll get the hang of it. Just remember, the case is in the details."

"Tell me again," I grumbled.

John ignored this. "Anyway, listen, there's operational security issues we need to discuss here. What do we do about this Cathedral City cop?"

"Crusher? Hey, man, that's your call. But he's goddamn scary. If it was up to me, I'd get rid of him."

"Yeah, I think you're right," replied John as he finished the download. "I'm going to talk to Stan Henry—he's the chief out there. I know he's got a huge interest in fighting gangs in the Coachella Valley. When he learns one of his men is working with the Vagos, he's gonna shit a brick."

Cops investigating cops. I was skeptical.

"You really think he'll go after one of his own?" I asked.

"Henry's a standup guy," replied John as he handed me a fresh device. "He'll get to the bottom of it. We've just got to step carefully and keep the source confidential. Last thing we need is your name floating around."

Couldn't have agreed more. One slip and George Edgar Rowe would crash and burn like the fuckin' Hindenburg.

11

My Love, My Nightmare

Back at the chicken coop, I was doing everything I could to get Jenna straightened out. I bought her a minivan and paid for her to go back to school to become a medical assistant. I also made sure she was clean long enough to pass her drug test with Child Protective Services, clearing the way to get her little girl back from Grandma, who still had custody.

Jenna's mom wasn't letting go of that kid without a fight, though. She loved her granddaughter and wanted to protect her, but she was also struggling mightily with demons of her own at the time. Grandma had been hooked on opiates ever since her two-week stay in a hospital burn ward, but there was something else I believe she got addicted to during the time she had custody of Sierra—the checks the state was cutting her for child care. The way I saw it, that woman just couldn't bear to part with that extra income, so we had to drag her to court.

"Know what one of my first memories of my mom was?" Jenna asked me the night before the first custody hearing. "I was six years old and my dad was driving me and my little sister around Big Bear looking for her because Mom hadn't come home the night before. He found her car parked in front of his friend's house and we all walked right into the bedroom and found them naked. My father left us right after that. We had this steep driveway with about two hundred stairs going down to it from the house, and I can still picture my mom standing on the deck and my dad walking down those stairs yelling at her, 'I'm finished. I am done with this,' and Mom's screaming, 'Please don't go.' I hated her for a long time after that."

"That why you left her?" I asked.

"I didn't leave because of Mom; I left because of the anal retentive asshole she married after my dad left. When I stopped listening to him he kicked me to the curb. Can't really blame him, I guess. I would have thrown me out too."

"How old were you?"

"Fourteen maybe. I called my dad and asked him to come get me. We ended up driving to Mexico because Mom called the cops and told them I was kidnapped."

I heard the rest of the story from Jenna's old man a few weeks later over beers and barbeque. If there was an "other side of the tracks" in Valle Vista, that's where Bill Thompson lived. The chief had a nice house out on Espirit Circle, where

Jenna's dad, Battalion Chief Bill Thompson of the Hemet Fire Department.

I'd occasionally go to prune trees as a favor. Afterward we'd head to the backyard and spend the hours drinking beer, eating burgers and trying to figure out his mixed-up kid—what some might call an exercise in futility.

Bill told me that after gaining custody of his daughter, he tried hard to make up for the time he'd lost with her. He bought Jenna new clothes, paid her an allowance—gave her just about anything she asked for. And because his little girl was a free spirit with the heart of a rebel, he allowed Jenna the freedom to find her own way.

Unfortunately her way was a total fuckin' disaster.

Didn't start out that way, though. Sophomore year in high school Jenna was taking advanced classes and nailing every one of them, getting straight As right down the line and setting herself up for a four-year college scholarship. But when she failed to make the cheer squad and was eliminated from the dance team ("Guess I wasn't peppy enough," she once told me) the girl latched on to the punk rock crowd instead.

One night at a party someone told her she could drink all night and never pass out if she just smoked a little meth. Well, that was the beginning of a very long slide. Didn't help that Daddy's work schedule was a drug abuser's dream. The chief was on duty twenty-four hours a day for eight days straight, which left plenty of time for his wild child to get naughty. By her junior year Jenna was heavy into heroin, and Bill Thompson had lost control.

"I was a hateful, selfish bitch who didn't care about anyone but me," Jenna once told me. "I didn't think about the future. I didn't want to think about the past. I just lived for the moment. And the moment I lived for was getting fucked up."

With her drug use spiraling out of control, Bill tried shipping Jenna to her mother. Her mother shipped her right back again. The situation at home went from bad to worse when the chief started finding bent spoons in the silverware drawer that his daughter was using to cook heroin. Money and valuables began disappearing from the house. Jenna even tried cutting the lock off Bill's Dyna Wide Glide, hoping to fence his motorcycle to finance her drug habit.

It all came to a head one day in 1998 when she stood on the second-floor balcony, picked up a potted plant and threw it over the banister, smashing it at her father's feet.

"What the hell is wrong with you?!" he shouted up at her.

"I'm a fucking heroin addict, that's what's wrong with me!" she screamed back at him.

That kicked off Jenna's first stint in rehab, but the girl's heart was never in it. Some old habits die hard, even for the young, and before long she was right back to using. Through the years that girl has been detoxed seven times, and seven times she's relapsed into drugs. I watched a friend suffer through that ten-day process once, and it ain't pretty. About six hours after last use the chills begin. And because heroin plugs up the internal plumbing, once the intestines clear it's bombs away. The mad shits are followed by nausea, wild temperature swings and intense body aches from head to toe. Hell, Jenna claimed even her hair hurt going through detox.

When she was eighteen years old she once tried detoxing on her own. Things got so bad that she asked her boyfriend, a Mexican drug dealer named Angel, to pack her in a moving box and seal it with tape. Jenna sat inside that box for six hours, curled up in a fetal position and shaking uncontrollably.

After rehab failed, Bill Thompson couldn't take it anymore. Rather than continue to enable his daughter, he finally put his foot down and kicked her out of the house.

"That ripped my guts out," he told me over backyard beers. "To watch my child walking down the street not knowing where she was going. That might have been the hardest day of my life."

Bill lost track of Jenna after that. She vanished into Southern California's underground drug scene. Before I entered the picture, he used to drive around the city in the dead of night, wondering whether his child was still alive. It was only after Jenna moved in with me that he quit those late-night rambles.

He said I let him sleep again.

"My daughter and I have this classic love-hate thing going on," Bill told me one afternoon. "I used to have to remind myself there were two Jennas. There was the free spirit with a kind heart that I just loved and adored, and then there was this other person that I absolutely hated."

"Yeah, I've met Satan's child a few times myself," I told him. "Especially first thing in the morning."

The chief laughed. "When we lived together I had a second phone line installed in her room just so I wouldn't have to go in there. I used to call to wake her up. It was safer that way."

"I hear you, man."

"That's pretty common with addicts," said Bill. "It's all part of protecting addictive behavior. Forces people to leave them alone so they can do whatever they want."

"Well, it sure works with me." I grinned.

Bill got quiet and sipped his beer. After a long moment he said, "Think I created a monster, George."

"Naw. It's not your fault, man. You've done your best. It's up to Jenna to help herself."

"Not sure she's capable," he replied. "I'm hoping maybe you can get through to her."

I smiled and shook my head. "I do what I can. But nobody controls Jenna but Jenna."

"You know what's sad?" said Bill. "I really believe my little girl could do just about anything she wants to in this life. She's that intelligent. But every time something good happens for her she seems to sabotage it. It's like she doesn't think she deserves happiness. I just don't get it."

With Jenna certified clean and sober by the state of California, regaining custody of Sierra from Grandma was just a formality. At the hearing, the judge awarded legal custody to the mother, and I had myself one more piece of Samsonite to add to my growing collection.

Man, if I could buy a ticket on the Wayback Machine and travel back in time, I'd bend over and boot myself in the ass. I mean, what the hell was I thinking? Here I was trying to infiltrate one of the most violent motorcycle gangs on the planet and I was wet-nursing a dope addict twenty-two years my junior and changing poopie diapers on a two-year-old.

While Jenna attended school, the job of minding Sierra fell to me and Old Joe. My buddy had had kids of his own and basically knew what to do, but I didn't have a fucking clue. When it came to diapers I was okay with pee, but whenever it shot out the other end my head went straight into the toilet. Got to the point where I couldn't pay the prostitute next door enough to come over and clean up the kid's messes.

So now it was "Three's Fuckin' Company" inside that shack at Valle Vista, with Old Joe stewing in the trailer outside, completely disgusted with the whole turn of events. My buddy loved little Sierra, but he was no fan of her mother, and Jenna wasn't thrilled with having him around either. I overheard the two of them arguing over me once—although Old Joe is so damn mellow it's a bit like quarreling with a fence post.

"I'm sticking by George no matter what," he was telling her. "We're partners."

"I'm the only partner George needs," Jenna fired back. "You need to move. Why don't you man up and go home to your kids and say I'm sorry I'm an alcoholic and a drug addict."

"Well, Buttercup," said Joe slowly, "I ain't exactly proud of where I'm at. But I can tell you this much. I've been through George's girl-friends before you, and I'll be here when you're gone."

That shut her up.

So now we were a family. A somewhat dysfunctional family, to be sure, but a family nonetheless. The all-too-infrequent stretches when Jenna was clean and feeling good about having her daughter back were a pleasure. But one or two pills would drive her right back over the edge again—a reality that weighed heavily on both of us.

"I know how I think of my mom and what her addiction has done to me," Jenna said to me as she was putting Sierra to bed one night. "And I think of how my little sister should look up to me but doesn't. I want to break that chain with my little girl. I don't want her doing to me what I did to my mom. I don't think I could bear it."

"Hey, it's a choice," I said. "I chose to stop. So can you."

She shook her head. "That might have worked for you, George, but that's not who I am. I'll always be an addict. If I touch heroin once I'll be strung out for three days. If I do it once today I'll do it twice tomorrow. I could get addicted to soap if I liked it enough."

"That's a cop-out," I told her.

She sat heavily on the couch beside me, looking much older than her twenty-two years. "I should be dead, you know."

"Join the club."

"I'm serious," she said in earnest. "I've lost five really close friends. We all made it out of our teen years, but heroin killed them right after that. So why am I still here? I've done just as much shit as they did. Maybe even more. I've tried overdosing a bunch of times and didn't care if I ever came back."

"You tried to commit suicide?"

She shook her head. "It wasn't like I wanted to die, but I really didn't care if that's how it ended, you understand? I never said I better not do too much because it might kill me. It was always, give me more . . . give me more."

12

Aspirin, a Tampon and a Gun

The story goes that back in the early 1980s the P of the Venice Beach Vagos, a one percenter named Crazy Johnny, was riding down Mexico way looking to get laid when he came across a bunch of Chicanos wearing handmade Vagos patches. When Johnny reported the news back to national, a fact-finding delegation was dispatched to find out just what the hell was going on south of the border.

Prophet, the national P at the time, was informed that as many as thirty Mexicans in the border city of Mexicali were practically begging to be anointed Vagos. After Prophet extracted a promise that they would faithfully observe all Vagos rules and regulations, he made their wish come true. Eventually another nine Vagos chapters would take root along the U.S.-Mexico border.

Almost from the moment those border chapters became established, Crazy Johnny and his Venice boys were running toys and stuffed animals down to the little bambinos. This turned out to be excellent public relations for Green Nation, and the club soon jumped on the good citizen bandwagon back in the States, adopting the Boys & Girls Clubs of America as their charities of choice. Members were expected to contribute food, clothing and toys to those organizations, but most of the younger outlaws hated that PR bullshit. They'd have preferred to blow a sawbuck on a few beers rather than on a stuffed pussy cat. But the family men had their hearts in it. Least I know Crazy Johnny did.

When Johnny announced another toy run to Mexico, this time to Mexicali, Big Roy decided to include the Hemet chapter. The ATF got a little nervous about that. United States jurisdiction ends once you cross into Mexico, which meant I was unprotected and on my own down there. But the situation couldn't be helped—wherever the P said to ride, that's where you rode. So off I went with the Hemet and Venice Beach boys, ready to party hearty with our Chicano brothers down Mexicali way.

Man, let me tell you about those Mexicali Vagos. If those dudes could scrounge two wheels together and strap on a lawn mower engine, they could ride for Green Nation. I've seen fat-assed Mexicans sputtering along on rusty mopeds, for chrissakes. It could get damn comical, but most of our amigos south of the border were dirt poor, barely able to rub two pesos together, much less afford a Harley.

When the Vagos thundered into Mexicali that day, it seemed like the whole town turned out to greet us like conquering heroes. They were especially hot for Crazy Johnny and his bad boys from Venice Beach, who wore trench coats when they rode, often with weapons concealed underneath. The Venice chapter was popular in the border towns because they always came bearing gifts.

"Viva Los Vagos!" cheered the townspeople. Then the city mayor and the chief of police threw us a big fiesta right on the main drag.

A pig was untied, its throat slit and the body dumped straight into a cauldron of boiling water. The Mexicans didn't even gut the damn thing. That little piggy bloated up so big its intestines came spurting out its asshole. Well, no way was I eating that rude shit, so I walked around the corner to a bar where some of the Vagos had gone to drink and raise a little hell.

I gotta tell you, man, there was nothing like those border town cantinas. Some crazy shit went on behind those walls. Over in Tijuana, I once saw Big Todd getting a blow job from a hot Mexican chick who wasn't all she appeared to be. Fuckin' Todd thought he was a lady killer, but when that "chick" bent over to suck cock, a pecker fell out of his dress that was longer than Todd's!

About thirty miles east of Tijuana, in the border town of Tecate, was another Mexican bar where Buckshot earned his Vagos road name at the business end of a shotgun. The way I heard it told, some drunk patch holder made the mistake of pissing off the bar owner. There was some yelling and screaming, mostly in Spanish, and the owner reached for his 12-gauge. Next thing you knew, those greenies came tear-assin' out of that establishment like rats deserting a sinking ship.

Right behind them, chasing them into the street, came the owner, waving his shotgun. As the Vagos were hightailing it out of town— BAWOOOM!—that pissed-off Chicano pulled the trigger and let fly a barrel of buckshot.

Only one bike caught that broadside—a brand-new Harley-Davidson that still had its paper license plate on the back. Needless to say, poor Buckshot's pride and joy was duly baptized and the man had himself a road name for life—or at least for the life he had left. Maybe that angry Mexican couldn't kill that ol' Vago, but cancer sure as hell did. Within three years Buckshot was dead and gone.

Long before Buckshot went into the ground, I attended so many Vagos funerals that I lost count. Members were always dropping like flies; cancer, heart attacks, bike accidents, car accidents—I once paid respects at three services in one day. When a Vago bit the dust, his chapter buddies would remove anything green from his house— anything and everything that had a Vagos logo on it, including T-shirts, bandanas, belts . . . even Vagos shit belonging to his old lady. Then the brothers would rummage through the pile, picking out what they wanted and burning the rest. I've seen send-offs where a fallen brother's cut was lit on fire and another where a motorcycle was doused with gasoline and torched like a dead Viking's longship. Once the ceremonies were concluded, the entire membership would jump on their choppers and ride for some bar to hoist a few farewell toasts—which, of course, was just another excuse to get shitfaced. One of Terry the Tramp's favorite spots for these solemn occasions was the Screaming Chicken Saloon.

The Screaming Chicken, found north of San Bernardino in the town of Devore, was a 1940s vintage gas station converted into a biker bar. A hard-core outlaw with a thousand miles of crud on him might walk in, take in the stink and the filth of the place, and think he'd died and gone to biker heaven.

Terry the Tramp liked the Screaming Chicken for a few reasons, but I suspect convenience had the most to do with it. The bar was easily accessible off the I-15, only thirty miles south of Tramp's home in the High Desert. The international P could cruise down in his Corvette, enjoy a few free rounds of beer on his brothers, then motor back home again.

On a scorching hot day in early summer, Tramp and another two hundred or so Vagos had jammed the saloon for another fond farewell to a fallen brother. But the sweltering heat and stink of dirt and body odor made staying inside unbearable. So I wandered out the door for some fresh air, passing a knot of old-timers in greasy Levi's gathered around an island where the gas pumps once stood.

The Screaming Chicken Saloon in Devore, home of "hot babes" and "cold beer."

Right away I recognized big Bubba, Tramp's biker buddy that I'd seen at the Yucca Valley bar a few months before. Bubba was standing next to Quickie John, the P of the Norco chapter, who was lounging on a bench seat ripped from a pickup truck. All sorts of discarded shit was spread outside the Screaming Chicken for lounging on: milk crates, fifty-gallon drums, even a rusty wheelchair. Kicking back in that wheelchair was the P of the Vagos Riverside chapter, an old-timer named Blackie. Standing next to Blackie was his longtime buddy 37, head of the Mojave chapter. Blackie and 37 were "forever brothers," a breed apart among motorcycle outlaws. Typically forever brothers had been riding with a club thirty or forty years. Like "nomads"—outlaws unaffiliated with any chapter—a forever brother often rode alone and answered to no one. In the world of the one percenter, be they Mongols, Devils Disciples, Hells Angels or Vagos, a patch on a man's cut that spelled out FOREVER marked him as a man of respect—a man whose words carried the kind of weight only a lifelong outlaw commanded.

"Hey, prospect!"

37 was waving me over. As a prospect, it was an honor to be hailed by a forever brother, so I strutted over with high expectations. What I didn't realize was that the mischievous old bastard was about to fuck with me, turning a leisurely afternoon of beer drinking into a goddamn three-ring circus.

"Check this out, prospect," 37 said to me. "I want you to get me some aspirin."

"Got one right here, 37," I replied, searching through my pockets.

As a prospect you were expected to always carry items that a patch might need in a pinch; needle and thread, bandages, spark plugs, aspirins . . . you never knew what those boys might ask for. I handed that graybeard two aspirins but wasn't prepared for what came next.

"Whoa, hold on a second," said 37 as I turned to leave. "Bring me a tampon too."

I stood dumbfounded as Blackie, Quickie and Bubba grinned and chuckled.

"That a problem?" asked 37, straight-faced.

"No problem," I answered and started off again.

"And a gun!" 37 shouted before I could enter the Screaming Chicken. I turned back, waiting to see if this was a joke. The old fuck wasn't laughing.

"What are you waiting for?!" he yelled. "You heard what I said. I want a tampon and a gun. Now get the fuck outta here."

Dutifully, I started on my fool's errand. I figured the tampon was just a matter of asking some Vagos old lady for a loaner, but the gun was definitely going to be a problem. I spotted Crazy Johnny, the P of the Venice chapter, over near the bar and hustled in his direction.

"Hey, Johnny, 37 asked me to bring him a gun."

"What for?"

"Dunno. I think he's just bustin' my balls."

"Well, you go tell 37 you ain't gonna put him in prison."

I knew that answer wouldn't fly, so I started making inquiries up and down the bar, getting strange looks from the clientele, as if a pecker had sprung from my forehead. But just when all seemed lost, some chick at the bar miraculously announced, "Hey, I have a gun."

She pulled it from her handbag. Granted, it was green plastic and squirted water, but I didn't give a rat's ass. Far as I was concerned, it was a goddamn gun.

Recognizing a desperate man, the bitch held me up for twenty bucks. But I paid that ransom, took the squirt gun and burrowed my way back through the crowded bar until I stumbled upon old Buckshot.

"37 asked me to bring him a tampon. Can you help a brother out?"

"Don't you ask me for no tampons, you dirty bastard."

"I'm not asking you, Buckshot. But how 'bout your old lady?"

Buckshot looked over to where his woman was chatting with some of the VOLs and grinned. "Be my guest," he said. "And good luck."

Buckshot's old lady declined my request with a playful slap in the face, but North's woman came through and handed me a tampon from her bag. Shopping list complete, I hurried outside to where 37 was waiting.

"Took you long enough," the old bastard groused.

"Sorry, 37," I said and proudly offered the items he'd sent me for. "Look, I got you a tampon and a gun."

37 took one look at the squirt gun and shouted above the din, "This motherfucker's trying to give me a gun! He's a fuckin' fed!"

That good ol' boy was screwing with me, but no one else knew that. Out of nowhere one of the Norco hang-arounds blindsided me with a sucker punch to the jaw. After I regained my bearings and realized who my assailant was, I beat that hang-around into the ground.

Now here came Big Roy and I was in trouble again.

The Hemet P dragged my ass around the corner of the building and started chewing me out. Quickie John soon joined the fun, pissed that the same guy who'd waylaid his vice president's nephew with a cast had now beat the snot out of one of his hang-arounds.

I felt a hand on my shoulder and turned to find 37. "Hey, relax, boys," said the forever brother. "I was just fucking with this prospect here. And you know, Quickie, he got hit pretty good by your boy. But I guess if you've got a problem with that you should talk to Tramp."

"Maybe I will," growled Quickie John.

Sure enough, in a few minutes the little garden gnome arrived, potbelly sticking out and that stringy white hair hanging to the shoulders.

"Prospect," Tramp says to me right off. "Is it true you hit one of Quickie's hang-arounds?"

"Yeah, but he hit me first," I protested like a first-grader.

Quickie jumped in with, "We should let all the prospects fuck him up."

Tramp thought a moment. "You know, that sounds like a pretty good idea."

Well, that was all Quickie John needed to hear. Wasting no time, he gathered all the prospects he could find for a good old-fashioned ass whooping. Before those boys could have at me, though, the international P issued a new directive.

"Now wait a minute, Quickie. All at once doesn't seem fair. Maybe we should have them fight one at a time." Tramp glanced over at me. "That work for you, prospect?"

"If that's the way you want to play it," I told him.

"Alright, Quickie," ordered Tramp. "Let's take this out back and line 'em up."

The crowd marched through the bar and out the side door into the open yard. Quickie John got to work making sure all his biggest bruisers were up front. It was time for a little one-on-one gladiatorial combat at the Screaming Chicken Saloon.

And those poor bastards didn't stand a chance.

Throughout my teen years and into my twenties, if I wasn't finding a fight, a fight was usually finding me. One night in the town of Winchester I got into a brawl outside a hamburger stand with three men, whipped two of them and ran off the third. Some dude ordering a burger saw the whole thing and suggested I should fight for a living. I didn't think anything more of it until I bumped into the same guy at a bar a few months later and we got to talking.

He told me about an underground fight circuit, illegal in the state of California, where bookies arranged bareknuckle matches. It was cage fighting before the cages . . . only more brutal. These were two men pounding each other toe-to-toe until one gave up or couldn't continue. There were no rounds. No referees.

"There's two hundred fifty bucks in it for you if you're interested," the man said.

I figured why not.

This was at the tail end of my U-Haul Bandit days and I was looking for a way out of the drug racket. I'd dabbled in landscaping and tree trimming, but not many upstanding citizens were willing to hire convicted felons, so the fight game seemed a sensible alternative. The man jotted down an address, date and time on a piece of paper and handed it to me.

And so began my bareknuckle phase.

That Saturday night I drove out to a bowling alley in Riverside that had closed for the evening. But the door was open, so I stepped inside to find a small crowd of maybe forty people gathered under a haze of cigar and cigarette smoke. Right away I recognized the dude from Winchester, hobnobbing with a group of bettors. He broke away and greeted me with a handshake. As we spoke, I noticed the others sizing me up like a colt at auction. In a moment the bookie approached, a chubby bastard with a stump cigar between his teeth, a Tupperware tumbler filled with whiskey in his hand and a stink about him that almost made me gag. There were only two rules, the bookie explained; no biting and no poking in the eyes.

My opponent was waiting for me in an open space in front of the snack bar, where the tables had been pushed aside to create a makeshift ring. The fighter looked to be in his late twenties—a little older than me at the time—wearing a tank top and shorts. I wore a T-shirt, Levi's and a new pair of Nikes, which I removed because I didn't want to get them bloody.

We shook hands, then someone clapped and the match was on.

As we circled each other I could tell by the cheers that the big money was on my opponent—nobody was giving the new guy much of a shot. I finally got tired of the dance and met the man halfway. He came in close, took a swing. As the punch missed, my foot flashed toward his temple and struck the side of his head faster than he could raise his hand to block it.

The kick that coldcocked my opponent was a move taught to me by my old martial arts instructor, Mr. Lee. I'd practiced it countless times when I was a kid, and countless more as I got older. I'd jump and kick door headers from a standing position . . . broke my toes doing that once. To condition my feet I walked through parking lots booting concrete barriers. For my legs it was broom handles, one in each hand, slapped up and down my calves and thighs. To toughen my torso I whipped nunchucks back and forth against my ribs.

See, the thing about fighting was you had to be able to take a hit. Of course, it was always going to hurt, but if your body could absorb the blow, you were golden. A lot of fighters couldn't handle the pain. I was never one of them.

After my opponent was lifted from the floor and got his head straight, the shit-stink bookie handed me my $250 and another slip of paper.

"Be at that address next Saturday," he said, "and I'll get you a grand."

The following weekend I grabbed my friend Magnum and we drove to Pomona for my next match. Magnum had been a close buddy all through my drug-dealing days, a tall meth-head who resembled Tom Selleck and didn't seem to know his own strength—like a big Baby Huey. Magnum first proved his loyalty when I was collecting on some drug money I'd fronted an ex-con. When the bastard went for his gun, Magnum clocked him. He became my trusted "road dog" after that, at least until he went to prison and Old Joe came along to take his place.

My next fight was after-hours in a Pomona bar, and this time there were maybe fifty or sixty bettors inside, including the fat bookie with his tumbler of booze. My latest opponent was a monstrous sonofabitch who had to outweigh me by at least a hundred pounds. And I'm thinking, *Holy fuck, now I'm in trouble.*

I removed my flip-flops and stepped into the open space near a couple of pool tables. This time there was no hand clapping to start the match. An air horn sounded and the fight was on.

My opponent was one of those lunkheads who throws a roundhouse from the ground up. When he tried that move with me, I quick-kicked him in the ribs. When he tried it again I booted him behind the knee, and now the giant was limping around like a lame dog. I was faster than he was. Much faster. The dude kept missing, and I kept working that bum knee over until he could barely stand. That's when I made a sudden move inside and drove the palm of my hand hard into his face, breaking his nose.

That bookie made some money that night. I think he must've cleaned up on most of those suckers in the bar.

I kept on rolling from there, and with each fight the number of bettors seemed to grow a little larger. Now they were calling me "Shotgun," my nickname before I was known as the U-Haul Bandit. I used to own a 12-gauge with a six-inch extension that my brother Keith had machined for me, and I used that shotgun to great effect. Before I made my reputation hauling furniture for delinquent junkies, I was the guy who blew their doors off the hinges and announced, "Where's my money, motherfucker?"

The bank I was making on the underground fight circuit was easy pickin's compared to the drug racket. For a minute of my time I was pulling in thousands of dollars. And that's all those matches usually went—minute, minute and a half. After three, both of us would be out of breath, so I wanted to roll up my opponent and get things over with as quickly as possible.

Man, I don't know how many bareknuckle matches I was in— there were scores of them. But for a long time I never lost. That cigar-chomping, whiskey-swilling bookie kept making money off me too. I recall him betting against me just once . . . and the stinky-ass bastard lost.

Despite the big paydays, I began to feel dirty about what I was doing—like some whore stripping on stage as those businessmen jerked off and laid their money down. I was done with the fight game, but Magnum was making too much money and having way too much fun . . . all at my expense, of course. So I promised him one more bout before folding the tent.

And it was a big one.

It was a daylight match held in the Southern California desert out behind a bar in the middle of nowhere. I was being pitted against an undefeated bareknuckle fighter from Louisiana—a dude with a lot more fights under his belt than I had.

The money was five to one against me.

I remember driving out to that desert bar with Magnum. The parking lot was jammed with vehicles, including a Cadillac Eldorado with Texas plates and the classic bull horns fixed to the hood. Bettors were coming from all over for that one.

Nobody recognized Shotgun Rowe as I stepped into the bar. So I took a stool, ordered a Corona from the barmaid and watched money change hands. Magnum left to find a bookie at five to one.

"You here for the fight?" asked the barmaid.

She was gorgeous. I wanted to fuck her.

"I am," I said, snatching the bottle from the bar before she could open it.

"It's supposed to be a good one," she said. "A high-dollar fight. How much you gonna bet?"

"Three grand," I said, then pried the cap off with my teeth—a little trick that used to freak my sisters out.

The barmaid wasn't impressed.

"Well, I hear it's going to be a great fight," she said. "Have fun."

I finished my beer and walked out the back door. At the rear of the building, surrounded by a crowd of close to two hundred spectators, was an elevated boxing ring enclosed by a single rope. My opponent was standing off to the side, chatting up some of the bettors. The man was older than me, and just about as tall. His misshapen nose and a road map of scars spoke of hard miles.

I went over and introduced myself. He struck me as a pretty cool guy—just a barroom brawling motherfucker, come from the bayou to put on a good show and make a few bucks. It wasn't personal for either one of us.

When it was go-time we stepped over the rope together and entered the ring.

A bell started the match. My opponent was quick. One of those fast jabbers—pop, pop, pop. Just flashing out that hard right hand. Right away he caught my jaw and split it wide open. I came back with a kick move that knocked him on his ass. He scrambled to his feet and got busy working my chin again until I put him down for good with a hard blow to the temple using the edge of my hand.

I could have put the boot to the man's head as he lay half conscious on the mat. I'd done it before to some of the assholes I'd fought. "Shit talkers" I called them. Dudes who thought they were badass and talked trash. Those were the fucks I put the boot to because I didn't want them asking for rematches. But I wasn't going to do that to this Louisiana boy. Too much respect. Besides, it was over. He'd lost.

I went back into the bar and took a seat while Magnum stitched the cut on my chin. I noticed the barmaid watching me with an amused smile. I asked for her phone number, figuring I'd made an impression. I was wrong.

"I'm sorry, no offense," she said, declining my request. "But I think what you do is stupid."

After that match I thought I was going to hang it up and call it a day. But I didn't. Magnum convinced me to keep the good times rolling, talking me into one more bout after another. The money and the crowds were growing, and so was my ego. I was still undefeated and getting cocky. Eventually I headed for Nevada, where bare-knuckle brawling was aboveboard and sanctioned by the state. That's where the big money was. I was looking at a twenty-five-thousand-dollar payday.

The Nevada match was held in a rodeo arena that still had a bunch of horse and bull shit on the ground. My opponent was a muscular black cowboy, a large man with a fight record as good as mine. But he got no respect from me at all. I walked out, refused to shake his hand and said, "I didn't know niggers were cowboys."

See, that's the man I was back then—a bigoted sonofabitch who said and did things that still turn my stomach today. Fact is, long before I'd been possessed by my addiction to meth, there was a two-headed beast lurking inside me called rage and hate. I look back now and recognize the person I once was, but I can't fathom the evil done in that monster's name.

As a young buck growing up in Hemet I was consumed by those ugly emotions. My little sister, Lin Ann, still keeps a poem I wrote in high school that speaks volumes about that dark time.

Staring out the window as the world passes by.
The dark clouds surrender to tears. I cannot cry.
Lightning flashes anger and thunder sounds my rage.
My heart screams to be out of this hell bound cage.
My soul cries out and yearns to be free far from this place.
Tears can be had so long before a heart explodes.
And emotions lead us down dark and lonely roads.

Not exactly Ralph Waldo Emerson, I know, but you get the picture. I was fucked up in the head. And unfortunately for my schoolmates, when I wanted to vent that bile, they were the easiest targets.

During my time at Hemet High I often spent free time in the school yard smoking cigarettes and hurling slurs at the handful of blacks who were bussed in from the nearby city of Perris. Hemet had become racially polarized back in the 1970s after the state tried to forcibly integrate the school system. Everyone I knew, including my brothers and biker friends, hated the "niggers." Of course, you're not born to hate, you're raised that way. And I was raised to despise those people with a passion that makes no goddamn sense to me today. It's a sad fact that the first morning those Perris kids showed up at our school, I culled one from the herd and beat the shit out of him.

Just because.

That earned another suspension from Principal Vanderwater.

And my issues with a man's skin color didn't end with high school. I took those prejudices with me into adulthood, where I could really do some damage.

I was clearing tree branches up in Orange County one day when I cut into a power line and electrocuted myself. Got zapped so hard my thumb nearly blew off. Doctors had to stick it back on using reconstructive surgery. Anyway, there was one black man on the work crew who I pointedly never spoke to unless it was to call him a nigger whenever he walked past. Got so bad the job foreman took me aside and warned he'd fire my ass if I didn't knock it off.

Turns out my heart had been weakened pretty good by that electrocution, not to mention all the coke and meth I'd been doing, because one day while on the job my ticker said "fuck you" and quit. I collapsed on the ground in cardiac arrest.

Only one man on that job site came to my aid.

Guess who?

He pumped my chest and gave me mouth-to-mouth. For all intents and purposes I was a dead man, but he brought me back to life again.

And I despised him for it.

Hard as it might be to fathom, I couldn't get past the fact he'd put his goddamn lips on mine. My first day back to work, the black man who had saved my life walked past.

I called him nigger.

And the depths of my unreasoned hatred didn't end there.

One summer night, when I was young, drunk and stupid, I got into a violent argument with a twenty-something black man outside a club in San Bernardino. I'd instigated the confrontation with some racist remark, and when he took offense I beat him down and knocked him straight out.

And then, in a life filled with shameful memories, I did the one thing I'm most ashamed of. I flipped that unconscious man onto his back, straddled his body, tore open his shirt and carved a Nazi swastika into his chest with my buck knife.

Oh, yes, I did.

I've never ended a human being's life. It's a goddamn miracle I haven't. But that night in San Bernardino I honestly thought I'd killed a man . . . and it didn't bother me in the least. I left him for dead in the parking lot and went on with my life. Yes, sir. I thought I was a real bad-ass motherfucker after that. Even got me some double lightning bolts tattooed on my arm to commemorate the occasion—the Nazi symbol for the Aryan Brotherhood.

Christ Almighty, the things I did in hate's name. I still have night-mares . . . and not a million Our Fathers, Hail Marys or I'm sorrys will ever make them go away.

That Las Vegas match, like most of my other fights on the circuit, didn't last long. I whipped that black cowboy, and Magnum and I walked out of that shit-strewn rodeo arena with thousands of dollars stuffed in our pockets. With that kind of cash coming my way, I put any thought of retirement on hold and signed on for another bout in Arizona, now as the heavy favorite.

Somewhere outside Phoenix, on a lawn manicured like a golf course fairway, I faced my next victim—a dude who was smaller than I was but built like a fireplug. Just seconds into the match, my opponent caught me with a blow to the jaw that shook me. I was surprised by the force behind that punch but figured I'd taken his best shot.

I figured wrong.

The fireplug followed with a left-right combination that I walked my cocky ass straight into. The first broke my jaw and scrambled my brain, the second knocked me down. I wasn't completely out, but I sure as hell couldn't go on. It was match over.

I'd lost my first fight.

A few months later my bareknuckle career ended in a hotel boxing ring in Tahoe. My opponent was an Asian dude who was just as good with his feet as I was. When I realized I was meeting my match, I did something I'd never done before—I tried to take him out for good. I avoided a roundhouse kick, slipped inside, and struck the man with a concussive blow to the chest.

And it nearly killed him.

Fire Department EMTs rushed into the ring and put the paddles to him. A helicopter was called in, and they airlifted the man out. He didn't die, but he came damn close—and it scared the shit out of me.

Tahoe was my last fight. It just wasn't worth ending another human being for a few lousy bucks.

So that was the opponent those unsuspecting Vagos prospects were lining up to battle one-on-one behind the Screaming Chicken Saloon. Big Roy and the Hemet crew knew about my brawling past, but no one else did . . . certainly not the poor bastards who were about to walk into an ambush.

Quickie John sent his first gladiator, one of the Norco boys, into the ring against Shotgun Rowe. I waited until he was close then . . . WHAP! WHAP! WHAP!

The other prospects had to help him off the ground.

The next challenger stepped forward looking more nervous than the last.

He went down even faster.

"Hey, Quickie John," said Tramp, pulling out his wallet. "How 'bout me and you bet this next one."

"Fuck you, Tramp," Quickie shot back.

Everyone went quiet, wondering what Tramp would do next. What he did was cancel the rest of the show and slap Quickie John with a thousand-dollar fine for mouthing off.

As the crowd dispersed, a familiar voice called out, "Hey, prospect!"

I turned to find 37 wearing an ear-to-ear grin. Blackie stood next to him, smoking a joint and giving me a thumbs-up. I approached timidly, wondering what wild-goose chase that old-timer was about to send me on next. But instead the forever brother laughed heartily and slapped my shoulder.

"Jesus, boy. Don't look so worried," chuckled 37. "I ain't gonna fuck with you."

"I wouldn't fuck with him either," added Bubba as he joined the group. "You got some real fast hands there, brother."

"He sure does," agreed Blackie, then he shouted at Quickie John as he passed, "Don't this boy have fast hands, Quickie?"

The Norco P scowled and kept walking.

"How long you been prospecting?" Blackie asked me.

"Four or five months, I guess."

"What's up with that? Most guys nowadays are patched in already."

"Well, least he's coming in the right way," offered Bubba, passing the joint along to Blackie.

"No doubt," agreed Blackie before taking a long drag. "None of that backdoor shit. Man's paying his dues."

I know it shouldn't have mattered, but I was flattered those boys had taken an interest in me. We talked a few minutes more until my eyes fell on Blackie's belt buckle. It was a large and impressive-looking thing, handcrafted in stamped silver and featuring Loki, the red devil himself, etched in the center between the words *Vagos* and *So. Cal.*

"Great buckle, man," I said to Blackie. "How can I get one like that?"

"You earn it, prospect." He grinned.

Blackie was a great guy. He'd been a hell-raiser in his early days, going to war against rival clubs just like most of the old-timers had. But age had mellowed the man. He unbuckled his belt and handed it to me for a closer look. There were three names scratched into the buckle's backside: Gator, Gargoyle and Harpo.

"Previous owners," explained Blackie. "That buckle's been handed down from one Vago to the next."

"No shit. Very cool."

"Only five like it in the world," Blackie said proudly.

"I'm gonna get me one just like this," I told him, handing it back.

"Hell, prospect," laughed the forever brother as he threaded the belt back around his waist, "just keep doing what you're doing and maybe someday you'll have mine."

13

The 2,000-Mile Pizza to Go

The months I spent as a prospect with the Hemet chapter were some of the most humiliating and frustrating of my life. Talk about miserable. I was over forty years old and I had a bunch of assholes calling me for stupid shit all hours of the day and night just because those patches on their backs said they could.

I washed their bikes. Did their errands. Lent money that never came back. Had my company employees mowing their lawns free of charge. Hell, once I even scooped dog shit out of Big Roy's yard. Whenever the Vagos called, whatever they wanted, I was expected to immediately drop what I was doing and get on it. Jenna was all over my case about it too.

"Big Roy called. He wants his dick sucked" was one of her favorite lines.

I was being run ragged, and my tree-trimming business was suffering. It was goddamn ridiculous. But the height of absurdity was the day Big Roy had a hankering for pizza and wanted me to pick one up for him.

In Oregon.

I figured Roy was just busting my balls, that he would never actually make me ride two thousand miles to fetch a pizza. But no. The motherfucker was serious.

"Put on your cape and ride, Superman," Jenna sniped as I threw on my cut and headed out the door.

I climbed aboard the Harley and took off on an epic pizza delivery. Up the Pacific Coast, through the day and into the night I rode. Sometime after midnight, saddle sore and dog tired, I pulled up at an address way out in East Bumfuck, Oregon.

I knocked. A Vago answered.

"I'm here to pick up a pizza for Big Roy," I said, as if that somehow made perfect sense.

"You George?" he wanted to know.

No, shit-for-brains. I'm the other asshole who just rode sixteen hours for a fucking pizza.

But I didn't say that.

"Yeah, that would be me," was the response I chose instead.

"Well, Big Roy don't want pizza no more," the Vago said. "Now he wants a Monster drink."

I could've murdered the sonofabitch.

But I didn't. I spared his miserable life, grabbed the can and rode back through the night and into the following afternoon to deliver Big Roy his fucking energy drink. And once I'd finished that fool's errand, I took a long, hard look in the mirror and asked myself if this undercover gig was really worth the bullshit that came with it.

I wasn't so sure. Not anymore.

That night I phoned Uncle Johnny Law and vented.

"I really don't know how much more of this I can take," I told him. "They're never gonna give me that goddamn patch."

"Don't fixate on the patch," John warned. "Keep your focus on the evidence."

But I was burning out, going through what John called "patch fever." Prospecting was such a grind that all you wanted to do was make it stop, and the only way to make it stop was to get patched. But there was danger in that mind-set. Informants suffering from the fever often lost focus, concentrating so hard on getting the patch that the mission became almost secondary.

"John, I'm telling you I can't do this. I'm busted, man. I've got no life. They've got me doing these stupid-ass errands, and I'm sick of it."

"I've been there," he replied. "I understand it's hard. But it won't last forever. You're tired right now, but you'll get through this phase, and once you do they'll ease up."

"I don't know, man," I said, discouraged. "These assholes might not ever let me out of this fuckin' phase. It's too good a deal. Todd's been withdrawing money from my wallet like I'm Wells Fuckin' Fargo."

The nightmare continued a few weeks later when Terry the Tramp decreed another Vagos run to Buffalo Bill's Casino in Primm, this time to celebrate His Royal Highness's birthday. It was mid-July and the temperature was cresting one hundred degrees on that desert highway to State Line, cooking the landscape in a redbrick oven. The pack of Harleys, which included bikers from several Vagos chapters outside Hemet, pulled off the road at one point so everyone could take a water

Big Doug Brown.

break and stretch their legs. As I'm leaning against my Touring Classic, squinting down the shimmering highway, I noticed a stumpy little mirage coming my way.

It was Quickie John, the Norco P.

Man, I couldn't stomach that roly-poly bastard, and I'm pretty sure the bastard felt the same way about me. I'd clocked his vice president's nephew, beat up one of his hang-arounds and cost the man a thousand bucks in fines, and now he was dogging my ass every chance he got.

"Hey, prospect!" Quickie barked at me from his chubby pie hole.

"What's up, Quickie John?"

He gestured toward his motorcycle.

"My bike needs washing."

That asshole had pulled this same stunt a few weeks earlier, and Big Roy had taken me aside and laid down the law.

"My P doesn't want me washing any bikes but Hemet's," I told him.

"Fuck your fuckin' P," barked Quickie. "I told you to wash my bike. Now get to it."

Quickie John was big on getting respect. He wasn't so hot on dishing it out. But I kept my mouth shut and went looking for water in the middle of the fucking desert. After scrounging it from a few sympathetic Vagos, I returned with a full bottle and wiped the road grime from Quickie's Harley. After I'd finished, and before I could get away, the sonofabitch called me back.

"Where the fuck you going?! You ain't done yet!"

Quickie took the bottle of soda he'd been drinking and slowly dumped it over his gas tank.

"Clean my bike, prospect."

Man, if not for the mission I would have ripped that squatty little fuck a new asshole. Instead I swallowed my pride and did what any true prospect would: I bent over and took it like the club whore I'd become. As I walked around begging more water, Big Roy intercepted me and slapped the bottle from my hand.

"Get your ass back over here with us," he snapped at me. "You serve Hemet, not Norco."

Now Quickie John came charging. In no time he and Roy were in a heated debate over whether one chapter had the right to tell another chapter's prospect what to do.

"He's club property," Quickie argued. "If I want him washing my bike, that's my right."

"He only washes our bikes," countered Big Roy.

"Oh, yeah?" Quickie retorted.

I could see this kicking all the way up to the Supreme Court. I almost laughed out loud it was so fucking stupid.

"We'll take this up with national when we get to State Line," concluded Quickie. "And we'll see what Tramp has to say about it."

And that's exactly what happened. The great bike-washing debate came to Buffalo Bill's when Terry the Tramp pulled me, Big Roy, Quickie John and several of the national officers into a room to hash out the whole childish mess. After Roy's opening statement it was Quickie's turn.

"This prospect's gotta pay his dues just like every other motherfucker in the club," he argued. "He's gotta earn his patch."

"Better back off, Quickie," Tramp warned. "Don't talk to me about earning it. Half the members in this club say your chapter's all decked out in patches they didn't earn. Hell, I've got guys that have been in for twenty years and don't have those patches."

It was thumbs-up for me and Big Roy, thumbs-down on Quickie John. Instead of Tramp's blessing, Quickie found himself lining up his chapter to face inspection. Then a couple of Vagos old-timers began cutting patches off those Norco boys faster than they could answer questions like, How'd you earn this one? and What the hell does that one stand for?

It had all backfired on Quickie. To add to the indignity, Tramp slapped the Norco P with another thousand-dollar fine and warned him to stay clear of me. Quickie John was never a fan of mine, but now he'd become an enemy. Which was fine with me. I couldn't give two shits whether that little bastard invited me to his birthday parties. Of greater importance was the valuable connection I was making with Terry the Tramp.

The emperor of the Nation invited me onto the casino floor with him and we played the slots together as Rhino stood guard with whatever chapter had been tapped for security that day. I watched Tramp load coin after coin after coin into those bandits, then I'd jump up and shout whenever he hit the jackpot. Tramp loved it, man. He called me his "lucky charm."

But the international P's true lucky charm was the club he'd been sucking dry for years. The Vagos MC was his bread and butter . . . his very livelihood. Tramp was fond of saying how he lived as a Vago and would die as a Vago. What he failed to mention was that he lived off the Vagos too. Tramp had recently shuttered Triple T Choppers, the motorcycle repair shop he'd owned for fifteen years, but there was no pension plan waiting when he retired. His only means of support was the club he ruled. The man had become a parasite, surviving on the sweat and blood of his brothers—a breach of trust that would go undetected for another seven years.

In theory, loyalty to the brotherhood was a commandment that ran neck and neck with respect. It was the glue that bound a club together. But there was little loyalty and no honor to be found among those thieves. For Terry the Tramp—as it was with the leadership of most outlaw clubs—the only true loyalty was to the almighty dollar. In fact, it was that same misplaced sense of loyalty that helped drive Hammer into the arms of the ATF a few years earlier.

Most outlaw clubs maintained a defense fund for members in trouble with the law. Sonny Barger and the Hells Angels, for instance, provided funds to bail their brothers out of jail. They ran a tight ship over there. You'd never see an Angel hung out to dry.

Not so the Vagos.

At a time when Hammer needed financial rescue, Tramp was too preoccupied on the casino floor to notice. Even Hammer's own chapter ignored him. From the moment the man was locked up, his brothers were out to rip him off—including a sleazy grab for his Harley and his old lady. So Hammer turned for the feds and stabbed them all in the back. His fear of the Nazi Low Riders might have driven his decision, but it was the disloyalty of his Vagos brothers that made Hammer's choice a no-brainer.

Eventually I got bored watching Terry the Tramp feeding club money into the casino slots and wandered outside for fresh air and a cigarette. But before I could fish the smokes from my pocket, I heard those two words I'd come to dread.

"Hey, prospect!"

Across the way a bearded asshole, standing with a knot of Vagos patches, was pointing me toward the giant Ferris wheel.

"Get on that thing and sing us the prospect song!"

Man, I was so sick and tired of hearing myself sing that stupid song that I'd actually started improvising, adding my own middle-finger salute to Green Nation that ended with ". . . and all you patch holders quit fucking with me," which Tramp liked so much he asked me to write it down.

So there I was, going round and round on the Ferris wheel, belting out the new-and-improved prospect song as hundreds of casino goers laughed, pointed and scratched their heads below.

No sooner had I finished than my Nextel was ringing.

Uncle Johnny Law was on the line.

I'd made it a habit of calling my handler whenever Green Nation moved as a herd. Before rolling for Buffalo Bill's, I'd followed the same protocol. And now John was somewhere down below, watching my back and judging my golden voice.

"You look like a pussy up there," was the first thing he said.

I scanned the sea of faces below.

"Where the hell are you?"

"Close enough to know you can't sing for shit, prospect."

The bastard was still laughing as I hung up on him.

Meanwhile all hell was breaking loose inside the casino. A former member of the Vagos Orange County chapter had shown up uninvited to Tramp's party. Weeks earlier the man had been run down the road, which meant the Vagos had confiscated his patch and motorcycle, then booted him out of Green Nation. Now his former brothers were stomping the party crasher between the slot machines as little old ladies leapt for their lives.

After that fiasco, Buffalo Bill's management banned the Vagos from their casino forever . . . which lasted right up until the next time the Vagos were banned forever.

When I arrived back at the apartment that evening, Jenna was waiting for me at the door. Guess she must've missed me, because I was barely inside before she pulled down my pants, dropped to her knees and got down to business.

Yup, that was a pretty satisfying welcome home. And it would have been even better had I remembered to turn off the recorder—an oversight I would later regret.

Jenna polished me off and I staggered weak-kneed for the kitchen, hitching my pants up along the way. As I reached in the fridge for a cold beer, there was a pounding at the door. Before Jenna could open it, Jack Fite came barging through.

Those who knew Jack best used to call him Satan, and everyone said he would die in prison. The man was a local legend when I was a teenager growing up in Hemet, a brutal sonofabitch who lived up to his name and had the long rap sheet to prove it. There was a time, before

Jack Fite.

I got my head straight, when I was an admirer of Jack's, but the day he beat the knees off a blind man with a ball-peen hammer was the day my infatuation ended.

The Hemet Vagos knew Fite's reputation, but Todd thought the chapter could use more muscle, so he convinced Roy to patch Jack into the club straightaway. Wasn't long before Big Roy realized his mistake. Jack Fite wasn't what you'd call a team player. He was a dangerous force of nature that did as he pleased, and nobody—not even the chapter president—could control such a man.

I was caught in the eye of that storm the day Jack came looking to kill someone. He knew I owned a .380 and wanted to use it to settle a score for a drug deal gone bad.

"Where's the gun?" he demanded, cornering me in the kitchen.

I looked past him to the living room, where Jenna stood frozen. She was well aware of Fite's reputation too. Billy, the father of her child, was related to Jack.

"Get the gun," I told her.

Jenna was smarter than me, though, and wasn't about to become an accessory to murder.

"I don't know where it is," she said.

Jack immediately sniffed the lie. "Give me the gun, bitch!" he exploded at her.

"I swear I don't know, Jack."

He pulled a pair of handcuffs from his jacket pocket.

"You don't know?" Jack fumed, wrapping the cuffs around his hand. "You're going to tell me you don't fuckin' know?!"

He took a threatening step toward her.

"Hold on, Jack," I blurted out.

The man spun quickly and hit me in the face with the cuffs, a blow felt in my back teeth.

"Run, Jenna!" I shouted.

The girl didn't have to be told twice. She bolted out the front door, and now that crazed Vago's anger was focused squarely on me.

"I want that gun!" Jack raged. "Give me the fuckin' gun!"

As he was saying this, the fucker was pummeling the snot out of me, splitting my head open and knocking me to the kitchen floor. Now I was lying helpless on bloody linoleum and Jack was stomping my legs. I couldn't defend myself, either. Jack Fite was a patch holder and I was nothing but a lowly prospect. Under the Vagos rules of engagement, a patched member had the right to kick a prospect's ass whenever he felt like it.

Of course, once I heard the bone snap in my leg all bets were off. Fuck the code, the bastard was trying to kill me. I managed to stand and escape out the back door, hopping and stumbling my way toward the backyard fence. There was no vaulting it like the bad old days. The best I could do was claw my way over the top and fall down the other side to safety.

A few days later Jack drove his panel truck over to the Soboba reservation to settle the score and got shot in the head by a terrified Indian. The bullet entered above one ear, traveled around his skull and blew out the other side. Jack got back in his truck, drove three miles and collapsed on a sidewalk in San Jacinto.

When I learned the sonofabitch who put my leg in a cast had been taken to the hospital with a bullet wound in the head, my first thought was *Gee, I hope he dies.*

No such luck. The man was out in two days.

It would take more than a bullet to kill Satan.

That ugly encounter with Jack Fite raised some alarming truths about this strange new world I'd signed up for. If I wanted Operation 22 Green to succeed, I had to play by outlaw rules. Trouble was those rules could get me killed. I was operating in a weird no-man's-land with my hands tied and a big target slapped on my back, one that invited any patched member to kick my ass.

And not only had I crossed into the Vagos' world . . . the Vagos had crossed into mine. Jack Fite was just one frightening example of that. Iron Mike took the apartment two doors down from me at the chicken shack. Big Todd would drop in uninvited at any hour to bend my ear and flirt with Jenna. And Todd's brother, Big Doug, was bunking in Old Joe's trailer. That wildman had appeared one day looking for a place to stay, and my buddy hadn't had the balls to turn him away. Poor Joe. He was so spooked by crazy Doug that he wouldn't even sleep in his own bed, crashing instead on a couch he'd dragged into the parking lot and left beside the trailer.

I'm not sure what the hell went on behind the walls of the Brown family home, but clearly something screwy happened with Todd and Doug; one was a certified asshole and the other was certifiably nuts. Big Doug was one of those dudes you tried not to make eye contact with, because if you stare into the eyes of a crazy fuck too long, they can do crazy fuck things.

He was among the first recruits patched into the Hemet chapter thanks to his little brother, but it wasn't long before the man became more trouble than he was worth. Doug was going around town beating people up, taking their dope and saying the Vagos were backing him up. The rest of the time he was high on meth, which, from Big Roy's standpoint, made him about as useless as tits on a bull. Fed up with Big Doug's erratic behavior, Roy finally dispatched Todd to pull his brother's patch.

When Todd showed up at the trailer to give his big brother the news, Doug didn't take it very well. He showed his displeasure by pulling a revolver and firing several rounds at Todd's feet. Once his brother was through dancing, Doug slipped through a hole in a chain-link fence and bolted into the Santa Rosa Hills. He returned a few hours later, lifted Joe's set of keys and stole my truck.

Doug was missing for three days, and the whole time Jenna had this creepy feeling the man was out there watching her. She'd stand in the window with a pair of binoculars and search the hills behind the apartments. I even buried a pressure plate outside the window where the air-conditioning unit was mounted and hooked it to an alarm in case the sonofabitch tried climbing through.

After three days the truck showed up in the parking lot with the keys in the ignition. Later that afternoon some of the Vagos spotted Doug strolling down a Hemet street and gave chase. Doug flagged down a police cruiser, jumped into the backseat and begged the cop to save his life.

Big Doug Brown had finally gone 'round the bend, and I'm not sure that whacky bastard ever made it back again.

14

Guns and Whiskey

The primary mission of the Bureau of Alcohol, Tobacco, Firearms and Explosives was first and foremost to get illegal weapons off America's streets. Special Agent Carr had emphasized that point when I first came aboard, and since then I'd been spreading the cheese to catch a few mice, hinting to the Vagos that I was in the market to buy weapons.

This wasn't raising any red flags with the Hemet chapter either. Most of those boys, including Big Roy and Big Todd, knew my history with firearms. I'd been a gun freak since I was a kid shooting deer and rabbits with a .22 rifle in the California Cascades. As I grew older I bought and sold weapons for profit. In the early eighties I was purchasing replica semiautomatic Thompson submachine guns through a pawnshop for three hundred bucks and flipping them for seven.

Despite the fact that I was a felon, I was usually packing some kind of firearm on my person too. If it wasn't the .380 strapped to my ankle, it was the modified shotgun with the six-inch extension. I'd used that shotgun as a drug dealer in the San Jacinto Valley, then later during a stint as a bounty hunter back in the days when you could kick in a door without a search warrant.

My love affair with guns was perfect cover during my time under-cover. Yes, I'd make drug buys here and there, but only when the opportunity presented itself. I never forced it. The Hemet Vagos knew I wasn't a drug user anymore, so I only bought on someone else's behalf. Firearms, on the other hand, were right up my alley. And the weapon I coveted most was a little beauty Big Roy made the mistake of showing me one day at the Lady Luck, a rare, Czechoslovakian-manufactured 7.62 x 25 caliber pistol.

"Hey, how much you want for that?" I asked him. "I'll buy it from you."

"It's not for sale. But if it ever is, I'll give you first crack," promised Roy.

Man, I wanted that pistol in the worst way. Didn't matter where it came from, Big Roy was a felon just like me, prohibited under federal law from possessing firearms.

There was an even bigger prize to be won, though. More than Roy's 7.62, I had my eye on the Vagos' war chest, a cache of weapons Buckshot kept stashed in his barn. That arsenal, contributed by Hemet's members, included revolvers, rifles, sawed-off shotguns—just about everything but a rocket launcher . . . and there were rumors the chapter had one of those squirreled away too. Hemet's war chest was the mother lode I was after for ATF, the giant pot at the end of Operation 22 Green's rainbow.

But until that day came, I kept busy buying whatever weapons crossed my path—like the stolen .30-30 rifle I bought from Big Todd, who had a felony conviction the same as Roy. At other times Vagos members knew someone outside the club who was in the market to unload a gun. The seller might come out to my shack in Valle Vista, or I'd go to a location of their choosing, all wired up for sound and picture. Because I was a convicted felon, selling me weapons was itself a felony. Once I paid for the gun and took possession, they were screwed.

The only snags I seemed to hit came in the month of September, the end of the government's fiscal year. That's when the money dried up for ATF and deals could slip away—including a fully automatic AK-47 and some Mac 10s I could have bought for five grand. Operation 22 Green fell under OCDETF (Organized Crime Drug Enforcement Task Forces), a multiagency program that provides supplemental federal funds for approved cases like ours. But when spending limits were reached and the fiscal year was done, getting additional money from the government was like prying a gun from Charlton Heston's cold dead hands.

John Carr was desperately trying to tear through bureaucratic red tape and put together the cash while I delayed the buy. But I couldn't stall for long. A few days late, he called the Nextel. Our conversation went something like . . .

"George, I've got the five thousand. Get those Mac 10s."

"What do you want me to do, shit them? Those Mac 10s are gone, jack."

But lost opportunities were the exception.

In early August I was contacted by one of the Vagos who had a friend looking to move some stolen firearms. The guns were being kept at an old farmhouse in Winchester, a rural community nine miles west of Hemet. I called Uncle Johnny Law on the Nextel and let him know I was heading out for a look. No need to wire up just yet—I was just window shopping, establishing a price then getting right out again. But John wanted someone watching my ass anyway, so he dispatched his right-hand man, Special Agent Jeff Ryan.

As I limped toward the door wearing my walking boot—I'd recently had the cast removed from the leg Jack Fite had busted—Jenna hurried to intercept me.

"Where you going now?"

"Got some business."

"Business, huh?" she sniped. "Business with who? Your Uncle John?"

She made sure to put the snide emphasis on "Uncle John."

Jenna had obviously been eavesdropping again. For the past few weeks she'd been probing me on this mysterious uncle I kept talking to, and when I stonewalled her it only made the girl more suspicious.

"I want to come with you," she insisted.

"You can't leave Sierra alone."

"I'll bring her with me."

I wasn't about to waste my time with pointless conversation, so I limped out the door. Jenna followed me to the truck, pleading her case at my backside.

"Between work and the gambling and your motorcycle pals, you never have time for me anymore. You go off for days, and then you come back like nothing happened. And you can't even tell me where you've been or what you're doing."

"We hang out plenty," I told her as I climbed into the cab.

"No, you and Joe hang out. He's another one," she said, nodding toward the trailer. "Why is it you always have time for him? I'm jealous of that stinky-mouthed motherfucker."

I slammed the truck door and snapped at her from the open window, "Watch what you say."

Jenna was close to tears now. "Are you listening to me? Are you even listening? What about me, George? Pick me for once. Pick me."

I turned the ignition and Jenna went wild.

"That's right! You go meet your Uncle John!" she raged. "What's that all about, huh?! You two a couple of faggots or something?!"

I backed the truck away, leaving her frothing at the mouth.

"Say hi to your faggot boyfriend for me!"

Later I found out Jenna was cruising the parking lots of gay bars in the San Jacinto Valley looking for my truck. She actually thought I might have gone homosexual. But what could I do? Better gay than dead, which is what I would have been had I told that girl the truth. Jenna was like nitroglycerin, man. One false move and . . . BA-BOOM!

About a quarter mile from the Winchester farmhouse I met up with

Special Agent Ryan. Jeff always struck me as friendly but a little preoc-cupied. Might have been a reason for that. A couple of years earlier, just two weeks before the World Trade Center fell, he'd seen an L.A. County sheriff's deputy get blown away right before his eyes.

Post-traumatic stress disorder wasn't exclusive to the military.

The farmhouse where the guns were stored was completely isolated, set back in the woods at the end of a long dirt road. Special Agent Ryan wouldn't be able to get close enough to back me up without attracting attention. At that point it wasn't a huge concern. I wasn't wired or mak-ing any deals, but things might get tricky when it came time to make the buy. This was shaping up as one of those complicated scenarios that gave an informant ulcers.

CIs worked alone on an island of hostile natives, often making criti-cal life-and-death decisions on the fly. Many of those decisions involved proper behavior in felony-type situations. See, when you were playing outlaw, people expected you to behave as an outlaw, doing things any run-of-the-mill bad guy would do . . . from snorting meth to putting a bullet in someone's ear. Difference is you were far from ordinary. You were working for the United States government. A real challenge for a CI was figuring out how to get around those pitfalls without exposing himself.

And there were no easy answers. Every situation was different.

John Carr once shared an anecdote about sitting in the back of a car with his informant, waiting on a drug buy, when a Mongol jumped in the front seat and cut three lines of coke. The biker snorted his line and handed the mirror to John, who pretended he was busy count-ing money for the transaction and passed the blow along to his infor-mant. Well, that poor bastard wasn't a drug user, but he took one for the team and snorted both lines. Looking to get higher still, the Mongol cut another three lines of coke and passed it around. John kept peel-ing bills, still stalling, and handed off to his informant, who hit both lines again.

"And now I see his eyes going wide," John told me. "Then that fuckin' Mongol cut another three lines."

I was laughing pretty hard now.

"After we'd made the buy I opened the door and my guy fell right out of the car," John continued. "I thought he'd OD'd. I called my cover team and said, 'I think we've got to take this dude to the hospital. I don't think he's breathing.'"

I knew it was wrong, but I couldn't stop laughing.

"You might think it's funny," John lectured me, "but get yourself in a tight spot and you'll find out how tricky things can get. That's what you need to understand, George. An informant who commits a felony hurts his case. Credibility goes right out the window, and the defense will jump all over that shit in court. We had a big problem with Hammer because of that—because of his drug use. So be careful. Don't let yourself get cornered if you can help it."

"What if I'm in a fight and weapons come out?"

"Just don't lead the charge, dude. If you have to get into it, then that's what you've got to do. But don't lead the charge."

That had my head spinning, but there was no point making myself crazy. I'd just have to figure it out as I went along.

I left Special Agent Ryan and headed down the long dirt road toward the farmhouse. The place was a shithole, and after I met the owner I immediately knew why. The man had been a carpenter once, but methamphetamine had taken control of his life and he couldn't keep his own home from falling apart.

He led me into the living room, where four of his spun pals were crashed on the couch and chairs. The place was being used as a tweaker pad—a location where meth-heads gathered to get high. And, man, did that place stink. Garbage was strewn everywhere, and a dog (least I think it was a dog) had taken a dump in the corner, which nobody had bothered cleaning up.

The carpenter pointed out six rifles leaning against the wall next to a fish tank filled with green water. On an end table beside the rifles were a couple of handguns. All were stolen. We negotiated a price, and I told him I'd be back with the cash. Then I got the hell out of there.

A few days later I was headed back to Winchester to make the gun buy, this time with Old Joe riding shotgun. I'd told him about the farmhouse and how ATF couldn't get a cover team close enough to help out in a jam, so my buddy had volunteered to come along as lookout. Guess a gun buy was more exciting than feeding branches into a wood chipper.

We rendezvoused with Carr at a remote location far from the farmhouse. I left Old Joe in the truck and climbed into the front passenger's seat of my handler's cover car, the same rusted-out shitbox I'd seen him driving on the way to Yucca Valley. John was busy copying serial numbers from the hundred-dollar bills he was about to hand me.

"See you brought your boyfriend," he said, pausing to glance out the window. "You two are thick as thieves."

Joe returned a wave and smiled, which he rarely did because of the condition of his teeth. The front set looked like a picket fence missing most of the pickets, and the back ones were mostly gone, thanks to a topped tree that had come down, pole-vaulted into his head and blown out the molars.

"Listen, I've got a chopper coming in," said John. "They have a telescopic lens that can pick out your moustache hairs."

"Lot of fuckin' good that'll do me at ten thousand feet."

John resumed jotting down serial numbers. "Yeah, well, you picked a hell of a spot to make a buy, dude. That lot's almost twenty friggin' acres."

He finished copying the serial numbers, then counted each hundred-dollar bill out loud into a recorder. When he was done he slipped the two grand into an envelope.

"Let's check your pockets," he said to me.

Standard operating procedure was to make certain an informant had no money on his person before a buy. The only cash you could have was supplied by the agency. After a thorough search, John hooked me up with sound and picture. That wasn't always the case, but with gun and drug buys my handler wanted all the coverage he could get.

"What's the code?" I asked once he'd finished.

There was always a code word or sentence in case of trouble. Usually it was "Big John isn't going to like this." If my handler heard that over the mic, the cover team would come in guns blazing. Of course, by that time I'd probably be toast.

"How 'bout . . . Jenna," John suggested instead.

I was instantly tongue-tied.

"Jenna?"

"Yeah, Jenna. As in thanks for the blow job, Jenna."

I hadn't told John about my girlfriend, mainly because I'd known he would disapprove. It was weird, man, but I felt like I was that special agent's snot-nosed kid, and I didn't want to let him down.

"How do you know about her?" I said sheepishly.

John pointed to the recording device.

"Do us both a favor and turn that thing off when you're done for the day, okay?"

I couldn't help the shit-eatin' grin on my face. But my handler wasn't amused.

"So who is she?"

"Just some chick who's been living with me."

"Is it serious?"

"She's got a kid. I'd say that's serious."

John's shoulders slumped and he turned away, shaking his head. "Christ, George."

"Don't worry about it, man. It's cool."

"Listen to me," John responded with a touch of anger. "Women are dangerous for someone like you. Women can get a CI killed. Didn't I explain about Hammer?"

"Yeah, you told me, but—"

"Dude. The girl is *living* with you."

"I haven't told her what I'm doing, and I don't plan to."

"Yeah, that's what Hammer said. Get rid of her, George. Nothing good can come of this. You need to get rid of the girl."

I wasn't in the mood for a lecture from Dad, so I climbed out of the car.

"Hold on a second," said John before I could close the door. He paused a moment before continuing. "Look, you're a grown man. But I have to tell you, George — and this is coming from years of experience — a relationship while undercover is a really, really bad idea."

"I got it," I said tersely and slammed the door.

As I headed for my truck I heard the window rolling down behind me, followed by John's mocking voice.

"Suck it, baby. Oh, baby, suck my cock."

I flipped the middle finger over my shoulder and climbed into the pickup. Then Joe and I drove off toward the farmhouse.

"So what should I do?" asked Joe as we headed down the dirt driveway.

"Don't do anything. Just stay in the truck. If there's trouble, honk the horn."

"Does it work?"

"Yes, it works."

We pulled up to the farmhouse and I crossed onto the porch and knocked at the front door. The carpenter answered, looking ragged, like he hadn't slept in a week. As we were about to head inside he spotted Joe sitting in the pickup. The man stepped out on the porch for a better look.

"Who's that in the truck?"

"Friend of mine. He's cool."

The carpenter considered Joe a long moment, then turned to me.

"I'm not sure we're gonna do this," he said. "Least not today."

This wouldn't have been the first time a seller got cold feet, and certainly not the last.

"Might not have the cash tomorrow," I warned him, waving the envelope.

The carpenter said nothing. I stood on the porch a few seconds longer, then started back down the stairs.

"Okay. Give me a shout if you change your mind," I told him.

When I was halfway to the truck, he called, "Hey, come on back!" and waved me into the house.

The rifles and handguns were arranged across the kitchen table. I checked each one to make sure they weren't loaded.

"Got something I can wrap these in?" I asked him.

The carpenter disappeared, and I took the opportunity to light a cigarette and look around. The house was quiet and appeared empty. All those tweakers had either cleared out or passed out, but the place still looked and smelled like a pigsty. The carpenter reentered the kitchen carrying some old bath towels.

"Man, I appreciate this," I told him as I rolled the rifles up. "When you've got a felony like I do, you can't buy these in a fuckin' store."

"What are you gonna do with 'em?" asked the carpenter.

"Flip 'em and make a little profit," I answered. "That's what I do. So if you've got more, just let me know, man. Anything you've got I'll be glad to take off your hands."

I pulled the envelope and started counting out the money on the table.

"One hundred, two hundred, three hundred . . ."

Every bill I counted was going on the record, and it was all adding up to a big fat bust.

A few minutes later we walked out the front door together, with the rifles bundled under our arms. The instant I stepped on the porch, I heard that ATF helicopter buzzing high overhead. Halfway to the truck, the carpenter checked his step and squinted into the bright noonday sky.

"What's that I'm hearing?"

I followed his gaze. You couldn't see the chopper up there—

must've been at a pretty high altitude—but the sound of its rotor was unmistakable.

"You hearin' that?" he asked me.

What was I going to do? Deny it?

"Yeah, I hear it. Could be a water pump. Or maybe someone's got a generator running at one of the farms around here."

This seemed to satisfy the man, because he shrugged it off and continued toward the pickup. We dumped the rifles into the bed, shook hands, and Joe and I drove away.

I would return three times to that farmhouse to buy weapons. And each time that carpenter pounded another nail into his own coffin.

When I got back from Winchester, I dropped by Shooter's Food and Brew to have a few beers. By this time Shooter had figured out that Big Roy was never going to let him join the Hemet Vagos, so he'd signed on with The Green Machine, the support club run by Sergeant Crusher, the crooked Cathedral City cop.

I was feeling sorry for myself that afternoon, which might explain why a few beers turned into a few drinks, which led to a fucking fiasco. Almost seven months into my time undercover I was starting to realize John Carr had been right all along. There would be no quick solution to Hemet's gang problem. Any illusions I had about cleaning up my hometown were vanishing with each month that dropped off the calendar. Yes, I was making the occasional gun buy, but Operation 22 Green was slogging along as if through waist-deep mud. Not to mention I was still a friggin' prospect, still stuck in that no-man's-land where I couldn't fight back, couldn't sit in on church meetings, couldn't gather the inside evidence I needed to get out from under the mission that was dragging my ass down. Some kind of spark was needed to get 22 Green's engine cranking, and before long I was convinced it was my responsibility, and mine alone, to make that happen.

For this I blame the whiskey.

There was a time, in my early days undercover, when I was drinking a whole lot of that rotgut. And once I started on Kentucky bourbon, I was going to finish Kentucky bourbon. I'd take a fifth of Wild Turkey and turn it right up . . . and still it wasn't enough. Once I got to where I was going, though, ol' Georgie didn't give a shit about nothin'. Things were even worse with tequila. Two shots of that devil water and I was looking to fight anyone, including my best friends.

Nobody wanted me drinking tequila.

A few beers led to lots of bourbon, and before I knew it the bar was crowded, a lousy band was rocking the joint and Crash and his wife had joined me for drinks. As I sat knocking back Wild Turkey and trying to ignore bad rock 'n' roll, an insane plan began to form in my booze-addled brain.

"I got an idea," I yelled at Crash over the din.

The brother emptied his glass and turned my way.

"Let's go to Elsinore," I said.

"What the fuck for?"

I lifted my glass and said, "The Sons of Hell."

This didn't register with Crash right away—that Vago was more fucked up than I was—but in a moment the lightbulb came on and a slow smile crept over his face.

"I hear you, brother."

The Sons of Hell was a support club for the Hells Angels, much like The Green Machine ran support for the Vagos. Because of their association with the hated Angels, there had always been friction between the Sons of Hell and Green Nation, but the sparks had never been quite hot enough to achieve ignition and liftoff. I figured if I could get those outlaws in Elsinore pissed off enough, they might retaliate, and if they retaliated, there was a damn good chance the Hells Angels would get involved. If the Angels jumped into the fight we just might be looking at a good old-fashioned gang war. And with a gang war you got criminal conspiracy, and with conspiracy you got RICO. Man, if I could give the ATF grounds for a RICO charge, I could get out from under Operation 22 Green and die a happy man.

My plan to make all of the above happen was masterful in its cunning simplicity. Crash and I would drive over to the Sons' favorite hangout in Lake Elsinore, a biker bar called The Hideaway, and we'd stir up a little chaos. This half-baked scheme, cooked up on Wild Turkey and executed by a couple of drunken assholes, was doomed to fail. But at the time, with a glass of Kentucky bourbon in my hand, I thought it was fuckin' genius. This was Shock and Awe, baby, and the joint chiefs had nothing on me.

The Hideaway Bar in Lake Elsinore had everything an outlaw biker could possibly want. There was a pool table, a jukebox with good old-fashioned rock 'n' roll tunes, an accommodating bartender willing to pour more shots of whiskey, and walls papered with customers' dollar bills, just like you'd find at the Screaming Chicken Saloon or The Crossroads in Yucaipa.

The only thing that biker bar didn't have was goddamn bikers.

Not a single one of those Sons of Hell was anywhere to be found.

I had to settle for tying a green bandana to a chain over the pool table, just to let those boys know we'd been there, then Crash and I stumbled back out the door.

Nothing had come of our bold probe behind enemy lines. There would be no biker war to end all biker wars. The Sons of Hell had tucked themselves in for the night, and all I had to show for my unrecognized genius was a splitting migraine.

On the drive back to Hemet our cell phones started blowing up with calls from Big Roy. Seems word had leaked that a couple of shitfaced Vagos prospects were cruising Lake Elsinore looking for trouble. We didn't answer those calls, but when we returned to our homes Big Todd was sitting outside my front door, and North was waiting on Crash.

We were both still half-cocked when our asses got dragged over to Big Roy's place in San Jacinto for a reaming.

"Who the fuck told you two clowns you could fuck with the Sons of

Hell?! I'm the P here. I say who goes where. You don't make a fuckin' move without my say-so, understand?!" He turned to Crash and shoved his chest. "Understand, motherfucker?!"

"Yeah, I understand," Crash answered dutifully but with little sincerity.

Now I spoke up. "It's my fault, Roy. Going to Elsinore was my idea."

"Your idea?" sputtered Big Roy, beet-faced. "Are you trying to make me look bad, asshole?"

"Hope not," I replied.

Now Roy shoved my chest too. "Well you are! This shit makes me look bad! Like I don't have control over my own fuckin' chapter!"

As Hemet's P, Big Roy was responsible for the behavior of his mutts, and yours truly had just slipped his leash and bit the mailman. To make matters worse, Roy had recently bought himself a new Harley Sportster and was worried Terry the Tramp might confiscate it—not an uncommon punishment among one percenter clubs.

Roy was pacing now, trying to contain the anger and keep his head from exploding. He stopped and stabbed a finger at the two of us.

"You assholes fuck up one more time and you're out. I'll run you both down the road, you got that?"

I bit my tongue and said nothing. Oh, happy day when I paid that bastard a visit in lockup. Oh, happy fucking day.

It was late when I got back to the chicken coop and slipped into the bedroom. As I pushed through the beads I almost tripped over Jenna. Sadly enough, buck naked and passed out on the floor was not an uncommon position for my girlfriend.

Neither was the excuse she usually gave for it: boredom.

Chief Thompson always said boredom was his daughter's worst enemy. And I think Daddy was spot-on. Jenna didn't want for anything. All she had to do was go to school, come home and take care of her kid.

But apparently that wasn't enough.

So after she'd gobbled all the pain meds in my medicine cabinet and lost contact with the prostitute who'd supplied speed and heroin, Jenna had hooked up with one of her old tweaker pals and started driving down to Tijuana, Mexico, for bottles of Soma, which are powerful muscle relaxants. She could be across the border and home again in two and a half hours and fucked up in three. And I couldn't stay ahead of her, man. Fast as I flushed those pills, the girl would be on her way to Tijuana to buy more.

Might not have been so bad if Jenna had known how to swallow one or two Somas. Unfortunately that was never my girlfriend's style. In true fashion, she'd pop a handful and end up flat on her back, drooling and vacant-eyed. Man, I hated that look—when you're trying to talk to someone and they're not even there. Old Joe and I would pick her nasty ass off the floor and pour it into bed, where she'd either puke between the sheets or shit in them.

That was the condition I found Jenna in when I came home from Big Roy's that night—fucked up on Somas and spread-eagle on the bedroom floor. I lifted her naked body into bed, then crawled in beside her. A few hours later I awoke to the mattress shaking—not uncommon with an addict like her. Usually when I got tired of the trembling I'd grab my pillow and sleep on the floor or boot her ass out of bed. But something different was happening this time. Jenna's body was twitching as though being poked by a cattle prod and her breathing was ragged. When I tried shaking her awake, there was no response. Her head just flopped around like a rag doll's.

Fuck. The bitch is dying on me.

I cradled her in my arms and rushed her into the shower, running the cold water full blast as I held her body against mine. When someone is that loaded, it takes hours to bring them back, but eventually Jenna came around and I had myself a shivering, wide-awake, fucked-up person.

That wouldn't be the last cold water slapping I gave my girlfriend. It happened often enough that I started leaving her in the shower with the cold water running and went back to bed. I never knew if I'd wake up in the morning and find Jenna drowned. As heartless as it sounds, there were times when I had my fingers crossed . . . I hoped and prayed that girl would die. I just couldn't take living like that anymore.

But it never happened.

The crazy bitch always survived.

15

Hell with the Angels

Any brother worth his colors takes a certain pride in being a Harley-riding, hard-drinking, gangbanging sonofabitch. Take away that patch and it'd be damn hard to tell one from the other—they're all cut from the same denim. But like many families, some brothers just don't get along.

That's how it is, and how it's always been, between the Vagos and the Hells Angels.

Since the day the Vagos (then called the Psychos) rumbled into San Bernardino during the 1960s and planted a flag on the Angels' home turf, the two clubs have been spilling bad blood. In fact, not long before I'd gone undercover, they had clashed during a motorcycle parts swap meet at the Orange County Fairgrounds, waylaying each other with mufflers, gas tanks, handlebars and whatever else they'd been able to get their hands on.

This mutual contempt between the Angels and Vagos spanned four decades and crossed three generations, leaving scores of bikers bruised, bloodied and sometimes buried. But then a strange thing happened.

Several months before I started wearing the green, the warring brothers struck an informal truce, and no one but me seemed anxious to break it.

Which is why it was unnaturally calm the day those two old enemies happened to cross paths at The Crossroads Bar and Grill in Yucaipa, a city that hugs Interstate 10 between Hemet and San Bernardino. The Crossroads was a biker-friendly establishment, more or less color-blind when it came to the patch on your back, but it was widely understood that the red and white from San Bernardino had adopted the place as their favorite haunt. In fact, some have claimed the Berdoo Hells Angels liked those digs so much that the place was later renamed Angel's Roadhouse Bar and Grill (which is a myth—Angel is actually the stage name of the stripper who bought the place).

The Vagos had a major bike run to Yucaipa that afternoon, and many of the chapter presidents and national and international officers were along for the ride. Some of the Hemet boys had been drinking before we hit the highway that day, but John Carr had warned me not to get pulled over, so I laid off the Wild Turkey and rode stone-cold sober into Yucaipa.

When we entered The Crossroads, the Angels were already inside getting hammered and shooting pool. I headed for the bar with my fellow prospect, Crash, and that tightly wound chapter president from Corona, Mumbles. There was tension in the bar that night—not unexpected given the amount of booze and testosterone—but the two sides were behaving themselves and minding their own business. Mumbles and I ordered drinks and shot the shit with the bartender, careful to steer clear of the Hells Angels in the vicinity.

Unfortunately, the Hells Angels wouldn't steer clear of me.

The green bandana around my head and the rocker on my back pegged me as a Vagos prospect, drawing unwanted attention from a scraggly bearded Angel wearing the infamous "death's head" patch on his back. As I tried to pass him in those tight quarters, he couldn't resist opening his mouth.

"Hey, boy," he said scornfully. "Why don't you get some real colors 'stead of that green shit."

That's all the man said. But it was enough. I might have only been a lowly prospect, but that sonofabitch was disrespecting me in front of a brother. And that just couldn't stand—not if I was to have an ounce of credibility with the Vagos. Like I've said, a top requirement among one percenters is giving and getting respect. And that afternoon at The Crossroads Bar and Grill, I wasn't feeling it.

I turned to find that Angel smirking back at me. But not for long. Faster than a cat can lick its ass, I coldcocked that fucker. The man hit the floor like a stunned mullet.

And that's when all hell broke loose.

Angels and Vagos came flying in from all directions, ready to throw down right then and there. The truce that had held for months was about to come unglued, and all because of little old me.

As I stood over that fallen Angel, daring him to stand up, powerful arms suddenly wrapped me from behind. I was in the iron grip of a man-mountain. He shoved me toward a group of rubbernecking greenies.

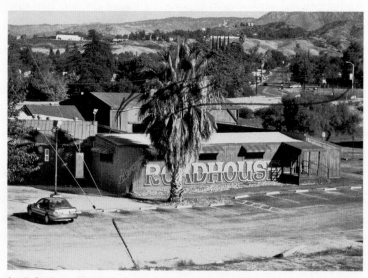

Angel's Roadhouse (formerly the Crossroads) where I decked the Hells Angel.

"Get him out of here!" the booming voice commanded. And when Rhino, the Vagos international sergeant at arms gave an order, people followed it.

Crash and some of the others did as commanded, hustling me to the far side of the bar while pumping my hand and slapping my back every step of the way. Few men have the balls to hit a Hells Angel, never mind in an Angels bar, and putting one on his back was cause for celebration.

"Fuck, yeah! That was beautiful!" shouted Mumbles, muscling his way through my crowd of admirers. Then he planted a kiss smack on my lips. "That's what I'm talkin' about! That's the way you do it!"

The little Tasmanian Devil was giddy with excitement, hopping around the floor with his hands on his knives, revved up and ready to slice and dice.

"Did you see that?!" he was shouting at anyone within earshot. "Did you fuckin' see that?!" He grabbed me by the scruff of the neck. "This fucker's got more heart than all you motherfuckers put together."

But not everyone was as gung ho as Mumbles. Big Roy appeared next, looking constipated with worry.

"You've got to leave," Roy said to me urgently. "Tramp wants you out of here right now."

"Fuck that!" barked Mumbles. "Did you fuckin' see what he did?!"

"All I know is the Angels want this prospect's ass and Tramp wants him out of here."

"Bull-fuckin'-shit!" Mumbles protested to deaf ears. "We should fight these cocksuckers!"

Big Roy ignored this, calling over Crash and a full-patch named Mickey, who had recently joined the chapter. "You two take George back to Hemet," he instructed. "And make sure he fucking stays there." Then Roy turned to me with a grave look. "You really fucked up, George," he said. "This time you fucked up good."

Oh, shit.

Cruising home down Interstate 10, sandwiched between Crash and

Mickey, I had plenty of time to consider just how badly I'd fucked up. All kinds of nightmare scenarios played out in my head. And it wasn't torpedoing the truce with the Hells Angels that concerned me. There could be worse things. But what if Tramp confiscated my Harley and ran my ass down the road? Losing that rat bike wouldn't be a catastrophe, but it would certainly signal the end of Operation 22 Green. Had I fucked that up too? And what if the Vagos decided on a more permanent solution . . . one involving shovels and sand?

Shit . . . shit . . . shit.

Sometime around midnight Big Todd showed up at the shack in Valle Vista. He shook my hand and told me the Hells Angels were buzzing like hornets and wanted a piece of my ass. Big Roy's orders were to stay put until Tramp figured out what to do.

I had that gnawing gut sense that something bad was coming—like a big ol' locomotive bearing down on me. If Tramp decided to hand the Angels my ass on a platter, I'd have to offer it up. To refuse would get me booted from the Vagos, in which case Operation 22 Green would become an early-term abortion. Course I wasn't thrilled with the idea of being dead, either.

"What do you think'll happen?" I asked Todd.

"Who the fuck knows?" was all he could offer. But as Todd left the apartment, I could tell that even he was worried.

Sometime in the early morning hours I grabbed my smokes and headed out to the parking lot to visit Old Joe. The Man upstairs is a damn good listener, but so was the man in the travel trailer. I needed a friend to talk to, get a few things off my chest, and Joe was the only person in the world I felt I could really confide in.

I sparked a cigarette, then knocked lightly on the trailer door. In a moment I heard his tense voice calling from inside.

"Who's that?"

Joe probably figured it was his old roomie, crazy Doug, back looking for a place to bunk.

"It's me, buddy."

The door opened and Joe appeared shirtless and wearing jeans.

"Hey, man, sorry to wake you."

"Not a problem," said Joe sleepily. "What's up, brother?"

"Could we talk?"

"Sure. Sure. Come on in."

He opened the door wider and stepped back.

"Out here's fine, if that's okay with you," I told him.

It was a warm evening in August, and I wanted to talk under the big night sky. Guess it felt like a more suitable stage for the large questions I'd been wrestling with. So I took a seat on the tattered couch Joe kept beside the trailer. He pulled on a T-shirt and joined me.

"Everything okay?" Joe wanted to know.

"Wish I could say it was," I answered, "but I think I'm in deep shit, partner."

"How deep?"

"I knocked out a Hells Angel at The Crossroads last night, and they're not too happy."

"Hang on," said Joe.

He disappeared inside the trailer, then popped out again with a handle of vodka. After taking a stiff jolt, he passed me the jug, and I hit it twice—one less than my limit for going screwy.

I didn't need screwy right now.

"I've got that bad vibe again, Joe. I just feel like this could be it, you know? Like maybe I might not survive this."

Old Joe was tongue-tied. I think his mind had seized. He'd never heard that kind of talk from me before. I was always the strong one. The guy who feared nothing and no one. But this? This was goddamn pussy talk, and my buddy couldn't process it. "I don't want to disappear, Joe," I said after a long silence. "I don't want to end up like David."

Old Joe took another pull on the jug.

"Know what I'm most afraid of?" I said.

He just blinked at me.

"That I'll get killed and no one will know where I'm at. I don't want to be buried in the desert without some kind of marker. That scares the hell out of me, you know?"

It took another jolt of vodka to free up Old Joe's pistons and get him talking again.

"Well, then fuck the patch," he said finally. "Fuck that patch, brother, and get out while you can."

I shook my head. "The operation's come too far. I couldn't bail on John."

Joe looked me square in the eye and said, "John ain't the one worried about gettin' buried in the desert."

That ended the conversation. In a few minutes I went back to bed to snuggle with Jenna, leaving Old Joe alone on the couch with his thoughts and his booze.

A lot of prayers went outbound during that long and sleepless night. I'm not what you'd call a Christian—I haven't been "born again"—but I do have strong faith in a higher power. I picture it kind of like this: I'm gripping the handlebars as my bike careens down life's highway with God holding on for dear life behind me, letting me know when to change lanes and what exits to take. Maybe that's the little voice that whispers in your head.

The one I was ignoring.

God help me.

Sometime before noon Big Roy called to say he was coming by to pick me up. Tramp wanted to see us at his place in the High Desert, and Roy was nervous.

"We're in trouble, George," he said ominously before hanging up.

Immediately I called John Carr. My handler already knew what had gone down at The Crossroads; I'd called him after returning from the bar. At first John seemed pleased. Great . . . George has stirred the pot. But as I described the aftermath, he began to understand the serious trouble I was facing.

"Roy's on his way over. We're headed for Tramp's house," I explained on the Nextel.

"Right now?"

"Right now, man."

"I can't get anyone over there that fast. Can you stall?"

"No way."

There was a brief silence on the phone.

"Alright, listen. I've got someone in San Bernardino. She's a detective with the county sheriff's department, handles gangs. I'll see if I can get hold of her. You call me as soon as you can and let me know you're okay."

A few minutes later Big Roy was honking for me in the parking lot. As I climbed into his truck I spotted Jenna standing in the open door of the apartment. I gave her a wave that she didn't return. I thought that might be the last time I ever saw her.

It was a long, quiet ride in Big Roy's truck as we headed for Hesperia—the longest ride of my life. When we pulled into Tramp's property about ninety minutes later, it looked like we'd stumbled on a wake.

Beyond the chain-link gate, ten to fifteen Harleys were parked in front of a gray stucco ranch. Grim-faced men in gang colors milled about, every one of them a Vagos officer.

This was some serious shit.

Roy left me standing outside the truck and headed over to speak to one of the Vagos. I lit a cigarette, tucked the lighter away, then looked up to find those outlaws gawking at me like . . . well, like I was the wake's guest of honor. Soon Big Roy started back again, trailed by Psycho, the P of the Victorville chapter. Those desert boys were insane. I think the heat boiled their brains.

"Alright, listen up," Roy said. "Tramp, Ta Ta and Rhino are inside with the Angels."

Fuck! The Angels are here?! I felt my chest grip.

"Tramp wants you to wait in the garage until you're called," Roy continued. "No one knows anything more than that, George."

Psycho shook his head. "I'd hate to be in your shoes, brother," he said. "Just don't let them see you shaking when you walk in."

"I ain't shaking," I replied as calmly as I could.

"Oh, no? Check out your cigarette."

Psycho was right. That Marlboro was shaking between my fingers like a dog shittin' tacks.

He and Big Roy escorted me into the attached garage, which was jammed with all kinds of well-organized tools and motorcycle parts.

"Good luck," said Psycho, smiling beneath his droopy moustache as he slammed the garage door shut.

Right away I was looking for a way out, but the only exit was through a single door leading into the house. Beyond it, the Vagos national leadership and members of the San Bernardino Hells Angels had gathered to decide my fate—and the longer I sweated in that garage, the more convinced I was they'd gathered for a lynching.

"Lord, this is your work I'm doing," I reminded the Man upstairs. "Keep me safe."

I paced the floor, puffing my cigarette, and stopped to examine an enormous black-and-white photograph of Terry the Tramp that he'd blown maybe four feet high and hung on the garage wall. Every Vago has seen that picture. In it Tramp is posing with his 1950s-vintage coffin-tanked chopper "Lady and the Tramp," while gripping a double-action western rifle in one hand like he's John Fuckin' Wayne. Tramp had reproduced that image on everything from T-shirts to playing cards and sold it at a hefty markup to his loyal subjects.

Christ. The man had an ego bigger than his beer gut. I was reminded of a night we'd spent in a hospital room playing dominoes a few months before as Tramp recovered from a heart condition. The man was a chain smoker and serial coffee drinker just like me, but what pushed his weakened heart over the edge was a blond bimbo that almost fucked him to death.

With Green Nation's international P flat on his back and vulnerable to being smothered with his own pillow, Crash and I were called in to take one of the round-the-clock security shifts. I swear, it was like guarding Don Vito Corleone. The nurses were laughing at us standing in the hospital corridor, arms folded, protecting our president from would-be assassins.

When Tramp called us into the room, we found Fearless Leader propped up in bed, hooked to a heart monitor and an intravenous drip. Immediately he pointed at Crash, who he must have overheard on the phone complaining to his wife about the shit-ass detail.

"Not you," Tramp growled. "You get the fuck out of here."

Crash ducked out fast, and Tramp smiled.

"Hey, George. What's going on?"

"Nothing much. Just here to watch you, Tramp."

"Well, sit the fuck down and let's play some dominoes."

Nothing bonds two grown men quite like playing bones into the wee hours. As we laid those tiles down, Tramp shared his war stories of the good ol' days, including how he came to be international P of Green Nation back in 1986.

At the time, the Vagos were a dying club, he explained, led ineffectually by a motorcycle outlaw named Leonard Berella. As membership withered, Tramp's older brother, Parts, heard of an upcoming officers meeting in Desert Hot Springs. Parts told his little bro—who was P of the San Gabriel chapter at the time—that he was just the man to turn things around and lead the Vagos back to glory.

"Lenny Berella sucked balls," Tramp continued. "Made a lot of bad decisions for the club. So I told my two buddies, Sonny and Jerry the Jew, that I was gonna take over the leadership, and we rode out to the officer's meeting. The Hot Springs chapter had parked all these shit-ass trailers in a big circle around the fire pit, and Lenny and I met in the middle to decide who would be the next international P.'"

Visions of classic Western showdowns danced in my sleep-starved brain, with Terry the Tramp as Clint Eastwood and Lenny Berella as Lee Van Cleef.

"I'd already warned Jerry the Jew, if that bastard comes at me, I'm gonna kill him," Tramp said.

"So did you kill the bastard?" I'd mumbled, barely awake.

"Didn't have to. Leonard stood up to me at first, but then all his support bailed out. Once that happened he was done. He left the club and never came back."

Tramp paused to sniff the air.

"Oh, fuck," he said. "I think I shit myself."

Standing in Tramp's garage, waiting on my moment of reckoning with the Hells Angels, I understood just how the man had felt in that hospital bed . . . because I was about to shit myself too.

I thought about calling John to see if that San Bernardino detective had made it up to Hesperia, but before I could reach for the Nextel the door to the house opened and Rhino appeared.

Fuck me. This was the same brutal bastard who'd zip-tied poor Shorty, that Vagos hang-around from Berdoo, then blown his brains out.

And goddamn was he big.

"Let's go," said Rhino, stone-faced.

I crushed the cigarette underfoot and followed that monster like a condemned man headed for the gallows. *Holy shit, Lord. This is where you've led me? What the hell's the matter with you? Why didn't you make me listen? I should have got off at the last exit, dammit. I should have turned right!*

I stepped into Tramp's kitchen—sauna hot and reeking of musty sweat and body odor. Jammed inside that cramped space and the adjoining dining room were seven grim-faced outlaws flying their colors, four of them wearing the red and white. A trio of Hells Angels was seated at the dining room table, each with a revolver resting in front of him.

Not good.

The fourth Angel was leaning his shoulder against the kitchen wall with a cocky grin on his face. It was the same asshole I'd decked at The Crossroads Bar and Grill.

"Take a seat, prospect."

Terry the Tramp was speaking. He motioned to the empty seat between him and Ta Ta. The moment I sat down, Rhino took a standing position directly behind me, blocking my exit.

Definitely not good.

"You know why you're here?" Tramp asked me right off.

I was about to open my mouth when one of the Hells Angels leaned over the table.

"Fuck this asshole. He ain't even patched."

"Don't matter," Ta Ta shot back. "He rides with us."

"He's a fuckin' prospect," spat the Angel. "Give him to us and we'll settle this right now."

I felt my heart jump. The Angels were going to drag me into the Mojave and do me right there. But I wouldn't go easy. Hell, no. Not without a fight. Now my brain went into overdrive. I needed an escape plan. I'd have to take Rhino down first. No easy trick. *Maybe a quick upward thrust into that thick neck might pop the carotid. And if the man-mountain falls . . .*

"You ain't takin' our brother nowhere," came Rhino's voice like a bullhorn above my head.

Man, I could've kissed that mullet-headed sonofabitch.

"He's no brother," the Angel snapped.

"I said it ain't happening," snarled Rhino, glaring down at him.

The kitchen grew pin-drop quiet. Strike a match in that tension and the whole damn room might've gone off like Mount St. Helens.

"Everybody just calm the fuck down."

This was the biggest and hairiest of the Hells Angels who spoke.

"Alright, prospect," he said to me, "why'd you hit him?"

I nodded toward the smirking Angel leaning against the wall.

"That dude said, 'Why don't you get some real colors.' I took that as disrespect, so I popped him."

All eyes now swung toward my accuser.

"That how it happened?" the big Angel asked.

"Fuck no. Like I told you. That prick swung for no good reason."

"You lyin' sack of shit!" I exploded.

"Fuck you, prospect!" he barked back.

"We ain't gettin' nowhere like this," interrupted Tramp. "Let's just stick 'em both in the backyard and let 'em fight it out."

Rhino clapped a meaty paw on my shoulder. "What about it, prospect? You good with that?"

"Yeah, I'm good with that," I said without hesitation.

"What about you?" Tramp asked my opponent.

The smirk was already wavering on that lying bastard's face. He squirmed for a moment, then shifted a nervous glance toward his brothers at the table.

"Check it out," said Rhino with contempt. "He's a goddamn pussy."

"I'll fight him," volunteered the Angel who wanted me buried in the desert.

"Fuck you will," bellowed Rhino. "If that's the way it's gonna be, let's just go four on four and settle it that way."

The Hells Angels weren't so hot on that idea, especially with Rhino fighting for the other team, so the two clubs bickered for the next few minutes—just like the good old days—until my gutless opponent finally caved under pressure and copped to the lie.

Now his three amigos were pissed. They'd put their asses on the line and been embarrassed.

As the Angels mounted their choppers and rumbled off toward San Bernardino, Rhino, Ta Ta and Tramp were grinning clear back to the molars. Tramp even wrapped me in a bear hug and asked if I wanted a drink.

Hell, yeah, I wanted a drink. Hand me the whole fuckin' bottle. I was a nervous wreck.

Not too long after that, the unofficial truce between the Vagos and Hells Angels began to unravel. The first crack appeared when the red and white jumped some greenies in Hollywood. Then, a few weeks later the Sons of Hell were turned loose on Green Nation in the San Jacinto Valley.

Of course, I couldn't give a rat's ass. If those two old enemies wanted to take turns pounding each other, that was fine with me. I was just happy to be alive and relieved 22 Green was still on track.

As an added bonus, I'd managed to get the best of the mighty Hells Angels—first at The Crossroads Bar and Grill, then again in Tramp's kitchen. As far as the Vagos were concerned, I was their flavor-of-the-month golden boy. Tramp later awarded me the "V" patch for my cut, emblematic of a member who brings honor to the club.

For seven long months my time as a Vagos prospect had been a humiliating and hellish ride—a stretch longer than most candidates were forced to endure. But within a week of that meeting in the High Desert, I was patched into Green Nation.

16

Riding with the Devil

On a Wednesday night toward the end of August 2003, about eight months after I'd first gone under, Crash and I were standing guard over the motorcycles when Big Todd called us into JB's garage. JB was a thirty-year-old army veteran and sales manager at Caterpillar, and he had offered his beautiful home for church meetings. And even though he kept us penned with the garden tools, that garage was a damn sight better than most of the places where the Vagos held church.

The patches were waiting when Crash and I entered. Besides Big Roy, Todd and JB, there was Doc, Sparks, Slinger, Buckshot, Swede, Jimbo, Ready, North and Chopper. And every one of those boys was looking grim.

What's wrong now? I thought. And did it have anything to do with the knucklehead standing next to me—my fellow prospect and personal albatross, Crash?

Right away Big Roy was in my grill.

"You motherfucker, I know what you did!" he bellowed at me.

"I don't know what you're talking about, Roy," I said, my mind racing through the possibilities.

"You don't know, huh?" Now Roy shifted his ire to Crash. "What about you, asshole?!"

"Uh, umm . . . ," stammered Crash before shrugging his shoulders.

"Swear to God, Roy," I said. "We don't know what you're talking about."

"Is that right?" Roy fumed, then turned and commanded, "Show 'em, North."

North, who had recently been promoted to vice president after Todd had gotten sacked for screwing up again, stepped forward with two manila envelopes.

"Here's what I'm talking about, motherfuckers," Roy growled. He reached into one of the envelopes and pulled out Loki, the Vagos center patch.

Hell, yeah!

Big Roy slapped the patch against my chest, then punched the spot as hard as he could. North did the same to Crash, and a cheer went up from the patches.

"Welcome to the club, brothers," laughed Roy.

The members swarmed us, hugging, slapping backs, shaking hands and kissing cheeks.

"Alright, assholes," Roy interrupted. "You know the drill. You've got five minutes to sew those patches on or lose 'em forever."

As I stitched Loki to the back of my cut, it began to dawn on me that the long and grueling march from prospect to patch was finally over. The door to the outlaw world had swung wide open. I'd be allowed to attend church meetings now, maybe even take over one of the leadership positions like sergeant at arms or treasurer. Man, there were real possibilities there for doing damage.

I followed the Vagos from JB's garage, then we mounted our bikes and headed out on a San Jacinto Valley bar crawl to celebrate the chapter's newest patches, Crash and Big George.

That's right. I had a road name now: Big George Rowe.

That's the nickname Big Todd had always hung on me, and that's how he'd phoned it in to national without Big Roy's permission. Roy wasn't happy about it, either. The man was of the opinion that two "Bigs" in his chapter was more than enough. He'd just gotten rid of Big Doug; now he had to deal with Big George. Far as Big Roy was concerned, I was one "Big" over the limit.

For now, though, it would be Big George making the rounds and showing off his new colors to a public that couldn't care less. They just wanted me gone with the rest of the Vagos. By the time we landed at Johnny's Restaurant, our final stop, we'd picked up a handful of patched members from some of the neighboring chapters, including a few boys from Norco—Quickie John's crew. The restaurant was practically empty when we walked in. In the year since the Vagos had taken over the place, business had dried up. The few patrons that remained watched us with nervous eyes and whispered urgently among themselves.

Look. The barbarians have arrived. Hide the women and children.

There were one percenters who would claim those civilians were showing respect for the patch. But that's not the way I saw it. If anything, what I saw in those faces was fear—fear of the patch. Of course, that was the seduction for many who joined motorcycle gangs like the Vagos. Punks like Roy and Big Todd got their rocks off on that power trip.

But there was something else I was aware of while laughing and drinking with the boys at Johnny's that night. Odd as it sounds, I felt their sense of brotherhood. I don't know. Maybe it had something to do with my past. I'd spent a good deal of it orphaned or adopted—never quite fitting in—and the Vagos offered a family where the misfit toys could find common ground and belong to something greater than themselves.

John Carr had warned me not to get chummy with that brutish clique. That's exactly what happened to Special Agent Billy Queen when he went under with the Mongols in 1998. The lawman got swept up in the motorcycle culture and found himself drifting over the line.

"Lot of times guys go under and start calling each other brother, and before you know it your focus gets lost," John cautioned during one of our Friday-night meetings at the Little Luau.

"Never gonna happen," I assured him. "I know the reason I'm here."

And I meant it too. I never lost sight of why I'd gone under with the Vagos. Why I'd worked so hard, risked so much and put up with such bullshit for that Loki on my back. I think it helped that I was never a greenie at heart. Guys like Hammer, who was a patch holder and bled green before turning for the feds, had a hard time breaking clean once the mission ended. For them it was gut-ripping to let go of their past, to permanently sever the closest relationships many of them would ever know.

I spent most of the night bar crawling with my back to the wall, guarding against any effort to tear

Sparks (top) and Buckshot, who left the Bros MC to join the Hemet Vagos.

that center patch off my back, which would bust me back to prospect. Crash, on the other hand, was drunk and careless—and he wasn't much of a seamstress either. Big Todd got his fingers under Loki and ripped it right off Crash's cut. Amid the yelling and screaming and finger pointing that followed, I slipped from the bar and punched the number for Uncle Johnny Law into my Nextel. I got John's away message and left one of my own.

"Hey, this is Big George calling. Don't you be giving me shit anymore, buddy. I'm a patch holder now."

I hung up and lit a cigarette. I'd smoked maybe half that Marlboro when a call came back from 818, the Los Angeles exchange.

"You think you're the balls now, don'tcha?" were the first words out of John's mouth. "Well, let me tell you something, Big George. You're just another piece of shit Vagos to me."

"This piece of shit Vagos is gonna make you famous, motherfucker."

"Bullshit," laughed John. "You want famous, ride with the Angels. Least you could have got the red and white."

I cursed my handler good-naturedly; he gave it right back, then the bouncer came charging out Johnny's back door.

"George! I need help in here!"

The Vagos had a stomp circle going, and some unfortunate civilian was on the ground in the middle of it. With the help of the bouncer I managed to get the man off the floor and away from that crazed bunch, then I dragged him out the back door and into the parking lot.

When I returned to the bar, the Vagos were laughing drunkenly and Big Roy was wiping blood off his boot with a napkin.

"What happened?" I asked Todd.

"I told him to move, but the fucker wouldn't move."

Roy tossed the bloody napkin onto the bar and grinned.

"He moved."

A "Code 69" is a war call. If a patched Vagos gets a Code 69 message at home or on his cell, it means there's an emergency and club business comes first. You drop what you're doing and get your ass to the location of that emergency. And if you don't make it, you'd better have a damn good reason why, because when it comes to ignoring a Code 69, the Vagos will definitely hunt you down.

As Big Roy so aptly described it, Code 69 is "serious club shit."

The day after my hard night celebrating the patch, I was draining my second cup of java and trying to ignore a splitting migraine when the phone rang.

"Code sixty-nine," said Todd the moment I answered. "Code sixty-nine."

"What's going on?"

"This dude just jumped my ass and fucked me up. I think my leg's broke. Code sixty-nine, bro."

I got an address and a general direction, then grabbed my truck keys. But before I could make the door, Jenna came out of the bedroom, half asleep and fully pissed off. The call had awoken Her Highness, and she was looking to tear someone a new asshole. I can tell you from personal experience that getting that woman out of bed in the morning was akin to poking a hibernating grizzly. You almost had to cover your nut-sack, because the bitch just might grab hold and tear it right the fuck off.

"Todd's in trouble," I told her as I rushed out the door. Whatever danger I was headed for couldn't be half as bad as facing my girlfriend in the morning.

I hopped in my truck and sped away, armed with nothing but an address. And for the life of me I couldn't find the fucking place. I finally rode across Highway 74 and went to Jack Fite's house for directions. Jack wasn't riding with the Hemet Vagos at the time. He'd grown tired of Big Roy's bullshit and left to join Nels Bloom, who we called Swede, as treasurer of a new Vagos chapter in Winchester.

There were no worries as I knocked on Satan's door. No concern about getting another broken leg. For one thing, I was a patch holder now. I could fight back. Besides, the evil one had apologized. Jack explained he'd just had a really bad day when he'd stomped me . . . and he was really truly sorry for that.

The motherfucker would be even sorrier once the takedown happened and Operation 22 Green was in the books. Because sometime later I grabbed my audio and video gear, went over to his house and bought fifteen grams of methamphetamine that he kept buried near his backyard shed. I knew this because I peeked through a hole in the garage when I wasn't supposed to be looking and saw where Jack dug up his stash.

The man came back bragging how he had a pretty good racket going. For a thousand bucks, someone was cooking meth for him, then Jack would turn around and resell it for ten, pocketing an easy nine grand. *Well, enjoy it while you can, motherfucker,* I remember thinking—*'cause you're going down, Jack.*

By this time my response to Todd's urgent Code 69 was pretty pathetic. If the brother was bleeding out somewhere, the tank had probably run dry. Fortunately Jack Fite knew which direction to point me. The homeowner who lived at that address, just around the corner, was a friend of his and one of Hemet's bigger dope dealers. At first Jack suggested I forget about the call and go home, but when I told him I had an obligation to help Todd, Jack sent me on my way with a promise to follow.

At the end of a cul-de-sac I found Todd and my ex-girlfriend Christie jawing with a long-haired mountain of a drug dealer named Dave. The story I heard later was that Todd had paid the dealer for crystal meth that was never delivered. Come to find out that was a crock of shit. Todd was trying to rip Dave off—maybe get himself another freebie like that transmission part he took after the Vagos gave Bro a beat-down at the Toy Box. Come to think of it, that was Todd's idea too. The fucker was getting real good at letting others clean up his messes. And being a Vagos was perfect for a guy like that. "You fuck with one, you fuck with all" was damn handy if you knew how to work it.

Of course, I didn't know any of that when I jumped from the truck and ran to help my Vagos brother. As soon as I got there, Big Todd launched one of his patented sucker punches at Dave. His swing missed, but Dave's didn't. The dealer cracked Todd good.

It was the last punch he would throw.

My first strike smashed into the man's third rib, breaking it off and puncturing his lung. The dealer toppled and hit the pavement like King Kong. But I wasn't finished yet. No, sir. It was no gentleman's game when you were in a street fight. My approach was always to beat my opponent until he couldn't fight back—no different from brawling bareknuckle in a bowling alley. Dave was a big sonofabitch, and I wanted to make damn sure he wouldn't get up again. In the heat of the moment Big George was living and breathing the green, baby, and there was no separating the government informant from the street brawling animal I was bred to be.

I was still pummeling the man on the ground when someone grabbed me from behind.

"That's enough, George!" yelled Jack Fite. "You're killing him!"

I didn't end Dave's life that morning, but the man was definitely out. Way out. A few days later Big Roy called me into the Lady Luck and ripped me a new one.

"The cops have been watching me lately, motherfucker. I'm trying to keep a low profile and you go and beat up one of the biggest dope dealers in town?"

"Todd called for backup. What was I supposed to do?"

"Todd said he never called you," Roy fired back.

I was speechless.

"I'm pulling your patch," he said. "In fact, I want your whole fuckin' cut."

I wasn't ready to call out Todd as a lying bastard. Not yet, anyway. I fetched my cut from the truck, turned it over to Big Roy, then drove back to Valle Vista, fuming. This wasn't the first time Todd had thrown me under the bus. When I was still a hang-around he'd done the same fucking thing at a bar we called The Bloody Bucket.

Sitting around getting hammered that night, Todd had given me a nudge and pointed out a group of twenty-somethings shooting pool. Don't know what it was about outlaws and pool tables that generated so much friction, but trouble was coming again—with a capital T and that rhymes with P and that stands for pool.

"See that asshole wearing the Hard Rock shirt?" Todd said to me. "I hate that cocksucker. Go fuck him up."

"What for?"

"Don't ask questions. Just do it."

"Yeah, but—"

"What the fuck? Are you down for this club or not?"

"You heard Big Todd," North jumped in. "Do what the man says."

It was one of those rock-and-a-hard-place moments John would later warn me about, where I was forced to choose between the long-term success of the operation and taking part in the exact same kind of abuse I'd gone under to prevent. I held my nose and chose the mission. On Todd's orders, I beat that kid down. The poor bastard never knew what hit him . . . or why. Of course, the irony of what I'd done hadn't been lost on me. I'd gone back to being a bully again, just like the bad ol' days at Hemet High.

When Big Roy learned what had happened at The Bucket he wasn't happy. It was okay to beat the shit out of people, but beatings had to be authorized. It was either Roy's way or the highway. Todd and North saved their own skins, denying they'd told me to beat the kid down, so all the shit got flung my way. Those fuckers hung me out to dry, but what the hell could I do? They were patch holders, and I was just a lowly hang-around. So I played the good soldier and took one for the United States of America.

Now here I was getting screwed by Todd once again. In less than twenty-four hours I'd earned my patch and lost it, which had to be some sort of record for ineptitude in the forty-plus-year history of the Vagos MC.

"This shit's going to national," Roy promised as I left the Lady Luck. "And if Tramp and I find out you're lying, it's gonna be your ass that's run down the road."

Fucking great.

So now I was faced with starting over as a prospect. Even worse, Big Roy was threatening to confiscate the ATF's bike and boot me out of the club, putting a stake through the heart of Operation 22 Green. When I called John Carr with the bad news, he couldn't believe it.

"You what?"

"I lost my patch."

"But you just got it."

"That's right. And now I've lost it."

There was a moment's silence while my handler processed this.

"How could you let that happen?"

I was in no mood for a pissing contest, so I gathered myself and told John not to sweat it. Yes, I was angry and discouraged, but I had a way out of that mess—an ace in the hole.

The hand was played a few days later when Big Roy called me back to the Lady Luck for a powwow with Todd and North. I didn't waste time bluffing when I got there.

"No more bullshit," I barked at Todd. "You called a Code 69 and you fuckin' know it."

That caught the bastard off guard. No matter what the circumstances, you didn't rat out a brother . . . which, believe it or not, didn't strike me as ironic at the time.

"That's what you say," Todd managed. "I don't remember that."

Now Big Roy broke in.

"If George is lying, what was he doing at that house with you?"

"How the fuck should I know?" Todd answered. "He just showed up. You know how he's always ridin' around and shit."

Man, I would have demolished that sonofabitch if he hadn't been doing such a good job of it himself. You could have driven a Freightliner through the holes in Todd's case. He looked to the jury for support, but North and Roy weren't buying his story either.

Big Todd wasn't what you'd call a sympathetic defendant anyway. He'd been hitting the meth pretty heavy and using club money to support his habit. All the lies, stealing and cheating had already got him busted from vice president down to sergeant at arms, and now he was one small step from joining the rest of us rank-and-file peons—or even worse for him, losing his patch and getting run down the road.

"You're going to take his word over mine?" Todd protested.

"Cut the shit, asshole!" I shouted.

"Fuck you!" Todd bellowed, giving me a shove. That Vago was used to barking like a tough dog and having people back down. But I wasn't a prospect anymore. I didn't have to take anyone's shit. I went nose-to-nose with that sonofabitch, daring him to throw a punch and put me in the mood to dance.

If Todd took the bait, I was ready to drill him. But the chicken-shit wouldn't bite. When he realized he was about to get a beat-down in front of Roy and North, he clucked once and stepped back.

And that's when I flipped my hole card.

Without realizing it at the time, I'd saved my own ass by getting lost on the way to Dave the dealer's house and stopping at Jack Fite's place for directions. I'd asked Jack to attend the meeting, and when he backed my version of the story, Todd was pretty much toast.

Next day Terry the Tramp handed down his ruling from on high in the desert. Big Roy was ordered to return my cut and pull Todd's patch. It was back to prospecting for the sergeant at arms. There was even talk of running Big Todd down the road because of all the chaos he'd been causing.

Few days later I drove back to the cul-de-sac and apologized to Dave the dealer for putting him in the hospital.

"I ain't mad at you," said Dave, talking with stitches in his face and his arm in a sling. "I understand it was just one brother looking out for the other. But I sure want a piece of that other dude. I'm gonna get that motherfucker."

I imagine there were quite a few people who felt that way about Big

Todd Brown. And odds were that someday one of them was going to follow through and "get that motherfucker."

Now that I had Loki, with all the rights and privileges that patch conveyed, I needed a Harley under my ass befitting my elevated status. I'd been complaining long and loud about that piece-of-shit Touring Classic that ATF had stuck me with, and finally Carr was able to wrangle me a new set of wheels. My second ride was a Harley-Davidson Heritage the government had confiscated from the Warlocks MC. Those outlaws must have said "Thank you, Jesus!" and laughed their asses off as that eyesore was rolled away. The bike came from Washington, D.C., looking like it had been left out in the weather for ten years.

But I didn't care. Even rust-covered, that machine was a damn sight better than the rat bike I'd been saddled with for nine months. As I loaded the Heritage into the bed of the pickup, I informed John Carr I intended to make a few alterations.

"My boss won't like that," warned John.

"Oh, yeah? Well then tell your boss to ride this piece of shit."

Soon as I got back to Valle Vista I went to work, stripping that Harley down to the frame. I threw on some ape hangers and got rid of the saddlebags. I retooled the motor and tranny, did a bunch of little tweaks, then rolled it back out again. Any one percenter would have been proud to ride that motorcycle. I'd built her outlaw through and through.

Now that I had myself a patch and a decent bike, I could finally take my girlfriend on some of the club runs. Jenna was actually happy with the idea of spending quality time with her suspiciously gay boyfriend. Our first opportunity to ride together came on a Vagos run down to San Diego. Hemet intended to make a show of force outside the Hells Angels' clubhouse, and a few of the VOLs were coming along for the ride.

A one percenter motorcycle club was a "men only" organization, and most members treated their old ladies as little more than meat.

Some even considered them communal property to be shared among brothers like a toolbox. But my experience with the Vagos was different. In Green Nation a man didn't touch another patch's property. Violating that sacred trust could get a member stripped of his patch and run down the road.

The patch on the back of a VOL's jacket told the world exactly who she belonged to. Jenna's jacket, for instance, would have said "Property of Big George" had she chosen to wear one. But in the early days that little rebel was fighting Green Nation all the way, so fiercely protective of her independence that she wore pink instead of green.

Jenna wasn't a fan of the Vagos Old Ladies at first either. She was barhopping one night with some of the VOLs when North's wife—a big woman Jenna called "Marmaduke"—started giving one of Jenna's old school pals a ration of shit for "brushing against her hair." My girlfriend didn't care much for Marmaduke's bluster, and she absolutely despised her lard-assed husband. North had once peppered an addict friend of Jenna's with a shotgun. The kid had survived the blast only to die later in a Chevron gas station bathroom from a heroin overdose.

Jenna fought against becoming a VOL for several months, but gradually she came to the conclusion that if she couldn't beat the green, she might as well wear it. In time she hung up the pink threads and threw on a denim jacket that announced "Property of Big George."

Of course, that didn't matter to a dirtbag like Big Todd. Property or not, that sonofabitch had a hard-on for Jenna from the moment I began dating her. Must have been some kind of ego trip trolling for another brother's woman, because he'd cruised that way before. Todd claimed to have fucked Crash's old lady and bragged that he knew Roy's wife inside out—and Big Roy was supposed to have been his bosom buddy.

During the months I was prospecting, Big Todd would send me on wild-goose chases for hours at a time just so he could snag some alone time with Jenna. And once he had her to himself, he'd whisper that I was cheating on her. Not only did that slippery bastard want to nail my girlfriend, he wanted to drive a wedge between us too. I knew what that snake was up to, but since Jenna swore up and down she wasn't interested in fucking Todd, I kept my mouth shut.

And that was my mistake.

As the Harleys were revving up for the run down to San Diego, I was informed by our road captain, Sparks, that Jenna couldn't ride with me, since the Heritage didn't have a sissy bar. The road captain was responsible for rider safety, and Sparks didn't want Jenna falling out of the saddle and bouncing down the I-15. If my girlfriend was coming to San Diego, she'd have to ride in the chase truck with Big Todd.

Well, shit, that was like walking a horny chicken into the fox's den. I should have sent her home right then and there, but Jenna had her little heart set on coming, so I made the trip solo while she rode with Todd behind the pack. On our way south we picked up some Vagos members from the Corona and Norco chapters, then rolled en masse toward San Diego.

When we reached the Angels' clubhouse, the Vagos revved their throttles, posed and postured and flexed their steroid-pumped muscles for the red and white, but that provoked a few bored yawns and little else. That was usually how these little club soirees ended—with a bunch of empty bluster. Yes, outlaws clashed, and yes, people got beat up—some even got killed. But more often than not, when it came to crunch time, those macho men turned into limp-dick pansies.

So after cruising impotently back and forth in front of the Angels, the Vagos left the city and roared north again. On the outskirts of San Diego the pack came across a biker-friendly bar, and everyone piled inside to slake their thirst. Jenna joined the VOLs at their own table while I took a seat with Iron Mike. In a few minutes Big Todd joined us, and we got to drinking.

"Hey, I've been meaning to talk to you," said Todd, leaning toward me.

I figured he wanted to borrow money again, but for once that wasn't the case.

"All that shit that went down between us? That was totally my bad, dude."

Well, no shit, asshole.

Instead of answering him, though, I took a pull on my bottle and said, "How you doing with Jenna? She giving you any trouble?"

"Jenna? Naw, everything's cool," said Todd, giving me that big horsey grin of his.

He paused to look around, then leaned back in again. "Listen, Big George, I've been thinkin'. You know about the guys in Van Nuys, right? They're making a killing off the dope dealers over there."

This was true. The drug-dealing entrepreneurs in that San Fernando Valley community were being shaken down by the local Vagos chapter.

"Well, why not us?" Todd continued. "Hemet's our home turf, right? So why shouldn't we take a cut of what the dealers are making in our backyard? We should own a piece of that action, don't you think?"

"I'm not so sure about that," said Iron Mike, shaking his head.

"What the fuck are you talking about, Mike? Think how much bank the club would make. We've got the numbers. Let's fuckin' use 'em, dude."

I have to say this about Big Todd. The man had great ideas for indictments. Shaking down drug dealers was called racketeering, and that was RICO, baby. As you can probably guess, I was a big supporter of Todd's stupid idea, but Iron Mike didn't share my enthusiasm. He left the table, leaving the two of us to work out the details.

"It's a good idea, don't you think?" muttered Todd, discouraged about losing Iron Mike's vote.

"Fuckin' A right," I said. "It's a *great* idea."

Todd took a drink. "Those pricks are making a fortune off us. I say fuck 'em all."

"I'm with you, brother."

"That's why we did Spun," Todd said. "Fuck that cocksucker."

My antennae immediately shot up.

"Spun" was James Butler, a forty-two-year-old heroin addict famous in the valley for leading cops on wild stolen-car chases. Typically, crazy Jim would either bring the one-hundred-mile-per-hour pursuit back to where it started or run out of gas trying. And then, just like my old high school buddy David, the man suddenly vanished.

The night Jim disappeared, his old man received an anonymous call claiming his son had been burned and buried in the desert. There were those who believed La Eme, the Mexican Mafia, was involved — Jimmy's girlfriend was a Hispanic dope addict with ties to that notorious prison gang — but the junkies in Hemet who knew the man best were telling a different tale.

They said two Vagos from the Hemet chapter had snatched Jim from Lake Elsinore. They'd driven him into the desert near the Southern California town of Anza, robbed him, put a bullet in his head, then torched the remains. James Butler was a drug addict and a fuckup, but he didn't deserve to go out like that. No one does.

Kevin Duffy, my detective friend from Riverside, had contacted me about Jimmy's disappearance. He'd wanted to know if I'd heard anything from the Vagos. But at the time I'd had nothing to offer him. I figured Jim was dead and buried in the Mojave, just like David, and no one would ever know what had become of him . . . until Big Todd got a little spun, poured a few drinks down his gullet and let slip the bombshell.

"Wasn't supposed to go down that way, but it did," Todd muttered, sounding a bit annoyed. "My bro really hated that dude. Things got a little fucked up."

"What happened to him?"

"Let's just say that motherfucker won't be coming back," said Todd before draining his glass.

Unfortunately I wasn't prepared to receive Todd's mea culpa. I never got the damn thing recorded — a huge opportunity lost. In the following weeks I tried getting him to confess again while I was wired, but that Vago never would talk. And then one day Todd said to me, "Why do you keep asking about Jim Butler?" and I realized it was time to fold the tent.

Eventually the Vagos piled back out of the bar, mounted bikes and roared north on the I-15 for Hemet. Somewhere along the way the pack lost contact with Big Todd's truck.

Which was exactly what that motherfucker had in mind.

Jenna had been a captive audience for Todd's relentless teasing and sexual innuendo. He'd worked her over pretty good on the way to San Diego, and now she was starting to warm up to him on the return trip.

So Big Todd went for the kill.

He explained to Jenna that she had an obligation to share herself with the brothers and prove she was down for the club. Other VOLs had spread their legs for him, Todd assured her, and now it was her turn. So my girlfriend went down for the club. She buried her face in Todd's lap and sucked his cock. At least she tried. That sleazebag was so spun out she couldn't get his dick hard. Eventually Todd pulled over and fucked her by the side of the road.

James Butler, who vanished from Lake Elsinore.

Somewhere up north, unaware of what was happening behind me, I followed the pack through Winchester and headed east on Highway 74. No sooner had we crossed the city line into Hemet than the all-too-familiar siren and flashing lights of a Hemet police cruiser were warning us to pull over. We stopped our Harleys by the side of the road with the cop tucked in behind us.

It was a short wait before Officer Spates stepped out wearing his pressed dark blue uniform.

I'd known Spates long before I ever signed aboard with the Vagos, and we'd always gotten along. I had no issues with the man. Spates was a good cop—at the time the only black cop on the Hemet police force. As he came toward us I noticed the camera in his hand. Every Vago knew what that meant.

Gang cards.

The Hemet PD wanted the Vagos gone from town almost as badly as I did, and one way to accomplish that was by getting them on record as gang members. The first step in that process was the traffic stop, pulling a biker over for just about any public safety violation. An infraction might include wearing a nonregulation helmet, missing turn signals, pipes that were too loud . . . any damn thing at all. And if one biker was stopped, then everyone riding with him became fair game. Each man would have his license, registration and evidence of insurance checked for violations, then the cop would write up the gang cards.

He'd start by taking the outlaw's photograph, then add his date of birth, Social Security number and driver's license information. And once the biker signed that card, the law had him by the short hairs. In effect, he was admitting membership in a street gang, opening himself up to those hefty gang enhancement penalties under the S.T.E.P. Act the next time he was arrested.

And those who refused to sign, well, some cops could make life pretty difficult. I saw motorcycles confiscated simply because a one percenter couldn't come up with evidence of insurance. For a lot of those boys the whole process was intimidating—especially for the guys on parole, who were afraid to disobey an order. Often the easiest solution was to just go ahead and sign the damn card.

"License and registration."

I gave Spates everything he asked for and answered his questions. But when he lifted his camera and pointed it at me, I drew the line.

"Get that thing away from me," I said, extending a hand in front of my face.

"I'm taking your picture now, Mr. Rowe," he said.

"The fuck you are, Spates," I told him.

Like I said, Officer Spates and I had known each other for a long time, and he'd never heard that kind of disrespect come out of my mouth. I hated to be a prick about it, but I was playing the role of the badass for the Vagos, and I didn't want my face on one of those fucking gang cards.

"What'd you say to me?" growled Spates, lowering the camera.

"I said you're not taking my picture. I've got rights."

"You tell that nigger!" someone shouted ahead of me.

I hated to hear that. I truly did. I never bothered taking a poll, but you could bet the bank that a vast majority of our nation's one percent-ers were dyed-in-the-wool racists. You certainly wouldn't find any dark faces among the hard-core outlaw clubs like the Vagos, Hells Angels and Mongols. They'd take the Mexicans, sure, but not a black man. No fuckin' way, jack. If you were black and wanted to ride outlaw, better look elsewhere—maybe the Soul Brothers or the Chosen Few over in Los Angeles, or the East Bay Dragons up in Oakland.

Most of the Hemet Vagos were proud to call themselves white supremacists. Big Todd had KKK tattooed on his right arm in bold two-and-a-half-inch letters. I myself had those double lightning bolts on my arm, the Nazi symbol for the Aryan Brotherhood and a reminder of a shameful chapter in my life that I'd sooner forget.

Sad truth is, there was a time when I would have been the first to call Officer Spates a nigger and probably raised my hand to it too. Took a lot of years and a ton of soul searching to purge all that mindless hate from inside of me. But once I started turning my life around, the old prejudices began dying away, and the painful reminders of that ugly time were pushed from my memory and left to the past.

Or so I thought.

Pumping gas on the outskirts of San Bernardino, just a few years before going under with the Vagos, I noticed a black man in a button-down shirt watching me from the next island. Before long he stopped filling his tank and approached me.

"Do you remember me?" the man asked.

I just looked at him. I didn't have a clue who this guy was or what the hell he wanted.

"Well, I remember you," he said. And I had no doubt he was right.

Then he started unbuttoning his shirt.

At first I didn't know what to think. I figured maybe the man was getting ready to fight, so I focused myself and got ready to rumble.

And then the last button was undone and his shirt fell open.

And at that instant I knew.

I fucking knew.

A swastika, scarred and faded but nonetheless recognizable, was there in front of me—carved right in the middle of that black man's chest.

"Now do you remember me?" he said defiantly, looking me square in the eyes.

I couldn't answer. I was too ashamed. But what could I say? Would *I'm sorry* really cut it? Would it make those scars disappear? Would I be absolved?

The man had probably imagined that moment a thousand times, dreaming of the day he'd face his bogeyman once more. But now that the moment had finally come, the asshole who'd scarred him for life had nothing to say.

He hung around long enough to watch me squirm, then returned to his car and the rest of his life. I never saw him again, but that little reunion messed with my head for a long time.

Anyway, Officer Spates never did take my picture. I had no legal obligation to allow it. The man had to swallow his anger and move on to the next Vago in line. Within an hour the pack was moving again and I was headed for home.

• • •

I already had my suspicions why Jenna was late returning from San Diego, but when she snuck back into the apartment and headed straight for the shower, I had a pretty good idea what had happened.

After scrubbing Todd's stink from her body, she climbed into bed with me. I asked where she'd been and was given some lame-ass excuse. Addicts are excellent liars, but I could see right through this one. A few days later Iron Mike, who was renting the apartment at the other end of the chicken coop, took me aside and said, "I'm not telling you nothing, Big George, but you might want to check out what happened with Todd and your old lady."

Of course, Iron Mike had just told me everything I needed to know—everything I'd already suspected. Turns out Big Todd had bragged to some of the brothers that he'd screwed Jenna—one more VOL notched in his belt. By doing so, the man had broken one of the biggest of the Vagos taboos: You can do what you want to a prospect's woman—after all, she's just meat—but you don't touch the snatch when Daddy's got the patch.

That night I got in the truck and drove over to the Brown residence, where Todd and Doug lived with their mother. When Big Todd answered the door I called him outside for a man-to-man. When his brother tried to intervene, I told Doug the matter was private and warned him to walk away.

"Word's out you fucked Jenna," I said to Todd, getting right to the point.

"Whoa. Where's this coming from? Did she tell you that?"

"No. Everyone else did."

"Well, everyone else is full of shit. I wouldn't do that to you, brother."

"That right? Maybe I should take this to national and let Tramp decide who's full of shit and who's not."

Had I followed through on the threat, I have no doubt Terry the Tramp would have run Big Todd's ass down the road. But I'd already made up my mind to keep that whole messy business in-house. Fact of the matter was, I couldn't afford to lose him. Because no matter how much of a scumsucking bastard Todd Brown was, he was an even better source of inside information. Get that man spun or drunk and he'd turn into a regular Chatty Cathy. With me, the bottom line was always the mission. So I swallowed pride and added "fucking my girl-friend" to the growing list of reasons why I couldn't wait for the day when I could get that man one on one. Someday soon we'd have our-selves a cage match.

In the meantime I'd keep Big Todd handy. Of course, I wouldn't tell him that. No way, man. I was having too much fun watching the bastard squirm.

"Alright, George, maybe it did happen," Todd finally admitted. "But it's not my fault, dude. Jenna asked for it. She's a fuckin' ho, brother."

I could have decked the sonofabitch, but he wasn't worth it. Hell, Jenna wasn't even worth it.

When word spread through the Hemet chapter that Todd had nailed Big George's old lady, the VOLs were pissed. And most of their righteous indignation was reserved for Jenna. Three of those women approached me at a grocery store one night and asked permission to give their wayward sister a butt-whooping. It was a sweet gesture, but I explained Jenna was my problem, not theirs.

As for Big Todd, nobody trusted that bottom-feeding prick anymore. The married Vagos, and even those with girlfriends, now viewed the man as a predator—a fox loose in the Vagos henhouse. When Ready noticed Todd coming on to his wife a few months later, he shoved a pis-tol against Todd's helmet and warned he'd kill the man if he ever came near his old lady again.

But despite the fact that the entire Hemet chapter and most of the free world knew what Big Todd had done, Jenna still refused to own up to it. The two of us danced around the question for weeks until I pinned the girl down one night and told her I could handle brutal truth but couldn't build a future based on lies.

Right from the start of her confession Jenna turned on the waterworks.

"He said I should make a commitment to the club just like you did," she blubbered. "I was afraid if I didn't do like he wanted they'd take your patch, George. And I know how hard you worked for that patch. I really did it for you."

"So you did it for me, huh?"

"Yes. For you, George."

It's not my policy to hit women. But if there was ever a time to start, that would have been it.

"I'm no fuckin' Einstein, but I'm not stupid either. So stop fucking insulting me," I said, biting back anger. "You're a big girl, Jenna. You knew what you were doing."

"I swear, George, I thought—"

"You screwed Todd because you wanted to," I snapped at her. "You did it for yourself—no one else. Not for me, not for the club and not for the good of the country. So stop wasting my time with all your goddamn lies."

I grabbed my truck keys and was about to head for Shooters when Jenna called me back.

"You're right, George. I'm sorry," she said, wiping away tears. "I don't know what's wrong with me. Guess I've always craved affection from men."

"Christ, Jenna, you're a child. Letting Todd stick his dick in you. That's your idea of affection?"

I swear I was channeling my old girlfriend. I heard Darlene's voice in my head saying, *Two dogs can fuck . . . that's not love.*

"I know it sounds messed up," said Jenna, "but I like it when men want me."

"I should be enough," I grumbled.

I couldn't believe I'd actually said it. Me, the guy who had screwed around his entire life, lecturing a chick who had screwed around even more.

What a fucking hypocrite I was.

What a pair we were.

For a brief moment I fantasized about dragging her cheating ass back to Todd, flinging her into his arms and telling him, "Take the bitch. She's your headache now." Only that would have been the end of Jenna.

Because it was the thrill of fucking the forbidden fruit Big Todd was after. He didn't care about my girlfriend any more than he cared about the other Vagos old ladies he'd slept with. Once Todd bagged his pussy he'd mount it on the wall and be done with it . . . and Jenna would be back on the street and on her way to joining her dead junkie friends. If that happened, a sweet little girl would be left without a mother.

I swear, taking care of the fire chief's daughter was like caring for a puppy. Let her out and life was sure to run her over. For her own good, I couldn't let Jenna go. Of course, I couldn't trust her either. Not any-more . . . and probably not ever again. Like my old flame Darlene used to tell me: once trust is gone, baby, it's gone.

17

A Promise of War

Operation 22 Green was barely plodding along in the summer of 2004, one year after I'd been patched into the Vagos. For me it was the dog days . . . every day, all the time. Sure, I continued making gun buys for ATF—even an occasional drug buy—but for the most part my life as a motorcycle outlaw was all about riding from one place to another, getting shitfaced, then riding back home again. Sprinkle that routine with even more drinking, the occasional fight and those Wednesday-night church socials, where the same tired bullshit was rehashed over and over again, and you've got a pretty good handle on life as a one percenter.

But every once in a while the seamy underbelly of that overgrown boy's club would be exposed; a big meth deal here, a shooting there and an occasional civilian beat-down thrown in for good measure. Some of the Vagos would be answering for those sins on the day of the takedown, but I wanted more. I was after the big score. My opportunity came that summer with rumblings of an impending gang war between the Vagos and the Hells Angels.

• • •

As I said, there was nothing like a good ol' fashioned gang war to break a few laws and get those indictments flowing under the RICO Act. You got one outlaw talking about rolling on the enemy, no one paid attention, but you got twenty of those bastards talking and you had yourself a criminal organization—which could go a long way toward a federal racketeering case.

The Hells Angels and the Vagos had been beating on each other for years, but even more so in the months since I'd decked that Angel at The Crossroads Bar and Grill. Those two enemies never needed much of an excuse to throw down with each other, but Big Roy decided to give them one anyway.

Eighteen months earlier the Hemet P had led his boys into Bro's Toy Box, chain-whipped Bro and made off with several members of his club, including Sparks, North and Buckshot. Now Bro had gone and done the unthinkable. He'd patched in with the Sons of Hell, a support club for the Hells Angels. These were the same fuckers that had been no-shows the night Crash and I had gotten shitfaced and gone looking for trouble in Lake Elsinore.

What chafed Roy's ass was that the Sons had patched Bro in despite pinkie-swearing never to bring any former member of the Bros into their club. Guess it wasn't enough to rip the man's head open with a chain and take his club apart. Big Roy wanted him banished from the outlaw world altogether. Much to his chagrin, though, that wasn't happening. The Sons of Hell were standing firm on club pride and allowing Bro to keep his patch—which wasn't that hard when you had a big brother the size of the Hells Angels standing behind you.

Outlaw motorcycle gangs went to war for many reasons, but personal slights fell pretty far down the list. And yet the Hemet P was demanding satisfaction. Big Roy felt betrayed, and among the one percenters' sacred commandments, betrayal touches on that most mortal of sins: disrespect. How Roy intended to avenge that insult would be the subject of our chapter's next Wednesday-night church meeting, to be held at the $300,000 home Jenna and I had just moved into . . . and which the feds had wired from top to bottom and one end to the other.

The new house on Espirit Circle came to us thanks to Jenna's dad, who had stepped down as Hemet's fire chief and was retiring as a captain. Jenna and I attended his going-away ceremony at the civic center in a room jammed with Riverside County firemen and cops. I knew quite a few of those officers and sheriffs' deputies. At one time or another I'd been handcuffed by most of them.

Toward the end of the evening, Jenna took the microphone and addressed the room. She told her father how much she appreciated all he'd done for her, how hard he'd worked to keep her off drugs and how much she admired him. As she spoke, the captain was moved to tears. He told me later that his daughter's courageous and heartfelt speech had helped bring some closure between them.

Bill had remarried around that time, and his new wife's home, just down the street from his own, was now standing vacant. During one of our backyard barbeques he asked if I might be interested in leasing the place to own it.

Hell yeah, I was interested.

"I think you deserve better than where you're at," Bill said to me. "A fresh start couldn't hurt, right?"

I knew where this was leading. Ever the counselor, Bill had often tried talking me out of the dead-end life of the motorcycle outlaw. I'd listen to the man's arguments, nod understanding, then go right back to riding with the Vagos.

"It's just that you always seem to have one foot in and one foot out," Bill said to me once. "From everything I've seen, I don't think your heart's really in it."

"You might be right, Pops."

"So why not get out?"

"It's complicated," I told him. "But believe me, it's not forever. Someday things are gonna change. You'll see."

"I really hope so. Because to be honest I don't see much of a future for you with those people."

Eventually Bill gave up trying to change my mind, a lesson he'd no doubt learned the hard way with Jenna. Besides, even a man who rode with an outlaw motorcycle gang had to be a step up from the drug-dealing, abusive sons-of-bitches his daughter had been shacking up with in the past.

Man, I couldn't vacate that shack in Valle Vista fast enough. Jenna and I went from living in a complete dump to a high-end property with a Jacuzzi bathtub and a spare bedroom for Old Joe. My buddy could finally move out of his Spartan fifteen-foot travel trailer.

Jenna wasn't exactly doing handsprings when she found out Joe would be following us to the other side of the tracks, but she sure was a happy piglet in her fancy new pen. That girl didn't want for anything. My Family Tree Service business was booming, so I paid all the bills and kept a little extra in her bank account so she had spending money.

By this time Jenna had graduated school and was working as a medical assistant in a family practice, so Old Joe became the designated nanny, shuttling little Sierra to preschool and dance lessons.

Yes, indeed. We were just one big all-American happy family. Jenna was still struggling with her demons, of course, but since the Todd episode she'd been making an honest effort to keep her shit together and be a good mother to Sierra and a faithful girlfriend to me.

Lying in bed together our first night in the new house, she snuggled close and whispered, "Thank you."

"What's that for?"

"For keeping me safe," she said. "I love you, George."

I didn't know what to say to that . . . so I didn't say anything.

It's true I still had feelings for Jenna, but I honestly couldn't say I loved her. Not after all the shit she'd put me through. I was just trudging my way forward, dragging her ass behind me. And let me tell you, man—between the lying and the cheating and the drug use, that five-foot-six, 120-pound load was some heavy weight to haul.

When I told Uncle Johnny Law about our new house on Espirit Circle, his eyes lit up with the possibilities. A homeowner with Loki on his back was an ideal setup for gathering intelligence—especially one with digs like ours. John's idea was to wire the entire place for sound and picture, then invite the Vagos in for their Wednesday-night church get-together. The Hemet boys were meeting in garages. Compared to that, my place would be like a boardroom at the Hyatt. They'd jump all over that shit.

ATF required a day and a half to completely outfit the house, so they had to maneuver carefully around Jenna's work schedule. As soon as she drove off in the morning, the technicians swooped in with their vans—one painted to look like an alarm installation company. These boys were surveillance specialists, and they were damn good at what they did. The techs moved fast but deliberately through the rooms, tearing up walls, placing electronics, then patching things up again. And, man, that gear was small. We're talking flea-shit tiny. Even if the Vagos knew what to look for, they never would have found it.

About midafternoon, while the installation was still in progress, I heard a motorcycle pull into the driveway and peeked out the window. It was Big Todd. He'd been reinstated as the chapter's sergeant at arms by this time and apparently considered us best buddies again. The sonofabitch never did apologize for screwing my girlfriend. The man just went about his business like nothing ever happened.

The garage was wide open, so Todd walked straight on through and entered the house like he owned the place.

"Hey, what's happenin', Big George?"

Todd still called me Big George, but to the rest of the Vagos I was now simply known as George. Big Roy had finally decided there were too many "Bigs" in the chapter, and since I was the last Big to come aboard, mine had to go. Roy tried to saddle me with the road name "Risky" instead, claiming it was because I was always on edge and you never knew what I might do. He even tried getting the rest of the chapter to call me Risky, but each time those bastards threw it out there I swatted them down. Something about working undercover with the name Risky didn't quite work for me.

Risky the Rat. Fuck that.

I knew of another patch holder who once drove a recycled police car. The name he got stuck with was "Cop," and members kept their distance from that dude like he was contagious. Nope, I might have been a snitch, but no way were they going to pin Risky on me. So I took Big George off the cut and settled for plain old George instead.

"You're putting that alarm system in, huh?" said Todd.

"Yeah. Finally getting it done," I told him.

On John Carr's suggestion, I'd spread the word among the Vagos that I'd be alarming the house . . . and surprise visitors like Big Todd were the reason why. He dodged one of the busy technicians and headed to the fridge for a cold beer.

"You hear the latest about Bro?" he said while fishing for a bottle.

"What about him?"

"The Sons of Hell said they won't boot him. Roy's fuckin' pissed."

"What's he gonna do?" I asked.

Todd twisted the cap off a beer, then nearly bumped into one of the installers on his way to hook up the garage.

"Well, you didn't hear it from me," he said, "but looks like we're goin' after them."

"Think so?"

"I know so, brother. And I can't fuckin' wait."

He plopped down in an armchair, swigged his beer and grinned at the activity around him.

"Fuck. Nobody's gettin' in here, huh?"

Big Todd stayed for another hour, drinking free beer and shooting the shit while saws buzzed and hammers pounded. The ATF boys never stopped working.

At 7:30 on Wednesday night, the Hemet Vagos gathered at the house to decide the fate of the treacherous Bro and those two-faced bastards, the Sons of Hell. Before the meeting got under way and club business was discussed, Big Roy took me aside and said he would have to take certain precautions. Next thing I knew, in walked some dude with one of those security wands you saw TSA using at the airport. This wasn't uncommon. The wand had come out before at other church meetings, even at Roy's place in San Jacinto.

I held my breath as the bug man started circling the room, moving the wand along the walls, the furniture, my stereo equipment, the lights and the fixtures—each time calling out, "Clear." It was clear this, and clear that. Well, one thing was perfectly clear to me . . . whatever the Vagos were paying that scammer, I wanted to double it. As I was watching him work, I was thinking, *Why, you dumb bastard. This whole house is infested. That thing should be screaming "BUGS!"*

But no. Instead the Vagos' so-called expert gave a final "all clear," packed his wand, stuck the check in his back pocket and walked out the door.

Let the intelligence gathering begin.

The situation with old nemesis Bro had Big Roy in a lather right from the get-go.

"It's gonna be on," he announced to the troops. "But if we make a move on that motherfucker, we make a move on all of them. If the Sons of Hell try to stop us, we'll fuck them up too and take their patches."

A little louder for the microphones, please.

"Someone could pull a gun," pointed out Big Todd.

"Maybe we should bring guns too," said Iron Mike.

"There are already brothers who carry guns everywhere we go," North assured the room.

Several heads bobbed in acknowledgment before Ready pointed out the obvious, "You know, we could lose a brother over a piece of shit."

That got Roy heated. "All I know is, those fuckers broke the agreement and they're not making him give up the patch. We need to start gearing up fast, because summertime is when this shit usually goes down."

"What does national say?" Sparks wanted to know.

"Tramp's talking with the Berdoo Angels now," Roy replied, "but they're backing the Sons of Hell like we back The Green Machine."

"You really think the Angels will get involved?" asked Ready, visibly concerned.

"Fuck the Angels," declared Big Todd.

"Hell, yeah. They're not gonna mess with us," said a cocksure Roy. "We fuckin' own California."

Man, I almost laughed out loud when I heard that one. Big Roy was delusional. If the Vagos went after the Sons of Hell, the Angels would almost certainly jump into the ring to defend their little brothers. And if that happened, a gang war could spread through the region like a brush fire whipped by the Santa Ana winds. I was keeping my fingers crossed.

After the meeting Roy took me aside.

"Remember that pistol I showed you a while back?"

"You mean the 7.62?" I said for posterity.

"Still want to buy it?"

The next afternoon I walked into the Lady Luck with a pocket full of money and a microphone. Roy went behind the counter and brought out the Czech-made pistol he'd shown me the year before. He didn't explain why he was selling it, and I didn't care. But the sale didn't come without stipulations.

"Here's the deal. I'll let you buy the gun, but I don't want you reselling it, understand? I don't want this thing coming back to bite me in the ass."

"Understood," I said. "Don't worry, man. I'll keep it safe."

As I counted out the money, I couldn't thank Roy enough for that badass gun—and for selling it to a man with a felony who couldn't buy firearms on his own. And when the deal was done, and that 7.62 was mine, so was Big Roy's ass.

Gotcha, motherfucker. See you 'round the prison yard.

I took the pistol back to the house on Espirit Circle, where John Carr photographed it, slipped it into a bag, then told me he was taking the weapon back to ATF as evidence.

"You can't do that," I said. "Roy told me to hang on to it."

"I can't let you keep it, George."

"Well what if he asks to see it? I'll be in so much shit."

"We'll figure it out," said John. "Maybe you can tell him you sold it."

"He doesn't want the fuckin' thing floating around out there. That's the whole point."

John shrugged. "Sorry, dude. I can't let you keep it."

End of topic. We were on to gang war, and John seemed confident the Vagos were headed in that direction. Apparently the Victorville Vagos had been making noise about riding against the Sons of Hell. Victorville was Psycho's chapter, and that High Desert region was Terry the Tramp's stomping grounds, so you know those two had to be in touch.

"Psycho's been talking about hitting the Sons of Hell to make a statement," John told me. "They're talking about pulling their patches and stealing motorcycles."

This was news to me. I'd heard nothing at the Hemet church meetings.

"Where's that coming from?" I wanted to know.

John paused, then said, "We've got someone in Victorville."

"What?"

"We've had someone under with Psycho's chapter since March."

Another informant? No shit.

I can't really explain why, but it was an oddly comforting feeling knowing someone else was out there doing the same crazy shit I was. I wasn't alone anymore.

"Do I know this guy?" I asked.

"Might. His name's Charles. They call him Quick Draw."

That didn't ring any bells. I might have bumped into this Quick Draw at the Screaming Chicken or any number of places, but I couldn't place him. Even so, once John gave me a little background, I felt like I had a pretty good handle on that government informant.

Charles was the classic CI, a man working off a plea deal to save his bacon.

He'd been convicted of armed robbery in Nevada, then busted by the DEA for running a meth lab in Pinon Hills, just over the San Bernardino Mountains. Charles had been facing serious federal time, as many as twenty years behind the walls, and hadn't been crazy about the idea. So he'd entered into a plea arrangement with the U.S. Attorney's Office in California. In return for his freedom, Charles had agreed to infiltrate the Mexican mafia for the DEA.

Once the DEA had finished with him, they'd turned him over to a sheriff's detective in San Bernardino. She was Shelli Kelly, a longtime veteran of the department who knew a thing or two about biker gangs. Detective Kelly's backyard was San Berdoo, considered the womb of outlaw country after delivering several infamous one percenter gangs like the Hells Angels and, some might claim, the Vagos.

When John Carr swore he'd send backup the day I went to Tramp's place to face the Hells Angels, it was Shelli Kelly who hustled up to Hesperia to cover me. Now she had a CI of her own to handle . . . and that was asking a lot.

John once described handling informants as "worse than having a kid." Being one of those kids, I wouldn't disagree. I sometimes called ten times a day looking for words of wisdom from Uncle Johnny Law. Over the course of a long-term investigation like 22 Green, there might be thousands of calls and meetings.

Shelli Kelly wasn't prepared to shoulder that kind of load by herself, and her department lacked the resources to babysit an informant 24-7, so she turned to the ATF's Los Angeles field office and Special Agent Darrin Kozlowski for help. For Koz it must have felt like old home week, coming back to the Vagos to handle Charles. Only a few years before he'd been on the inside looking out as a patched member of the Hollywood chapter.

Getting patched hadn't nearly been the ordeal for Koz's CI as it had been for me. Those desert chapters were like the Wild West, man, and infiltrating was as easy as hanging around the same bars. From there it was a quick run up the ladder. Charles, aka Quick Draw, had been under a year less than me and was already a sergeant at arms in Victorville. And according to John Carr, those desert boys had already given Quick Draw plenty of indictable material.

In July, just a few months earlier, two Victorville Vagos had walked into a meth dealer's home in the Lucerne Valley intent on robbery. Both those boys were spun on crank, armed with revolvers and acting on a tip that a buyer with six grand in his pocket was coming over to score some dope. But the only person in the house was a forty-three-year-old tweaker named Little Jimmy, who freaked out when the Vagos walked in and ran for the door. One of the Vagos, a twenty-six-year-old dimwit named Twist, turned his gun sideways gangsta-style and pulled the trigger. The bullet tore through Jimmy's back, then his heart. He made it out to the front steps, where he died.

The two Vagos fled the town and thought they'd gotten away with murder. And they would have too, except a few nights later Twist was cruising the High Desert with his new buddy, Quick Draw. And Quick Draw, it turns out, was an excellent listener. He wanted to hear every thrilling detail of Twist's robbery gone bad, and that dumb-ass Vago was only too happy to put it on the record.

But now ATF had a dilemma. Charging those two Vagos with murder would mean revealing Quick Draw as the undercover source, and that informant was too productive to lose. For the long-term sake of the mission, John Carr and ATF made the decision to hold the evidence and keep fingers crossed that nobody else got hurt while those killers roamed free. It was a gamble. A big fuckin' gamble. Eventually when Operation 22 Green wrapped and the takedown happened, Twist and his partner would answer for Little Jimmy, a dead man who only wanted to get high.

"It's a checks and balances thing," John told me. "We can get information from Charles that we check off with you and vice versa. This way one hand knows what the other is doing. Koz and I think it would be smart to get you two together and coordinate our efforts. What would you think about meeting him?"

"You want me to meet the CI?"

"Yeah."

"Does he know who I am?"

"Not yet."

"Good. Because that's the way I want to keep it. He's a doper, John. And I don't trust dopers. That's all I fuckin' need is for this guy to flip on me. It ain't happening, man."

My handler tried to convince me the Victorville CI had cleaned up, just as I had. But I wasn't going for it. In my experience addicts rarely changed. Sooner or later the old Charles would rear his ugly head and I'd be fucked. Like I told John, it came down to trust, and I didn't trust that ex-tweaker CI. No. I wanted to keep the circle as tight as possible. Already with Detective Shelli Kelly aboard, it had widened more than I was comfortable with. Those in the know now included Detectives Kelly and Duffy, John Carr and some of his ATF colleagues, my buddy Old Joe and, last but not least, the mysterious undercover cop from the Los Angeles County Sheriff's Department who rode outlaw but my handler refused to identify.

Terry the Tramp didn't want any part of a gang war. Wars cost money, which meant fewer funds in the club account, which meant fewer coins for the slot machines. The Vagos international P was anxious to find a way around Hemet's call to battle, which was why he was busy trying to talk through the impasse with the Hells Angels in San Bernardino. But the natives of Green Nation were restless, and as the drumbeat for war grew louder, Tramp had no choice but to act.

So he threw Big Roy a bone. He green-lit a hit on Bro himself. It was a move that risked pissing off the Sons of Hell and the Angels anyway, but it was a risk Tramp had to take.

When Roy informed the chapter that Tramp had given a thumbs-up on Bro, they were immediately into it—all revved up and ready to go.

"We going to Bro's house to handle this?" asked Chopper, a husky young Mexican. He was a former high school classmate of Jenna's and Doc's stepson—the dentist I'd sold my bike to for gambling money.

"I think we should get him when he's leaving for work in the morning," offered Big Todd. "We could use baseball bats."

Better get a sledgehammer if you plan on taking down Bro, I wanted to say. That boilermaker was a huge, no-necked motherfucker—the kind of guy you'd have to shoot to stop, as Freight Train used to say. I was hoping that wouldn't happen, though. I liked Bro. That big boy could get along with just about anybody. But because he'd stood up to Todd and Roy (and got a chain wrapped around his head for his trouble) he was number one on the Vagos shit list.

Roy decided whacking Bro with Louisville Sluggers was a pretty good idea. So he directed Big Todd, Iron Mike and Chopper to grab some lumber, ambush Bro on his way to work, and take batting practice on his head.

This is what Big Roy was good at, firing up the troops and sending them into battle while he watched the carnage from yonder distant hill. Hemet's P was one of those generals who led from behind, and in my book that made him a pussy. But it also made him smart—smart enough to understand the danger of leading a charge where laws were being broken. Club officers were prime targets for the feds, who saw cutting off the heads of leadership as an effective way to cripple outlaw gangs like the Vagos. If Big Roy wasn't careful, the United States Justice Department could take away everything.

Including Big Roy.

Better the peons go down, he figured.

But at the end of the day, as was usually the case, nothing happened. The hit squad hung around Bro's house a few times but always returned dragging their baseball bats, claiming their target never showed up or they couldn't find him. So as the summer months waned, Bro was still out there flying the Sons of Hell colors, and it was driving Roy to distraction. Bro was an itch he just couldn't scratch.

Big Roy wanted to go after the Sons of Hell, and Tramp had run out of time to broker a deal. In mid-October of 2004, the Vagos international P sanctioned a war against the Sons, notifying Vagos chapters in Venice, Southside, Victorville, Pomona, Norco and Corona to stand by with Hemet for the coming fight.

Tramp also warned his rank and file they should be prepared to go toe-to-toe with the mighty Hells Angels if they wanted to remain in the club. If they weren't prepared for bloodshed, he told them, they should turn in their patch immediately or face physical punishment.

"Tramp says we're gonna roll on those motherfuckers," Big Roy announced during church at his home in San Jacinto.

"Are we talking guns . . . knives?" North wanted to know.

"It would be guns, knives, bats, chains, everything," Todd chimed in. "If they have their gunners, we'll have our gunners on the side."

"The Sons and the Angels are gonna be in war mode," Roy warned. "Tramp may roll us in club strong to Hells Angels and Sons of Hell functions. This won't be like a bar fight. You could be in a situation where you have to decide if you're going to take a life."

Big Roy then refreshed memories by laying down the guidelines again for a Code 69. He was wasting his breath, because while Code 69s sounded cool in theory, they seldom came off the way they were drawn up. Maybe it was just too involved for those geniuses. If a member received a Code 69 on his cell phone, he was expected to immediately drop whatever he was doing. He had to wear dark shoes and dark clothes (no club colors), and pack an extra shirt and Levi jeans (in case one pair got bloody and had to be tossed). Gloves would be required, either rubber or the cotton gardening variety. Members also had to travel alone in a private vehicle (no motorcycles) and without weapons of any kind. Everyone had one hour to show up at Buckshot's barn, where the war chest was stored. Instructions would follow.

How 'bout instructions for the fuckin' instructions?

"This is serious Vagos shit," Roy reminded the troops, as if they were headed for the shores of Normandy. "A Code sixty-nine comes before everything else. And you'd better fuckin' show up at Buckshot's place. If not, you'd better have a damn good reason."

Me (blurred) with the Vagos in 2005.

A discussion followed on which chapter members would be "slingers" and "shooters." The slingers would fight, the shooters would carry iron. I was designated a shooter because I owned a gun. Todd was a shooter. Iron Mike was a shooter. Even Crash was a shooter.

A few days later members of the Vagos support club, The Green Machine, were brought into my garage for a briefing by the sergeant at arms. I'd been forced to boot the Vagos out of the living room after they'd treated the floor like their personal ashtray and Jenna had had herself a hissy fit. House or garage, though, didn't really matter. Those ATF techies had wired the whole damn place for sound and picture.

At the briefing Big Todd did his best General George Patton impersonation, slapping around one Green Machine member who was slow to take his seat, then warning the rest they should just turn in their patches if they weren't prepared to face the vaunted red and white.

One of the Green Machine members in attendance that night was Crusher, the sergeant detective from the Cathedral City PD who had been tasked with running background checks on Vagos prospects. At that point Crusher was on borrowed time, the subject of an internal affairs investigation probing his relationship with the Vagos. So far the man had managed to stick around longer than I would have liked, but John Carr assured me Crusher had one foot out the door and the other on axle grease.

I won't get into the details of how the ATF nailed that dirty cop. Suffice to say some of the names handed to the sergeant for background checks were tagged by the feds and traced right back to the Cathedral City PD. Sergeant Crusher had shot himself in the foot.

In the end that crooked lawman would never be prosecuted for betraying his solemn oath; to do so would have exposed me as the informant. With Operation 22 Green active and with bigger fish to fry, ATF decided against blowing my cover—not unlike the situation with Quick Draw. Sergeant Crusher would eventually be squeezed like a pimple on the ass of law enforcement and wiped from the Cathedral City PD.

• • •

October slid into November, and still all was quiet on the western front. At that point it was trench warfare, with all of us hunkered down in our holes on either side of no-man's-land. Nobody, it seemed, was willing to come out and fire the first shot.

Leave it to Rhino, that mullet-headed man-mountain from San Bernardino, to toss the boys over the top and into the fray. The international sergeant at arms instructed the Hemet chapter to begin surveillance on the Sons of Hell, gathering member's addresses so the Vagos could pick them off one by one. Big Todd was handed the assignment, but he didn't waste much gas in the effort. All he came up with was one fuckin' address.

That was enough, though, to at least start things rolling.

I got a call one night from North, who by this time had ditched the Hemet chapter and signed on with Quickie John's bunch over in Norco. I was given an address and told to meet him there right away. He wouldn't say why. When I arrived in my truck I found North, Big Todd and Junior, the Winchester chapter's sergeant at arms, holding baseball bats and tire irons on a residential street.

"See that truck there?" said North, pointing me toward a house down the block where a pickup was parked at the curb. "That belongs to a Sons of Hell patch. Tramp gave the order to take him. Once he comes out, we're gonna fuck him up."

Oh, shit.

These idiots were going to ambush that poor bastard—maybe even kill him—and I didn't know what the hell to do. It was one of those no-win scenarios John Carr had warned me about. I couldn't leave, but I couldn't get involved either. And to try and convince those guys not to beat their intended target would be futile and suspicious.

No, man. All I could do was stick around and hope for the best.

Within minutes of my arrival, Chopper, Sparks, JB and Iron Mike showed up carrying bats and metal pipes. But Mike also carried something more worrisome—a .45 caliber semiautomatic tucked under his belt. It wasn't exactly shaping up to be a fair fight, but then again, nobody ever accused an outlaw of fighting by the rules.

Less than an hour later the Sons of Hell member left his house and climbed into his truck.

"Handle it," Big Todd commanded Iron Mike.

"I'm going to shoot him," the little Vago announced.

Iron Mike scrambled into a pickup driven by Junior, the Winchester sergeant at arms, and the truck roared off with Mike ready to blast away from the passenger's-side window. The Sons of Hell patch saw them coming as he started his truck. He slammed into gear and veered sharply around the oncoming pickup, then sped past us like a frightened rabbit. In a moment came the hunter, tires screeching against the asphalt as the truck turned the corner and disappeared.

I never heard gunshots, or anything else for that matter, until later that night, when I got word that the rabbit had managed to evade his pursuers and escape with his skin. Later when I was wired up, I spoke to Iron Mike about what happened that day.

"That was a pretty tough situation they put you in, brother," I told him.

Mike turned to me with a serious gaze and said, "If I could have, I would have shot him."

And I have no doubt that little Chicano spoke the truth.

18

A Snitch in the System

It was a Code 69—drop everything and get to the barn right away. I was supervising my work crew on a tree-trimming job when Big Todd called my cell phone and told me to get to Buckshot's place. Apparently Terry the Tramp had just authorized the Hemet chapter to roll on the Sons of Hell in Lake Elsinore, and my work truck was needed to carry the war chest.

Just when I was starting to think the gang war had been pushed to the back burner, the heat had suddenly been cranked up again. Here might be one last chance to nail the Vagos on a RICO, one final opportunity to put a stake through the heart of the operation that refused to die. I left the job site, hopped in my truck and called John Carr on the road to Buckshot's place.

He didn't pick up.

Shit.

I punched in the ATF field office and found myself talking to Special Agent Jeff Ryan.

"Where's Carr? I need to talk to him, man. It's important."

"Special Agent Carr is unavailable," said Jeff.

"Where the hell is he?"

"I don't know."

"Well, what should I do? We're about to roll on the Sons of Hell."

There was a brief pause before Jeff replied, "I'll call you back."

Just minutes from Buckshot's property I still hadn't received a return call from Special Agent Ryan, so I rang ATF on the Nextel again. This time there was an anxious edge to Jeff's voice when he picked up the phone.

"I can't get hold of John," he said to me. "I'm trying to contact someone higher up."

"There's no time for that, man. We're rolling at seven."

"What do you want me to do?"

"You're asking *me*?"

I couldn't believe it. Here was a golden opportunity to wrap Operation 22 Green with a nice, fat RICO bow, and my handler had gone missing.

"Alright, man, here's the deal," I said after a long pause. "We're rolling at seven o'clock for The Hideaway Bar in Lake Elsinore. We'll be coming in on Railroad Canyon Road. You got that? Railroad Canyon."

"Yeah. Yeah, okay," replied the special agent.

When I pulled into Buckshot's driveway I found most of the Hemet boys already gathered—maybe sixteen in all, which was just about the entire chapter at that time. Per Code 69 stipulations, they should have all been traveling incognito. But there were no dark shirts and pants, no change of clothes, no rubber gloves and no private vehicles. Everyone was mounted on bikes and flying their colors. Everyone, that is, but our fearless leader.

Once more, Big Roy Compton was commanding from the rear.

Two of the Vagos emerged from Buckshot's barn hauling the chapter's war chest. They slid the arsenal into my truck bed. Big Todd climbed into the cab beside me, and the green army rolled with a burst of dirty thunder. I trailed the pack for several miles down Highway 74 before we turned off and headed in the direction of Lake Elsinore.

The closer we came to The Hideaway Bar, the more nervous I got. John Carr was AWOL, and one of his recurring themes was to avoid trapping myself in felony situations. Yet here I was, driving a pickup loaded with illegal weapons on my way to commit felony assault.

Just remember John's advice, I told myself. *Don't lead the charge.*

Now I was hoping and praying for a miracle—that once we got to the bar the law would be there to jump in at the last moment and stop the rumble before anyone got hurt.

About a half mile out, a Riverside County Sheriff's Department cruiser went rushing past. Then came two more with lights flashing.

Fuck. The cops are red-lighting us.

Now I'm crapping my pants. I've got a war chest filled with weapons in the truck bed behind me and three sheriff's deputies out front. Two of those lawmen stepped from the cruisers and approached Slinger, our VP at the time, who owned a Chrysler dealership in Hemet. After talking with the cops, Slinger strode back to my truck and spoke to me and Todd through the open window.

"We're screwed," were the first words from his mouth. "The cops said we should turn around. They know we're headed for The Hideaway. They know what we're doing."

The instant I heard that my balls shriveled like pecans.

"How the fuck could they know that?" Todd wanted to know.

Later I found out the answer. Special Agent Ryan had called the ATF contact at Riverside County, who then rang their Lake Elsinore station for a heads-up. Somewhere between ATF and Lake Elsinore there was a monumental brain fart. What the cops should have done was intervene once we entered The Hideaway Bar, not made a goddamn traffic stop before we got there. Not only had this catastrophic blunder threatened the operation but it had also put my life in serious jeopardy.

"We've got a snitch," Todd fumed. "We've got a fuckin' snitch."

"Think so?" said Slinger.

"How else do you explain it? They knew which direction we were coming. Only our guys fuckin' knew that."

This was bad.

"Could've been the Sons of Hell," I said, trying a little misdirection. "Maybe they saw us coming in. We've used spotters when we thought something was coming, right?"

It was lame, but it was the best I could do on short notice.

Believe it or not the Hemet chapter was baffled by that bullshit for a couple of weeks. But it wasn't long before their focus turned inward again, and the question on everyone's mind was . . .

Who's the rat?

"We've got a snitch in the system."

It was our first church meeting since the traffic stop in Lake Elsinore, and you could feel the tension in JB's garage that night. As Big Roy scanned the faces of the guys he'd brought into the chapter, you knew he had to be thinking, *Which of you fuckers is the one? Who's the snitch?* I thought he was looking my way more often than the others, but that could have been my imagination.

"Someone's feeding law enforcement information," Roy continued. "And I think it's coming from this chapter. So starting tonight, we're tightening security. I want all of you to take off your shirts and pants. We're doing a strip search before we start."

A couple of the patches spoke up in protest, but Roy steamrolled them.

"I'm the P of this club, motherfuckers. If something happens, it's gonna be me going down, not you. So get the fuck out if you don't like it. The rest of you, everything off but the underwear."

I was wired for sound that night. I was always wired on Wednesday nights when church was held anywhere but the house. As I stripped down to my socks and boxers, I honestly didn't know what was about to happen. Chopper and Big Todd came out with one of those security wands. I prayed it was the same worthless hunk of junk that had failed so miserably at my home a few months earlier.

One by one, the ugliest mix of stripped-down, steroid-pumped, overweight, out-of-shape, hairy-assed men in recorded history shuffled forward for inspection. When it came my turn, all I could do was hold my breath.

Todd ran the wand over my crotch.

Nothing beeped.

He ran it over the clothes I'd handed Chopper.

Nothing booped.

Sue the manufacturer . . . I was "all clear" again.

It took over an hour for the line to move through security, but all sixteen of us passed with flying colors. After everyone was seated, Roy stood before the group and held up one of the local Riverside County newspapers.

"See this?" he said, tapping the front page. "There's a story in here about how the Vagos went looking for members of the Sons of Hell to get into a war. And if you read this fuckin' story it's gonna say everything we've been talking about in church."

Roy rolled the paper and continued. "So here's the deal. From now on we watch what we fuckin' say. No one talks to cops if they get stopped. All these careless comments about going to war or killing somebody or stealing motorcycles are what the law can use against us. All they have to do is link a few things together and we're busted. Every one of you needs to assume that any time you talk to someone face-to-face or on the phone it's being recorded and will be used against us. So new ground rules. From now on we run this chapter from inside the room. Everything stays in-house, you got that? And nobody discusses club business on the phone or cell phone."

Roy held up one of those throwaway cell phones.

"Get one of these instead. This is a virgin phone. I've got it under a fictitious name and a fake address. This is the phone I'll be using. But remember. I don't want anyone calling me about club business because it shows a structure, and that's what the feds want. If you have questions, ask them in church."

He lifted the rolled newspaper and shook it at us. "Listen up, motherfuckers. I'm not sure exactly what the fuck is going on around here, but I'm watching every one of you. If there's a rat in this chapter, I'm gonna find him . . . and I'm gonna fuckin' bury him."

Was it my imagination again, or was Big Roy looking at me when he said that?

The next time I saw Special Agent Jeff Ryan would be the last meet-up until the takedown. We were meeting in the Little Luau parking lot so he could swap out my recording gear. As he was approaching, the agent had the hunched posture of a whipped dog.

"Listen, George," he said. "I want you to know that when I called our contact at Riverside I told him not to divulge any information. Somewhere along the line we had a breakdown."

A breakdown? Yeah, I'd say so, buddy. Because of someone's fuckup, the opportunity to nail the Vagos had been blown and now I was under suspicion and getting strip searched. There was heat on my back and a draft on my balls.

"I won't be seeing you for a while," Jeff continued. "My supervisor is taking me out of the field. I've been assigned to the shooting range."

"Is that a good or a bad thing?" I asked.

"Doesn't matter," he said. "I'm okay with it."

I almost felt bad for the poor bastard. But I'd been this goddamn close to getting out from under Operation 22 Green, and now Big Roy was too scared to move and the Hemet chapter had gone underground. Hell, Roy was even forbidding us to wear our colors around town.

And the fallout didn't end with Hemet. At least two other operations being run through the Riverside Gang Task Force had also ground to a halt. It was dead calm out there, man. You could almost hear the crickets chirping.

As weeks turned into months and Operation 22 Green continued to flounder, frustration was mounting. It cost hundreds of thousands, sometimes even millions, of dollars to run an undercover case, and John Carr's superiors needed to see results in order to justify the huge investment of money and man hours. My handler was starting to come under pressure to get things moving again, and he, in turn, was laying that pressure on me.

"What the hell do you want me to do?" I bitched at him over the phone.

"I don't know, George, but we need to do something. My supervisor's dogging me to pick up the pace."

"Well, then tell your supervisor to get his ass down here and make something happen. I'm doing everything I can, alright? Everything you guys have asked me to do, I've done. But these assholes are watching me now. Until everything calms the fuck down I'm not pushing a goddamn thing, okay? And if your supervisor doesn't like it, well, all I can say is fuck him and fuck you."

Whenever I behaved badly, John Carr's punishment was to withhold my chicken katsu at the Little Luau and force me to drive sixty miles to a McDonald's in Pomona. Following our heated exchange that's exactly where I was headed for our next Friday meeting.

I finished my last cheeseburger, then sat in my yellow plastic booth chewing on a straw as I waited for my handler to arrive. John was always chronically late, but two and a half hours was obviously some added punishment for being naughty. I was close to walking out of the place when the man finally walked in.

"You're as bad as a fuckin' tweaker," I told him as he plopped down in the seat opposite me. "I've been sitting here over two hours, man. I've eaten four fuckin' cheeseburgers and an apple pie."

John leaned forward and said straight-faced, "You give me any more shit, Rowe, and I'll throw your ass in jail."

Then he gave a sly grin, and that broke the ice.

"Go fuck yourself," I cursed under my breath.

"Don't worry about it," said John. "We're both under pressure, dude. I've got other shit I'm dealing with too. Our CI in Victorville just got arrested. It's a big mess up there."

Charles, aka Quick Draw, had been in a bar called Mickey McGee's with a handful of patches and prospects when a dispute had arisen with a civilian over—surprise, surprise—a pool table. Per international FW1-UFWA regulations, the Vagos had gone berserk and stomped that civilian bloody while Quick Draw had roamed the sidelines warning those greenies that the cops would come.

And sure enough, the cops had come.

A San Bernardino County Sheriff's Department sergeant had been watching the bar from the parking lot, knowing the Vagos had been inside. He'd come in like the cavalry and arrested the whole bunch, including ATF's inside man. Now Quick Draw was cooling his heels in a cell, slapped with a two-hundred-thousand-dollar bail, and special agents Kozlowski and Carr were looking for a way to spring him without compromising the case. It would take them a month.

It was a mess, alright. But to be perfectly honest, I didn't give a rat's ass about Quick Draw McGraw and his problems up in Victorville. I had worries of my own. After more than two years undercover and months of stress, I'd hit the wall.

In the past when I'd come to this point, John would pump my tires with a pep talk. *Keep it going, George. The goal line's in sight. We're in the home stretch. Rah, rah, rah!* But I wasn't listening anymore. I was done with the grinding pressure, the long hours and being pushed around and treated like a child by Big Roy, a punk I could have bitch slapped with one hand—make that two hands—tied behind my back. I wanted the whole fuckin' thing over and the Vagos out of my life . . . whatever that life was going to be.

And that was the big question.

My eyes were finally opening to a future beyond 22 Green, and I couldn't see any. Life would change once this was over. I realized that now. This wouldn't be as simple as removing my cut, exiting the Vagos and merging back into my old life in Hemet. I'd detoured onto a fucking road without an off-ramp. I'd never get back to the place I'd been.

Fact was, I'd eventually have to testify against the brothers I took down, and once George Rowe's name was out there, his ass would be grass. And the lives of those closest to me would be in danger too. Certainly Old Joe was screwed, just like he'd warned from the beginning. And even though I'd kept Jenna in the dark, no doubt the Vagos would assume her guilty by association.

I'd dug everyone a big-ass hole . . . and no matter how hard I thought it through, I couldn't figure a way out.

"Let me ask you something, John," I said, stirring what was left of my shake with a bent straw. "What happens to me when this ends?"

"I don't follow."

"When this case is over, I'm fucked in Hemet, aren't I? I can't ever go back."

John didn't answer right away, but I could read the look on his face.

"Maybe not, George," he finally said.

It was almost a relief to get it out there—to finally address the elephant in the room. The big bastard had been standing there all along, and I'd been ignoring him. Well, not anymore. *Hey, there, Jumbo. Nice to finally meet you.*

"Okay. So what can I do?" I asked. "What are my options?"

"Well . . . we could move you. Put you someplace safe."

"You mean like Hammer?"

"Hammer killed himself, dude."

"What else we got?"

"Well, there's always WITSEC. Witness security. What they used to call witness protection. The U.S. Marshals Service runs that program. We'd have to apply, but there's no guarantee they'd take you."

"But if they did?"

"Then you disappear. They'd move you, give you a new name, new Social . . . a whole new identity."

I considered this a long moment.

"What about Joe? Could he come?"

John shook his head. "Not unless you're legally married."

I returned a wry smile. "Joe's a great guy, but . . ."

"Listen, George. Don't worry about your friend. If WITSEC is the direction you decide to go, you have my word Joe will be protected. Far as I'm concerned, when you signed up for this operation, he came with the package. But here's the thing you need to know about the Witness Security Program. If the marshals take you and you do go in, you're basically cut off from the past. You can't have any contact, any communication, with anyone you might have known. If the marshals find out you've compromised your new identity, you'll get thrown out of the program. It's a big step, dude. A life changer."

I leaned back in the booth to watch a young family across the way chowing down on their Happy Meals. Sometimes it was easy to forget there was a world out there where people didn't worry about things like getting buried in sand or rebooting their entire fucking lives. Man, I just wanted to live in that world again. But I couldn't. It was gone.

"This was the deal right from the start, wasn't it?" I said matter-of-factly. "I was never going back to Hemet."

John leaned closer. "It's just how things worked out, George."

Yeah. It's how things worked out, George. And now here I sat in the land of Ronald McDonald. Totally fucked.

"I need to think about this," I said after a moment.

"Yeah, you do. It's a big decision," agreed John. "But I'll do whatever I—"

I put up a sudden hand, stopping him midsentence. Someone familiar had just entered the restaurant. I'd watched him knock down beers with Terry the Tramp and hung out with him at the Screaming Chicken. I knew this long-haired bruiser. It was Bubba, that big, friendly biker who refused to join any outlaw club.

"Fuck," I hissed at John under my breath. "I don't believe it."

"What's wrong?" John said, turning to follow my look.

"That's Bubba, man. He's a friend of Tramp's. What are the fuckin' odds?"

Bubba spotted me.

Oh, shit.

He walked up to the table, hovering above it, and offered me his big paw.

"Hey, George. Good to see you, brother."

"What are you doing here?" I answered as calmly as I could, pumping the big biker's hand.

"Working, brother. Always working."

Then he extended his hand to John Carr.

"How goes the battle, John?"

I was floored.

John slid over, and Bubba pushed into the seat beside him.

"Wait. You two know each other?" I said.

Bubba turned and smirked at John. "Look at this handsome son-ofabitch. I hate sitting next to this guy. He always makes me look bad."

"Show him where you work, Bubba," said John.

Bubba discreetly reached under his shirt and pulled out a gold star hanging from a chain. The badge was stamped Deputy Sheriff, Los Angeles County.

"This is where I work."

"No shit" was all I could manage.

"No shit." Bubba smiled.

Born and raised in Long Beach, California, Bubba was turned on to law enforcement at an early age watching television cop shows, much like John Carr. Only where John was a fan of *Miami Vice*, Bubba loved *Adam 12*. He'd entered law enforcement in 1969, then gone undercover as Bubba the biker, buddying up to motorcycle outlaws and gathering intelligence for over twenty years.

For a good chunk of that time he'd worked with Special Agent Carr as a core member of ATF's One Percenter Task Force, taking an occasional hiatus to travel the country, speaking at law enforcement seminars as an expert on outlaw motorcycle gangs. In fact, it was Bubba, I found out later, who had introduced my friend Detective Duffy to John Carr. This man was the matchmaker behind my marriage to ATF.

Now pushing fifty, Bubba was nearing retirement and looking forward to rejoining his family, including a long-suffering wife who had pretty much raised their four kids during her husband's long absences.

"I wanted you to meet Bubba because he's going to be helping me out more—exchanging gear, delivering money for the buys . . . that sort of thing," said John.

"Yeah, if I'm still around," I replied.

"Having a tough time in Hemet, huh?" Bubba said.

"Big Roy's been riding me pretty hard lately," I told him, still trying to wrap my head around the fact I was talking to a lawman.

"Roy thinks you're the informant?"

"He hasn't said that, but I've got a feeling he's thinking it."

Now John cut in. "There's always somebody who thinks somebody's a cop, George. Don't worry too much about it. There's nothing they can pin on you."

"Listen to the man. He should know," said Bubba, nodding toward John.

Then that big biker leaned his elbows on the table and shared with me the most important bit of advice I'd ever receive on the art of surviving undercover.

"Listen. Here's all you need to remember if someone accuses you of being a rat. Whatever happens, never cop to it. You understand? Even if they claim they've got you dead to rights, never admit who you're working for. They'll try to bluff you out, and that's how guys get caught. No matter what they say. No matter what they do. Never cop to the truth, brother. Never."

For six months a chill hung over the Hemet Vagos. Never mind that Operation 22 Green was floating facedown, our chapter's weekly church sessions had become painfully uncomfortable exercises in paranoia. Every Wednesday night suspicion seemed to fall on someone new, passing from one member to the next like a loaded gun in a game of Russian roulette. There was a chambered bullet with the snitch's name on it, and everyone was wondering whose head would get blown off.

First in line was Mickey. Someone in the chapter had been whispering to Roy that Mickey was the rat. After all, he'd shown up at the Lady Luck out of the clear blue one day asking to join the Vagos. So Big Roy ordered Todd and JB, the chapter's resident computer whiz, to pull the man's phone records.

The trigger was squeezed and . . .

Click.

Mickey checked out.

Big Todd himself was up next. Because of his past history with the ladies and all the drug abuse, nobody in the Hemet chapter trusted that bastard . . . nobody, that is, except Big Roy. The Hemet P loved Todd like a brother and remained his ally throughout. Roy didn't believe for a second that his best friend would rat on the Vagos.

Click.

Jimbo was suspect for a few days. The man who supplied steroids to some of the crew, including Roy and Todd, got the third degree, but nothing panned out.

Click.

Loki's turn.

Loki was a tattoo artist who worked for Roy at the Lady Luck, bought a Harley-Davidson on a payment plan from the chapter and became patched. His girlfriend, Krissy, was a porn queen from Orange County. When Krissy's spurned ex-lover spread a rumor that Loki was a government snitch, some of the Orange County Vagos tried to take him on a one-way trip to the desert.

The attempt to abduct Loki happened on a club run to Lake Havasu on the California-Arizona border. Outside the motel where we were staying, I heard Loki's cries for help. Five of the OC Vagos were trying to wrestle him into a van. I sounded the alarm and the Hemet crew came rushing to the rescue.

"He's a fuckin' snitch," one of the Orange County boys protested to Big Roy.

"Got the paperwork to prove that?" Roy barked at him.

Turns out they didn't. All they had was the word of some jealous ex-boyfriend.

"Loki is with Hemet," Roy warned them. "Unless you've got something that proves he's an informant, you're going to leave him alone. If it turns out he's a snitch, we'll be the ones to take care of it."

Click. Loki was spared.

Crash was next in line.

Crash had been living life as all true outlaws should: abusing crystal meth, failing to show up at church meetings and beating his old lady on a regular basis. And every time he whipped that rail of a woman, she called the cops on him. What made the Vagos suspicious was the fact that their brother never seemed to get hauled off to jail. And they didn't trust his old lady either.

"Crash tells that bitch everything," Todd pointed out at church. "Maybe she's the one talking."

Of course, I had to agree completely with the sergeant at arms's assessment. You bet your ass I pushed the heat that way. I was like the drug addict who picked the baggie off the ground, put it in his pocket and said, "Let me help you look for that."

Crash was always in trouble, man. I'd lost track of how many times that crazy bastard got busted from patch to prospect. Seemed like the dude was forever washing motorcycles. It was just a matter of time before the Vagos said enough.

The straw that broke it came at Shooters Food and Brew one night when some teenager accidentally spilled his drink on Jenna. Crash was really spun and went ballistic on the poor kid, beating and stomping him bloody. When Tramp found out about it, he called me and Crash up to his place in the High Desert for a little face-to-face. Sensing trouble, I put an urgent call in to John Carr, who sent Detective Shelli Kelly up from San Bernardino to cover my ass.

When Crash and I were escorted into Tramp's kitchen, Rhino was there waiting. Right away the international sergeant at arms pointed a warning finger at me and snapped, "You stay out of this." Then he proceeded to knock Crash off his chair and slapped him around the kitchen. I felt bad about it—like maybe I should have stood up for my Hemet brother. But getting between him and Rhino in Tramp's kitchen would have been suicide.

When the beating was over and Crash was nursing a split lip, I noticed activity out the sliding glass doors. A couple of Vagos in Tramp's backyard were wrapping what looked like a dead St. Bernard in a blanket. One of them hoisted the animal onto his shoulder and, swear to God, that thing looked just like a body. Then they headed around the side of the garage toward the front of the house.

Oh, shit. Shelli Kelly was probably out there somewhere. *What if she thinks it's me wrapped in that blanket?*

In fact, Detective Kelly told me later she was just seconds from drawing her service revolver as that dead dog was tossed into the bed of a pickup. But before she could pull the gun, Crash and I came strolling out of the house.

Far as Terry the Tramp was concerned, it should have been Crash wrapped in that blanket. Because following our meeting, he was as good as dead to the Vagos. Tramp called Big Roy and told him he wanted that fuckup run down the road—to take both his patch and his motorcycle. So at our next church, Big Todd cut the threads from

Crash's center patch and Roy booted him out the door, warning him they'd be coming for his bike.

Confiscating a member's Harley-Davidson was like kicking a dead St. Bernard. What was the fucking point? Well, the point was money. Bikes could be bought, repaired and sold for a hefty profit, or leased to a member at a big interest rate. And if the member defaulted, he'd get run out and lose the bike. But in Crash's case, Big Roy was just going to confiscate that stock Harley and sell it for cash. So a few days later Todd and I were dispatched to take possession.

Crash was expecting us. The man was tweaking when we got there and didn't give a shit about much of anything in the condition he was in.

"Can I take your bike, Crash?" asked Todd apologetically.

"Over your dead body." Crash grinned.

"Sorry. National told me to take it."

"Oh, yeah? Well then why don't you go in the garage and get it, motherfucker."

When we entered the garage, we found the Harley lying in pieces across the floor. Crash had taken the whole damn machine apart.

What a piece of work.

In a strange sort of way, I was going to miss that crazy sonofabitch . . . maybe because he was no longer the man under Roy's microscope.

Happy trails, Crash.

Click.

Finally, inevitably, with just one pull of the trigger left, it came around to me.

As he'd already done with Mickey, Big Roy ordered Todd and JB to check my phone records. And, of course, a hundred fuckin' calls to Uncle Johnny Law immediately showed up.

"Oh, that's just his uncle's number," Todd explained to JB. "I know that for a fact."

Holy shit. That was close.

That Wednesday after church, at the end of a long and tiresome stretch of strip searches and paranoid accusations, Roy pressed his hand against my chest.

"If I ever find out you're a rat . . ."

"Just kill me now then, Roy," I said, remembering Bubba's advice. "If you're thinking I'm a rat, just kill me now and you won't have to worry about it."

Roy and I faced off for a long moment, but I never flinched. He finally broke it off and moved on. A few seconds later Big Todd approached me, looking anxious.

"Tell me it's not you, George," he said confidentially.

I looked him straight in the eye.

"It's not me, Todd," I told him.

He patted my shoulder, looking relieved. I think Todd just needed to hear me say it.

Shortly after that the inquisitions ended. Don't ask me how—it defied logic—but the bullet with my name on it never did fire.

Click.

19

Something in the Oven

Must be nice to come home after a hard day at the office and find a sympathetic ear to bend . . . maybe get a few "poor baby's" and a nice foot massage. I came home to a woman passed out on the floor, buck naked and spread-eagled with her face in her crotch.

Jenna had lost her job as a medical assistant when she and the head nurse had been caught writing each other prescriptions. The DEA had gotten involved, and Jenna would have been prosecuted if the doctor had decided to press charges, but he'd just wanted her gone. So now she was bored at home and high all the time. And that girl didn't just get high, man. She got *really* high. It wasn't enough to do just a little heroin, or pop one or two pills like the Somas she'd been swallowing. With Jenna it was always a handful.

"What the fuck is wrong with you?" I asked when she was coherent enough to comprehend English.

"Guess I was bored," she muttered.

"What the fuck, Jenna? You can't keep using boredom as an excuse."

"You sound like my dad."

"Well maybe your dad's right. Look, you either choose to get high or you don't. It's as simple as that. I had a problem and I quit."

"Well good for you, George," she snapped at me. "Why don't you tell me another thousand times how fucking amazing you are? That's you, isn't it? I choose to get high."

"Then I guess you choose to die young."

"Maybe so."

"And you don't care, do you?"

"I guess not."

"Well, fuck you then, bitch. If you don't care, why should I?"

I flushed all her pills at the end of that argument, and Jenna spit in my face. When I grabbed her by the ponytail and told her never to do it again, she called the cops on me. That was Jenna's way. Get her pissed off enough and you were pretty much guaranteed a visit from the local PD.

After the cops heard both sides, decided it was bullshit and left, I made a decision of my own. I was going to leave Jenna. Truth was, if it hadn't been for little Sierra, I probably would have bailed months before. For two years I'd dealt with the addictions, the cheating and the mood swings. But now I was done with that crazy bitch, and not even her little girl could save Mommy now.

I dropped the bomb that night after Jenna finished her shower. I was waiting for her when she came into the bedroom, tying off a robe.

"I just wanted to tell you that I'm leaving," I said.

"What are you talking about? Where are you going?"

"Doesn't matter. Away from you."

My friend Shooter had an extra bedroom he'd offered me. I'd crash at his place until I could figure out my next move. Jenna chased me out of the bedroom, telling me how much she loved me and how sorry she was for calling the cops. But I knew that desperate apology was only temporary, and that her addictions were stronger than love. I understood this because I'd been the same animal in the days when I'd been abusing coke and meth.

Jenna trailed me through the house and into the garage, now cursing me every step of the way. I guess when "I love you" fails, the next best thing is "Come back here, cocksucker." I opened the garage door, strapped on my brain bucket and fired up the Harley. Even the roar of that 96-cubic-inch engine did little to drown out Jenna's wild ranting. She got in front of the bike and grabbed the handlebars.

"You can't leave me!"

"Get the fuck out of my way!"

"You can't go!"

"I'm done. Move your ass!"

"George, I'm pregnant!"

My brain seized. I eased off the throttle.

"Bullshit" was all I could think to say.

"It's not," swore Jenna. "I missed my period. I did the test. I'm pregnant."

Goddammit! I kicked the Heritage into gear and nearly knocked Jenna over as I blasted out of the garage. In my mirrors I saw that pissed-off woman chasing me down the street with her bathrobe flying open and her naked body out there for the entire neighborhood to see.

I'd been trying to get off the hard booze back then, but I figured this was one of those special occasions that called for a good old-fashioned drinking binge. So I bought a bottle of Wild Turkey and blew past my limit in no time. Then I stumbled into Shooter's Food and Brew, where I bumped into Big Todd and Iron Mike. Even in the drunken state I was in, I recognized the irony of having Todd on the stool next to me, but at that point I figured why not buy a few rounds for the proud papa.

Of course, my girlfriend could have been tapped by any number of guys, given her history, including a part-time fuck buddy named Spike from tweaker days. Hell, for all I knew it could have been Pedro down the block who'd knocked her up. I just couldn't imagine that baby being mine. Never mind all the dicks that had been shoved between

Jenna's legs, there were the doctors who'd told me I was probably sterile after all the chemo and radiation cancer treatments I'd been forced to endure. I'd never bothered to use protection after that, and none of my girlfriends had ever gotten pregnant . . . until now.

I found myself flashing back to my old man. There had always been a nagging doubt in my mind whether I was really his kid. Dad was a pureblooded redskin, and my mother was dark-skinned too. My older sister, Carol, had their same coloring, but my little sister and I were both lily white. Lin Ann insisted we were the by-product of artificial insemination, but I always figured I was spawned by one of Mother's boyfriends from her bar-crawling days. Whatever the pedigree, I'd lived my life with the cloud of illegitimacy hanging over my head, and I didn't want any part of that with Jenna.

I slept off the drunk in Shooter's spare bedroom, then popped some aspirin in the morning and made a beeline for the pharmacy. I bought one of those home pregnancy test kits and headed for Espirit Circle so Jenna could piss on the stick. I wanted to see for myself. I had to be certain.

The color changed. She was pregnant, all right.

I asked her point-blank if I was the father. It was a valid question, but despite the odds stacked against her, Jenna insisted the baby was mine. At that point I didn't know what the hell to do, so I asked her to get an abortion. When she refused, I went out and got shitfaced all over again.

That afternoon and into the early evening I sat on a barstool at Shooter's, drowning myself in Kentucky bourbon while trying to think through my latest predicament with a booze-addled brain. With a few more drinks under my belt I called John Carr and gave him the headline. I couldn't say he was thrilled by the news. There were no "Congratulations" or "Thatta boy's." It was more like I'd punched my handler in the gut and knocked the wind out of him.

"George, you're killing me, dude," he moaned. "You've basically sealed our fate with Jenna. I warned you a hundred times to get rid of her."

"Spare me the lecture, okay? She says she's carrying my kid. What the fuck am I supposed to do?"

"Are you sure it's yours?"

"Thanks, pal," I snapped. "That's just what I needed to hear."

Truth be told, I already had one kid out in the world that I wasn't taking care of, and I didn't need another, especially one who might not be mine. But having been such a monumental piece of shit in the past, I felt an obligation to step up to the plate.

For better or worse, I had to do the right thing.

So after work the next evening I walked through the front door at Espirit Circle and tossed Jenna a box with an engagement ring.

"You're going to marry me, right?"

"Yeah, sure," said Jenna.

"Cool," I replied, then walked back out again.

Yes, sir, I was a romantic sonofabitch.

Not long after we got engaged, a specter from Jenna's past walked through the open garage and appeared unexpectedly in our kitchen.

It was Billy, her old boyfriend—and the sight of him froze Jenna with fear. She didn't know what her ex was capable of. It wouldn't have surprised her if he'd pulled a gun and started blasting away. But the man had come with a different purpose in mind. He'd recently finished an eight-month stint in prison, and his sister had driven him over to visit Sierra. Billy was bound, drunk and determined to let that kid know who her real father was.

He strode through the house like he owned the place, saying, "Where's my daughter? I want to talk to my little girl."

That's when I intercepted him.

"Whoa, whoa, whoa. You need to back the fuck up," I warned him.

Billy had always been afraid of me in the past, but he was hammered that night and feeling his oats. I could also see he'd been lifting weights in the prison yard and was pretty jacked.

"Get out of my way, George."

"Come back when you're sober, Billy."

"Fuck you," he spat back. "I'm her father, and I'm gonna talk to her."

He pushed past me into the living room, where Sierra was watching television, and knelt in front of her.

"Don't screw it up, Billy," I hissed at him under my breath.

"Hi, Sierra," he said to her.

"Hi. Who are you?" Sierra wanted to know.

That's when I grabbed Billy and pulled him out of the room.

"In the garage. Now."

As I followed him through the kitchen and into the garage, I remember thinking this was the same prick who'd beaten Jenna unconscious in Arizona and dangled Sierra out the window of his car, asking, "Anyone want a fuckin' baby?"

And now he wanted back into that baby's life?

I'd given that sonofabitch every opportunity to do the right thing by his little girl. He lived only half a mile away but had never come to see her until that day. I'd even offered him money to buy her birthday presents. I'd wanted Billy to be part of his daughter's life, but he'd blown it. Now it was too late. Sierra had adopted me as her daddy, and that arrangement was working out just fine.

"There's no way I'm gonna let you come back here and fuck with that kid's life," I warned him, trying hard to keep my anger in check.

"I'm her father," he growled at me.

"And I'm her dad."

"Fuck you, George. Anyone can be a daddy, but Sierra's only got one father, and I'm gonna tell her that."

He tried moving past me into the house. I pressed a hand against his chest.

"No, you're not. You're gonna come back when you're sober, and we'll talk then."

"Fuck you," he said, slapping my hand away.

That's when I hit him.

Billy bounced off the cement floor and somehow got wedged between the washer and dryer. Wasn't much of a fight after that. I went crazy on the sonofabitch, kicking him in the head until he was nearly unconscious. Far as I was concerned, I was dealing with one of those "shit talkers" from my bareknuckle fighting days and was putting the boot to him. I didn't want that abusive bastard ever coming back into our lives again, and I was making damn sure he got the message.

When the lesson was over, Billy's own sister didn't recognize him. She pushed his bloody wreckage into her truck and hauled it away.

That was the last time Jenna and I ever saw him.

20

Aloha, Brothers

In September of 2005, the ATF paid my way to Hawaii for the annual Labor Day run to Kona on the big island of Hawaii. It was supposed to be a working vacation on the government tit, traveling to make a gun buy from a member of the Vagos chapter in Puna. But after buying weapons from a patch named Woodstock, I ate bad shellfish and spent the next five days with my ass and head in the toilet.

If I was going to be sick and flat on my back for a week, though, at least the room was nice. The four-star hotel overlooked the beach, while the rest of Green Nation were slumming it in the cheap seats farther inland, forced to endure the clatter of tired air conditioners.

Only one other Vago shared my luxurious accommodations on the Kona coastline, some big ol' goober-looking dude I spotted kicking around the parking lot. I thought it was curious that we were the only two greenies in that particular hotel, but I didn't bother thinking it through. I was more concerned with running out of toilet paper.

Problems had followed Green Nation across the ocean. The Puna Hawaii Vagos were having issues with another motorcycle club on the island called the Kinsmen. You would've thought with soft sandy beaches and tropical breezes those Hawaii boys would have been a mellower brand of outlaw. But no. They were making plans to remove the Kinsmen's patches by force. What seemed to bother the Vagos most was the "81" patch the Kinsmen wore on their cuts; the eighth letter in the alphabet is *H*, and *A* is the first. That would be the Hells Angels.

It was always about those fucking Angels. Not sure why there was so much contempt for the mighty red and white. Could be the Vagos saw them as a bunch of prima donnas who walked around thinking their shit didn't stink. Or it just might have been a chronic case of Angel envy. There are a ton of one percenters out there who get a stiffy at the mere thought of an Angel's death's head on their back. Big Todd, for one, had himself a huge man-crush on that outlaw club.

Whatever the reason, because the Kinsmen were advertising support for Green Nation's archenemies, Tramp had given those Puna boys the green light to rip the patch off any Kinsmen that crossed their path. I got that same order direct from the big kahuna himself, who told me I could keep the patches as battle trophies.

But taking scalps was the furthest thing from my mind as I lay roombound with my stomach cramping and nasty shit blasting from every orifice. John Carr had come knocking . . . and he'd brought company. Standing with him on the second-floor walkway was ATF Special Agent Kozlowski and that big ol' goober-looking Vago from the parking lot.

Fuck!

"No way, man. No fuckin' way," I cursed at John. "This ain't happening."

"Just listen to me a minute," he said, extending his hand to stop Koz from following him into the room.

"I don't fuckin' appreciate what you're doing, man. You know how I felt about this."

"George, I'm sorry. But this had to happen. You and Charles have seen each other around the hotel. Koz and I thought it'd be best to have you two meet instead of looking at each other sideways the whole time you're here."

That smelled like bullshit. I just sat on the bed and slow cooked.

"You know I would never jeopardize your safety. I wouldn't do that to you," John insisted before gesturing toward the door. "I'm just telling you Charles is a good guy."

I looked past him to the CI from Victorville. Quick Draw didn't seem particularly thrilled to see me either. I knew right away this was one of those arranged marriages, and already it wasn't working.

"Have I ever steered you wrong, dude?" asked John.

"Not until now," I told him.

It took me a while to warm up to Charles. Like I said, I didn't trust dopers, reformed or otherwise. We finally ended up having a long phone conversation the day before I headed back to the States. I'd been undercover a year longer than him, but a lot had happened up there in the High Desert. Those boys were crazy, and Psycho, the Victorville P, let his inmates run wild.

Charles had stories to tell.

We talked about "Twist" Foreman, the asshole who'd shot Little Jimmy in the back during that home invasion in Lucerne Valley and how Charles was moving significant quantities of marijuana for Psycho. Just before coming to Hawaii, in fact, he'd bought fifty pounds of it on the P's dime.

By the time we were done talking I decided I actually liked that CI. And I have to admit it felt pretty good having someone in similar shoes, sharing an experience only a handful of people will ever know.

But I still didn't trust him.

The next day I was at the airport, and my perfectly miserable Hawaiian vacation ended as it began. As I stood in line with other Vagos waiting to fly off the island, I met a businessman who wanted to get home worse than I did. So I told the gate attendant I was willing to switch to the next flight. She took one look at my paperwork, then said something that nearly buckled my knees.

"I'm sorry, sir, I can't help you. This ticket was bought at a government rate."

Ho-lee shit.

"Let me see that," said a Vagos national officer behind me.

I handed him the ticket and pulled the starter cord on my brain.

"Where'd you get this?" he wanted to know, trying to figure out what he was looking at.

Hard to believe, but the first thing that popped out of my mouth was, "ATF bought it for me."

I don't know where the fuck that came from. I just blurted it out. But I have to tell you, man, that comeback saved my ass. All those Vagos started laughing, which bought me just enough time to scramble out of that mess.

"Got an uncle in the military who gets that discount for me. Couldn't fly without it."

Thank God those brutes weren't rocket scientists. Still chuckling, the Vago handed back the ticket and I got on that plane and settled into my government-discounted seat as fast as I could. I'm not sure if it was the remnants of shellfish poisoning or that near fiasco at the gate, but my guts were on spin cycle. I checked the seat pocket in front of me for a barf bag . . . just in case.

When I returned from Hawaii I learned Buckshot was near the end of his road, dying of cancer. This wasn't a surprise; for months the poor bastard had looked like death warmed over. But as he was exiting Green Nation that ol' Vago left me a parting gift, recommending that I replace him as the Hemet chapter's secretary-treasurer. With my business experience it was a good fit . . . especially for the ATF. Now I had access to the chapter's books, and that made Special Agent Carr a happy handler.

Before he dropped out of the club, Buckshot warned that Big Roy's hand would be in the strongbox on a regular basis and that he'd never pay back a dime of what he borrowed. The chapter's books would get wiped clean three times while I was treasurer. Each time the bank was empty, Roy would badger members to get their dues paid up. For a patch holder that added up to eighty bucks a month. With twenty members in the chapter, as much as sixteen hundred dollars was going into the strongbox every thirty days. Far as I could tell, Big Roy built his new, custom chopper without a word of thanks to the schmucks who paid for his parts. And you know what? That was cool with me. I wasn't saying nothin' to no one. Who was I but a lowly treasurer, and he the mighty P?

On the flip side of the hyphen I was also the chapter's secretary. Go figure. Me, the guy who couldn't read or write in high school, was now a secretary. Once a month every Vagos secretary, maybe twenty to thirty guys, would gather in a Fontana restaurant to hear Ta Ta hand down the latest commandments from God of the High Desert. Charles was Victorville's secretary-treasurer at the time, so we'd sit together at those boring-ass meetings, just a couple of federal informants kicking back and recording whatever leadership decreed, including where runs were headed and any snitch alerts.

As Ta Ta was droning on, Charles gave me a kick under the table and leaned closer.

"Did you hear that?" he said under his breath.

"No. What?"

"We're looking for an informant with the initials JR."

I sat up straight and was mentally sorting through the possibilities when I suddenly realized they got the first initial wrong. I believed it then and I still believe it now. Those two letters were close enough to GR to shrivel my sphincter to the size of a BB . . . and how anyone could get that close I haven't a fuckin' clue.

So now I'm swallowing hard and Charles is nervous because, since returning from Hawaii, he's been seen hanging around a lot with this guy GR. I called Big Roy on the ride back to Hemet and shared the initials with him, which he relayed to the membership at our next Wednesday-night social.

Right away Slinger said, "I knew it wasn't anyone in this chapter."

He had plenty of patches agreeing until Roy threw a wet blanket.

"Tramp still thinks there's a cop or informant in this chapter, so let's not congratulate ourselves just yet," he told the boys. "He wants all of you to submit new paperwork and photographs for background checks. We'll be taking pictures after church. It's all going back to national. Everyone's being reinvestigated."

I couldn't count the number of "fuuuck"s I heard. I added one of my own.

"And one more thing," Roy cut in. "We need someone to video-tape when we make the run to Warner Springs. Tramp's looking to identify anyone who doesn't fit in. Anybody have a camera and want to volunteer?"

I raised my hand immediately.

Warner Springs in San Diego County is an area of scrub pine and chaparral tucked between Mount Palomar to the west and Anza-Borrego Desert State Park to the east. At the turn of the century the place was a stage coach stop, but in the years since it has become a resort area known for its hot springs. On the outlying acreage were the cheap seats—a camp-ground with RV hookups, a country store and a bar, perfect for a bunch of saddle-sore outlaws looking to party hearty at the end of a long run.

I packed my things, including a video camera on loan from the United States government, climbed into the truck with Jenna and hit the road hauling our fifth wheel to Warner Springs, leaving Old Joe be-hind to watch little Sierra. By now my fiancée had become a true VOL, fully embracing Green Nation and the outlaw lifestyle. Jenna had made friends with most of the Hemet patches and their old ladies, sported a Property of George jacket and went to bed wearing black VOL pajamas with green stripes down the legs.

We arrived at the campground to find the party already in full gear. I grabbed the camera and immediately headed out to do some video-taping. Here was a golden opportunity, courtesy of Terry the Tramp, to put names to some faces the ATF had never identified as gang members before, especially those Northern California boys who were mostly anonymous to law enforcement. While a prospect worked the camera, I shook hands and collected names. *Hey, thanks for the ID, brother. The ATF might be in touch later.*

As I'm glad-handing my way through the crowd, the sound of cat-calls and whistles grabbed my attention. A young girl, no more than thirteen years old, was passing a group of shitfaced Hemet boys on her way to the general store.

"Hey, sweet thing! Come here and gimme some!" shouted one moron.

"Oh, baby, I could fuck you up the ass right here, right now!" yelled another.

And it only got raunchier. The terrified kid put her head down and kept walking into the store.

As I turned away, I spotted a familiar face. Bubba was coming my way with a beer in his hand and a big grin. I took the camera from the prospect and shooed him away.

"Still alive, huh?" said Bubba, watching the prospect walk off.

"Still breathing, man. Aren't you worried being seen with me?"

"Should I be?"

He slapped my back and turned to study the pride of Green Nation mingling across the campground, smoking their weed, getting drunk and raising hell.

"So how you making it, brother?" Bubba asked.

"Doin' okay," I told him, lighting another cigarette.

"What's it been now? Two years?"

"Closer to two and a half."

"Long time."

"Sometimes it feels longer."

"Try doing it as many years as I have, young man," Bubba grinned, then took a long pull on his bottle. "Must be getting close to the end, though. These cases usually don't go beyond two or three years."

"Well, I'm ready whenever the fuck they are."

"Are you?" Bubba said cryptically, then nodded toward the Vagos. "It's not so easy for some people, brother. I'll bet you're friendly with some of those boys. But when the takedown happens, a lot of the guys you think are cool are gonna go down. That's always the tough part. Taking down your buddies."

As Bubba spoke I was scanning the campground, picking out the faces I'd hate to see busted. Like JB over there. I liked that dude. Slinger and Ready were cool too. I hated to think of them getting caught up in the net when the feds hauled it in. Then there was Blackie, 37, and JJ—forever brothers who were no longer full of the same piss and vinegar as in the early days. Those old-timers were just hanging out, smoking weed and laughing at the world going by.

I knew what Bubba meant. As much as I'd enjoy seeing assholes like Big Roy and Todd bite the dust, at the end of Operation 22 Green there was bound to be collateral damage. Both friend and foe would crash and burn together.

"You just have to remember who you work for," Bubba was telling me. "And sometimes that's not so easy. Guys lose themselves. I've known undercover cops who infiltrated and had that problem."

Bubba glanced over at me and took a swig of beer, looking for a reaction.

"Like I told John. I know why I'm doing this. I know who I am."

The big man saluted me with his bottle just as a shrill whistle sounded from across the campground.

"Hey, prospect!"

37 was hailing me. No doubt that graybeard was out to bust my balls again.

"Not anymore, brother!" I shouted back at him. "Fuck your tampons, and fuck that fuckin' song!"

The old Vago grinned and waved me over to where he, JJ and Blackie were passing a joint.

"Better go see what he wants," said Bubba. "I'll see you 'round."

Blackie offered me a hit as I joined the group, but I waved it off.

"We could use more weed, George," said 37. "Can you fix us up?"

"Sure. How much you need?"

Jenna had bud for sale. My fiancée had become the de facto pill and weed supplier for the Hemet chapter. As it turned out, though, the forever brothers had no interest in buying pot. Those stoned fools were merely buying time, grinning and winking at each other like grade-schoolers dying to share a secret.

"What's so funny?" I asked.

37 tugged at his belt and nodded me toward Blackie. When I turned, Blackie was removing the silver Loki buckle—the beauty handed down through the years from one Vago to the next.

The belt slipped from his waist, and Blackie held it out to me.

"I know you've had your eye on this for a while, brother. I've been around for a long time, and if anyone deserves this buckle, it's you."

"Seriously?"

"I want you to have it," insisted Blackie. "Just make sure the belt comes back."

I swapped out my own belt so he could hold his pants up, then dug

Blackie's belt buckle.

a new hole in Blackie's with a pocket knife and strapped it on. Did I maybe feel a pang of guilt taking that old-timer's prized possession? Me, an informant for the feds? Sure . . . a little, I guess. But not enough to give it back. No way, jack. That buckle was fuckin' cool.

• • •

Maybe a half hour later, the uncle of the young girl that had been harassed by the Hemet boys came charging down in his vehicle. From the moment he jumped from his car the man was giving the Vagos an earful, demanding to know who was in charge of the savages that had accosted his niece.

"Who the fuck you yelling at, motherfucker?" barked Roy as he stepped forward.

"You, if you're one of the jackasses that told my niece you wanted to fuck her."

Big Roy threw a punch and the rest of the Vagos pounced. Todd was stomping away along with Mickey, Charlie and a few others. It was the usual outlaw gangbang: brutal, overwhelming and unfair. The battered uncle tried to escape, scampering on hands and knees up a small hill, but the Vagos knocked him back down again. The man finally broke free of the frenzy, made it to his car and took off like a wildman. He nearly ran down a few Vagos on the way out. They were goddamn animals, he probably figured. The bastards deserved to be roadkill.

A while later, an older dude, maybe early sixties, showed up on a motorcycle and told the Vagos it wasn't right for them to come in, take over the campground and start beating people up.

So they beat him up too.

Later John Carr tracked down the uncle who'd been stomped defending his niece. John told him there was a witness to the assault, and that he could have the Vagos prosecuted for it. The uncle was grateful and might have pressed charges if he hadn't gotten shitfaced a few months later and driven the wrong direction on the freeway.

And that was the end of that.

21

End of the Road

Operation 22 Green had dragged on for almost three years, and that was enough for John Carr and the ATF. I'd been stumbling my way toward the finish line for months, at times so worn out I was crawling on hands and knees, but when I finally broke the tape and collapsed, I couldn't believe the damn thing was over.

The end came unceremoniously over the usual lunch at the Little Luau. I was talking to John about the assault at Warner Springs when he cut me off.

"I'm shutting down 22 Green."

And there it was, just like that. ATF was cashing its chips and getting out of the game.

"This has been in the works for three or four months," John continued. "I just didn't want you thinking about it until the time came. Well, now it's time."

"When?" I said after a moment.

"If all goes according to plan, we're looking at early March."

Man, I should have been dancing on the tables at the Little Luau and singing the "Hallelujah Chorus." I'd been waiting a hell of a long time for that moment. But now that it was here, I wasn't sure how to feel. I'd been married to the case for years—long enough for it to become a huge drag on my life. And yet there was this insane part of me—one that probably needed to be lobotomized—that still wanted to make the marriage work, to keep 22 Green going and see how far we could take it.

In fact I was just days away from telling Big Roy to go fuck himself and hooking up with a chapter in the San Fernando Valley. Hell, I'd even thought of going after a charter of my own. And with Charles up in Victorville, we'd been making grand plans to bring all of Green Nation to its knees.

But none of that was happening now. Once the plug was pulled, I'd have to be satisfied with whatever washed down the pipe. John could tell I was less than enthused.

"What's up with you? This is what you've been waiting for."

"I just think there's more we can do," I said lamely, and the words sounded nuts leaving my mouth. "I've been hanging with Southside. If I could—"

"Whoa, hold on, dude," John interrupted. "This is my call. We can't go on forever. ATF won't let that happen. I had to pick a date. It's done. So let's just take what we've got and call it a day. It's time to end this."

"We got enough for a RICO?" I muttered after a long pause.

"So far that's the plan. We've got evidence of racketeering in weapons, drugs and murder. We'll proceed on that basis and see what happens."

I nodded. "Just remember. When this is over, I want in that cell with Roy and Todd."

"And just like I told you before, I can't promise that," he answered.

John went back to his teriyaki.

"I'm about to start pulling warrants," he said as he ate. "Things will get tricky now, especially on a case this size. There'll be a lot of communication with a lot of different agencies. Lot of paperwork crossing desks."

The operational security issues would be enormous. John Carr was pulling eighty-six search-and-arrest warrants for Riverside, Los Angeles, San Bernardino, Orange and Ventura Counties, covering Southern California towns and cities as far north as Port Hueneme, south to Murrieta, west to Manhattan Beach and east to the High Desert. Every Vagos president, sergeant at arms and secretary-treasurer in Southern California was on the list to have their homes searched. Operation 22 Green was shaping up as the largest gang takedown in United States history.

Because of its unprecedented magnitude, John's biggest concern was the threat from within the ranks of law enforcement. Cops talk to cops, and there were a shitload of lawmen in my neck of the woods who had grown up around the Vagos, gone to school with them, even got shitfaced with them. There were big question marks about an officer in Apple Valley, a couple from Hesperia and six from San Bernardino—one who was later terminated for passing information along to the Vagos. Charles had once shared drinks with a Barstow deputy who'd tipped him off to a search of Psycho's home over a stolen motorcycle. Because of these operational security concerns, it had been decided that only team leaders would be told of the takedown beforehand. The rank-and-file officers would be kept in the dark until the takedown was under way.

"You might want to think about getting out of the house," John continued. "If things break bad, you want to distance yourself from Jenna so she doesn't get caught up in it. Spread the word you've split with her. I think it'd be best for all of you, including the kid."

We finished lunch and headed into the parking lot, where I immediately reached for my smokes.

"There's something else we need to talk about," said John as he fished for his car keys. "What do we do about WITSEC? If you want me to start the ball rolling with the marshals, now's the time."

Since John had first mentioned the Witness Security Program, I'd spent plenty of time thinking and praying on it. And the more I did, the more WITSEC appealed to me. I could start over again. My entire shameful past would be wiped out. In my next life no one would know the drug-dealin', multiple-felon, racist asshole I'd once been. I'd be the phoenix rising from the ashes of a man once known as George Rowe.

But the question was, with all the baggage I'd collected, would this bird even fly? I was way the fuck over the weight limit, man. And John Carr had his doubts as well. He wasn't sure I'd ever get off the ground.

"Look, George," he was telling me. "We both know Jenna's a party girl. Your fiancée loves her drugs. I don't see her giving up that lifestyle, do you?"

Instead of answering the obvious, I lit a cigarette.

"And here's something else to think about," he continued. "Even if Jenna is willing to go into the program with you—and that's a big if—there's no guarantee her little girl can go too."

"What? Why not?"

"Because you're not her biological father. Whoever the father is would have to sign off. He'd have to give up all parental rights to Sierra."

Billy? The asshole whose head I'd used for soccer practice?
Oh, shit.

"And you're just telling me this now?"

"Hey, I've never dealt with this kind of crazy situation before, okay? Everything's a lot more complicated. And to be honest, even if everything works out the way you'd like—Jenna's gung ho to go and Sierra's dad signs off—I can't promise the marshals will even take you. This is a family package now, and that's a lot more work and expense for the marshals. You're a hard sell, George, see what I'm saying?"

Yeah, I saw what he was saying. And it was a goddamn mess. There were just too many questions without answers. The easiest thing to tell John was . . .

"Fuck it. What have I got to lose? Let's go for it."

•   •   •

Joe was in the back bedroom, shuffling through Family Tree Service paperwork when I got back to the house. In a few weeks I'd be walking away from the business I'd built over fourteen years, and six employees would be headed for the unemployment line. More collateral damage . . . man, the body count was really piling up.

Me and Old Joe cracked a bottle and talked until Jenna came home. I started by telling him ATF was pulling the plug on 22 Green, which he was relieved to hear. Then I told him the rest: that I was applying for witness security but he couldn't come.

I saw the air go out of my friend like a pricked balloon.

"So what happens to me?"

"You can come with me when the takedown happens. We'll hang together until the marshals come for us. John says that could take months."

"And what then?"

I squirmed a little, then said, "John promised he'd look out for you. He'll get you to a safe place."

"Sure. He says that *now*," said Joe ruefully.

My buddy was feeling down, and I hated to do it, but I had to kick him in the head one more time.

"Listen, man. I need you to look after Jenna for a bit. Nothing permanent, it just has to look that way until the takedown. If she won't leave with me, it'll be better for her if it looks like we broke up."

He shook his head. "You're putting me in the middle, brother, and you know that's not a place I like to be."

Old Joe was right, of course. But in the end the man did as I asked. Joe used to say all he ever wanted from life was a 1954 Ford F-100 pickup and a new set of teeth. I hope someday that boy gets everything he's asked for, because after all the shit I've put him through, he sure as hell deserves it.

• • •

Finding an excuse to leave Jenna was just a matter of letting her nature take its course. I don't remember what the fight was about. I do remember throwing a trash bag full of clothes into the truck bed and heading for Shooter's house. I planned to lay low at my friend's place until the take-down—about a month out.

First night away my cell phone started blowing up with calls from Jenna. I didn't answer, letting voice mail pick up. The first went something like "You left me?! I'm delivering your baby next month, mother-fucker!"

I didn't listen after that.

Swear to God, Jenna called me every damn day, several times a day, alternately begging and cursing at me to come home. When she realized she was getting nowhere, she had her daughter start leaving messages. That beautiful little girl had recently celebrated her fifth birthday.

"Come home, Daddy. I want you to come home."

Man, it was gut wrenching.

Found out later that Jenna was strapping Sierra into her Dodge Caravan and driving around town looking for Daddy. She had a notion I might be at Shooter's place and would sit in the minivan for hours outside his house waiting for me to appear. She never did catch me, though.

And I wasn't the only one getting harassed. Jenna was so pissed off that she was running a scorched-earth campaign with the Vagos, calling their old ladies and sharing all the gossip about who was fucking who. Guess she figured if she couldn't have me in her life, neither could the Vagos. The situation got so out of hand that Big Roy pulled me aside after church one night and asked me to put a stop to it.

"Your girlfriend is making a fuckin' mess," said Roy. "You've got to do something."

"You handle it, man. I'm done with her."

"Just go back to her, would you, please? The bitch is out of control."

I couldn't, though. Not until the takedown.

Meanwhile Old Joe was miserable, getting an earful from Jenna day and night. He'd sneak out of the house just before sunrise and meet me on the corner, where I'd pick him up and drive him to work. In my experience, there was no man more straightforward and trustworthy than Old Joe, and he was having real problems with all the deceit—one of my former specialties. The guilt was chewing him up.

"How's she doing?" I asked one morning as he settled into the cab.

"Not good. She sits around the house crying all the time, George. And she doesn't eat."

"If it helps, tell her I'll be coming home. I just need time."

"She thinks you've gone back to Christie."

Jenna's old man was calling me too. His daughter was burying him with distraught calls and making him crazy. I stayed in touch with Bill during my time away, occasionally dropping off money for rent, bills and groceries. I tried to reassure him the split was temporary—that I wouldn't abandon his daughter and Sierra.

"She's hard to live with, isn't she?" he said to me while flipping burgers one day on the backyard grill.

"I guess you'd know about that, Pops."

"You know, I have to tell you, George. I didn't know what to make of you when we first met. Still don't. I never have understood this road you're taking with the Vagos. There's the tough guy George who rides around with bikers and acts like a gangster, and then there's this other person who cares about people and tries to help them out. I really don't get you, but I like you. Just wanted you to know that."

Bill's little speech was heartfelt, and I decided to give him something back. It was the reason I'd asked for our meeting that afternoon.

"Listen. Some shit is gonna be coming down soon. I think you might be happy about it . . . but then again maybe not. Whatever happens, though, I just want you to know I've never done you any wrong . . . not intentionally."

"When have you ever done me wrong?"

I paused a moment, then said, "I'm not who you think I am."

I reached into the pocket of my Levi's and pulled out a folded piece of paper—the same paper John Carr had handed to me at his office almost three years before.

"If something happens to me, call this number. The man that answers can explain everything."

Bill took the paper and glanced at the scribbled phone number.

"What's going on, George? Are you in some kind of trouble?"

"I'm sorry, Pops. I know it sucks, but that's all I can tell you right now. Just don't share that number with anyone. It's only for you, okay? And only if something happens to me."

Bill studied me a long moment, visibly concerned. He was trying to read between the lines but couldn't. I wouldn't allow it.

"Okay," he finally said, and shoved the number into his pocket.

Jenna had her baby shower at Bill's place a few nights later. Billy's sister was there. So was Jenna's mom, her dad's new wife and several of the VOLs, including JB and Buckshot's old ladies.

Must have been a bittersweet experience for my fiancée, because when she got home she told Old Joe it was time for him to hit the road. To have him around was like "holding on to the past," Jenna explained, and she couldn't live that way anymore. It was too hard. So my buddy showed up at Shooter's place that night looking for a place to crash. Shooter gave him the travel trailer parked at the side of his house—which was roomier, at least, than the fifteen-footer he'd once called home.

During the four weeks I remained separated from Jenna, I occasionally snuck back to the house on Espirit Circle to grab the things I planned on taking once the takedown happened. Usually I conducted those stealth operations when Jenna's minivan was gone, but a few times I tried going in during the early morning hours before she rolled out of bed.

And that's how I got caught.

I left the truck in the driveway and crept into the garage to root through some tools, unaware little Sierra had seen my arrival and had run to tell Mommy I'd come home. All of a sudden the door from the kitchen swung open and there stood Jenna in her VOL stretch pajamas, belly pushed out like a python digesting a pig.

Baby Bear had awakened Momma. And Momma Bear was pissed.

"What are you doing here?" she growled at me.

"I'm not staying. Just came to get a few tools, that's all."

"You're not leaving me again," she warned, coming toward me with claws out. "You're gonna be here when your baby comes."

"I'll be back for the baby, Jenna. But right now I'm taking these tools and I'm going."

"No, you're not," she said.

There was no talking to that woman once she got her back up. Especially at that hour of the morning. I could see where things were headed but couldn't stop it. Jenna threw a tantrum that would have made any five-year-old proud. Meanwhile, the actual five-year-old was trying to contain the situation, pleading, "Mommy, be quiet" and "Daddy didn't do anything."

"It's okay, baby," I told Sierra. "Daddy's leaving, but I'm coming back, okay? I promise."

"You're not leaving me again, you piece of shit!" screamed Jenna.

I refused to play her game, especially with Sierra watching, so I reached for my truck keys on the workbench. Jenna got there first and snatched them away. When I asked for them back, she kicked me. When she tried again, I lifted my foot to block it, and she ended up flat on her ass.

Jenna immediately went to DEFCON 1. Nuclear war imminent.

"You're going to jail, motherfucker!" she exploded. The girl dusted herself off, disappeared into the house with my truck keys and called the cops.

When the Hemet police arrived minutes later, my fiancée waddled out to the driveway to meet them and demanded I be hauled away for assault. Now from across the street came cockeyed Pete in his jeans and

T-shirt. Pete was one of those neighbors who always seemed to know what was happening around the hood. You could fart and that dude could tell you what time it went off. We'd been friends since the day I'd saved him from a Vagos beat-down at an Italian restaurant in town. Iron Mike had resented the way Pete's lazy eye had been looking at him, so I'd been forced to step between them.

"You saw what he did to me, Pete!" Jenna railed. "You saw George hit me."

"Didn't see it that way at all," Pete told her. "Saw you hittin' and kickin' George, though."

When Jenna realized I wasn't going to be dragged away in cuffs, her next move was to jump into my truck and lock the doors. While the cops knocked on the glass and politely asked her to step out, Jenna was frantically rifling through my glove compartment, the center console, under the seats and behind the visors. I don't know what the hell she was looking for, unless it was some evidence I was cheating on her . . . or maybe drugs the law could bust me for.

When the girl realized there was nothing to be found, she stopped tearing the cab apart and emerged from the truck. I think those cops might have hauled her off to the nut ward if she hadn't been so pregnant. Instead they returned my keys and told me to hit the road.

Glancing over my shoulder, the last thing I saw was Jenna standing in the driveway, barefoot and pregnant, still jawing at those poor cops.

22

Down an Empty Highway

The takedown had been pushed back twice—the complexities of the operation were just too enormous—but the ATF finally settled on a date, and John Carr shared it with me one week out: Thursday, March 9, 2006, at 6:00 a.m.

For me, the homestretch would prove the hardest. Now that I knew the end date, I just wanted the damn thing over with. I'd been effectively off the grid for a month now, walking the high wire without a net. There were no cover teams, no backup at all. Kevin Duffy, my old friend from the Riverside County Sheriff's Department, had asked for increased patrols around Shooter's place and the house on Espirit Circle. John Carr was calling every day to make sure I was still alive.

I felt like a soldier on short-time, nervous about getting picked off in the waning days before leaving the war zone. Whenever friends asked me to join them for a night on the town I'd decline, worried about getting ambushed. I was getting a stiff neck from looking over my shoulder.

By Wednesday, one day before the takedown, everything was set. I would be waiting at the house Thursday morning at 6:00 a.m., when lawmen from the ATF and the Riverside Sheriff's Department would arrive to escort me, Jenna and Sierra to a safe place—provided, of course, Jenna wanted to go. That was still a big question mark, given the bomb I was about to drop on her.

If all went according to plan, we'd head across town to Shooter's place and pick up Old Joe, whose marching orders were to pack a bag, stay sober and meet us outside the trailer between six and six thirty. John Carr had cleared my friend to stay with us until the U.S. Marshals could make a decision on whether to take us into the WITSEC program.

And then I phoned Jenna.

"I'm coming home tonight."

"Fuck you. The locks have all been changed and your garage door opener doesn't work."

"I'm coming home, Jenna."

"You're not welcome here," she said, and hung up on me.

If something was going to happen, I wanted to go down protecting my home and family—such as it was. Melodramatic, maybe. But that's how I was feeling on the eve of the takedown.

On Wednesday night—as over seven hundred lawmen from across the country were converging on Southern California—I went to my last Vagos church in JB's garage. I was nervous as hell as I sat in that meeting, and I wasn't even wearing a wire. I was so close to getting off that wild fuckin' ride, and yet coincidence had put me in a room with every member of the Hemet chapter just hours before the shit hit the fan. Most of these boys would be staring through bars come this time tomorrow.

I looked around at the faces in that garage—faces of men who had called me brother for the past three years. Some of these boys were friends, decent people who'd made the mistake of throwing in with bullies and assholes. I wasn't out to hurt all of them, and I'd asked John to spare a handful of those Vagos come judgment day. But my handler had made no promises. If free passes were to be handed out, Special Agent Carr wasn't saying.

So there I sat in JB's garage stressed out of my mind. It was an eternal hour and a half of paranoid thoughts and jangled nerves. *Someone knows. Big Roy is looking at me funny. I'm too quiet. I'm fidgeting. My armpits are drenched. They're gonna fuckin' kill me, I just know it.*

The rational part of me laid this off to an overactive imagination, but, man, the damn thing was galloping wild. And it didn't help that it was the weirdest friggin' church I'd ever attended. I mean, nothing got done. It was just one big party in the garage that night. Everyone was in a great mood.

I asked Big Roy if I should read the minutes.

Don't bother.

Should I collect the dues?

Naw, we'll do it next week.

Motherfucker, there is no next week.

After church adjourned, the whole chapter wanted to keep the party going and raise some hell around town. Come on, George, ride with us, pleaded the boys. I told them thanks, but I had things to do. Truth was, I was worried I'd end up taking a sand nap.

I motored over to Shooter's place and left the Heritage in his garage. The ATF would collect that bike later. Then I gathered the leaf bags stuffed with belongings I'd been collecting over the past month and tossed them into the truck bed.

When everything was ready, I called Jenna again.

"I'll be home in a few minutes," I told her.

"I'm shutting the lights off and going to bed," she snapped, then hung up.

As promised, the house was dark when I pulled into the driveway.

It was late. Close to midnight now.

I snuck in through the garage and entered the kitchen, pulled off my boots and headed into the hallway. I passed Old Joe's bedroom and noticed Jenna had turned it into a nursery. There was a crib and a changing table in there now. I moved quietly past Sierra's room and entered the master bedroom.

After stripping off my clothes, I slipped beneath the covers next to Jenna, mentally wrung out yet too wired to sleep. If my fiancée knew I was there—and I suspect she did—she wasn't letting on. Waves of emotion washed over me, from relief to hope to anxiety to happiness to sickening, sweat-popping fear. Sometime after 5:00 a.m. I got tired of staring at the nightstand clock, climbed from bed, threw my clothes back on and headed into the kitchen to brew coffee and smoke a cigarette.

John Carr's orders were to stay put and wait for a police escort out of Hemet, but I was never good at following orders. I was dying to know what was happening out there, and Jack Fite's place was less than a mile away. Jack was on the ATF's target list, specifically his little meth stash out near the backyard shed. Curiosity had me by the shorthairs, so about twenty minutes before takedown, I finished the coffee, lit my third cigarette and slipped from the house.

As I drove through the dim streets of Valle Vista, headed toward Highway 74, I realized disobeying orders had been a mistake. Two Riverside County cruisers sped past, flying in the direction I'd just come. I arrived at Jack Fite's house a few minutes later. The ATF had hit him early. There was an armored truck parked at the curb and federal agents swarming the property carrying automatic weapons and wearing bulletproof vests.

Those SRT boys weren't playing around.

At that moment my Nextel rang. It was Special Agent Jeff Ryan on the line—apparently released from shooting-range duty—calling to say he was on his way. Shit. No time for sightseeing, I had to get back to the house fast.

In just the few minutes I'd been gone, four deputy sheriffs' cruisers had arrived on Espirit Circle. The street was sealed now. With that much protection I felt like the president of the United States.

As I jumped from the pickup and made a beeline for the house, Special Agent Ryan emerged from his unmarked SUV to intercept me. Behind him strode a stocky Mexican deputy and a ponytailed female officer, both wearing the pressed tan and drab green uniform of the Riverside County Sheriff's Department.

"Everything okay, George?" asked Jeff as we walked toward the front door.

"I'll let you know after I wake Jenna," I told him.

"Better hurry. There's not much time."

I flipped on the living room lights and left Jeff and the two deputies while I headed down the hall to wake Jenna. I didn't know what to expect. I mean, on the best of mornings, waking that woman was like waking Satan himself. And this was nowhere near the best of mornings. My fiancée was about to get the mother of all wake-up calls.

I clicked on a lamp and sat on the edge of the bed.

Man, I felt like I was lowering my ass on a lit keg of dynamite.

"Jenna," I whispered, giving her shoulder a gentle shake. "Hey, Jenna. You've got to get up."

She rolled over and blinked sleepily at me.

"Baby, you've got to get up," I said softly. "The cops are here."

She pushed herself up on her elbows, instantly awake.

"Where's the warrant?"

That girl had sold and used just about every drug imaginable, and she must've figured the law had finally caught up with her.

"They can't come in here without a warrant," she insisted.

"It ain't like that," I said.

"What do you mean it ain't like that? Tell them they need a warrant or get the fuck out."

Jenna was building up a head of steam now. She threw off the covers and lurched from bed, revealing her black Vagos Old Lady pajamas. Later she would claim she sniffed something different in the house that morning. Not the usual scent of coffee and cigarettes. This was something different. A sterile, antiseptic smell was how she described it. The smell of cops.

She charged from the bedroom, blowing past the female deputy in the hallway with a "What the fuck?" then storming into the living

room, where the Mexican deputy and Special Agent Ryan were waiting. The law was ill prepared for the coming of Satan's child.

"What the fuck?!" Jenna raged at the two strangers. "Where's the
warrant?!"

Jeff gestured toward the couch. "Have a seat, Jenna, and I'll
explain—"

"I don't fucking know you," she flashed, cutting him off. "Get the
fuck out of my house!"

Then she turned to me. "What's going on, George?"

"Just listen to the man, baby," I said.

"Listen to what? Somebody better tell me what the fuck is going on."

Agent Ryan took his cue, addressing Jenna as if he'd been practicing
in front of a mirror.

"For the last three years George has been working undercover in
conjunction with the ATF and local law enforcement to bring down
the Vagos motorcycle gang."

My fiancée stood there blinking at the man, looking as if she'd been
sledgehammered. She was trying to process what she'd just heard. Only
she couldn't. It was too much.

Ryan kept flogging the dead horse. "Right now there are seventy-
two raids taking place throughout this city, Riverside County, Orange
County and San Bernardino County," he informed her.

Jenna turned to me with a look of stunned disbelief.

"Is this true, George?"

"It's true," I said.

It took a few more seconds to wrap her mind around it, but once
reality clicked in, I thought the girl's head might explode.

"You're a motherfucking snitch?!"

I honestly hadn't known what would come from Jenna's mouth
when she learned the truth. Maybe I'd been naive, but for some reason
I'd never expected "motherfucking snitch." When we'd first met, she'd
had a needle hanging from her arm, bruises all over her emaciated

body and no shoes. I was paying for a $300,000 roof over her head and had given her a safe place to stay. I'd cared for her little girl, cleaned the shit from her sheets and taken cold showers with that woman to keep her alive.

And now I was a snitch.

Check that. I was a "motherfucking snitch."

I hung my head. I was at a complete loss for words, so Special Agent Ryan spoke for me.

"First of all, it's not like that . . . ," he began.

"Not like what?!" Jenna exploded on him. "You tell me this. That he's a snitch? It is like that! I want all of you out of my house right now! Get the fuck out of my house!"

"I'm sorry, but we can't do that," said Jeff. "It's not safe for you here anymore. You'll have to come with us."

"What are you talking about?"

"You have fifteen minutes to gather your things, and then we're going to escort you, George and your little girl to a safe place."

"When am I coming back?"

Jeff fidgeted, then said, "You're not."

As reality crashed down on her like an avalanche, Jenna freaked.

"Oh, my God! Oh, my God!"

I tried to hold her, but she pushed me away.

"Oh, my God!" she shouted again before bolting out the front door in her pajamas screaming, "They're going to kill us! We're all going to die!"

Right about then John Carr called me on the Nextel. He wanted to know if I'd broken the news to Jenna yet.

"Yeah, we told her."

"How's she taking it?"

"Not well."

"Let me talk to her."

"You can't."

"Why not?"

"Because right now she's running down the street screaming, 'We're going to die.'"

I hung up with John and put in a call to Jenna's dad. Nobody was better at getting that girl under control than Bill. I woke him from a sound sleep.

"I know it's early, Pops, but I have to tell you something. Something important."

"Yeah, okay. I'm listening."

"I've been working undercover with the federal government to take down the Vagos. That's why when you were asking me what was going on I couldn't tell you."

Silence followed, but I could hear Bill scrambling out of bed.

"You still there, Pops?"

"Yeah. Yeah, I'm here," said Bill, trying to shake the cobwebs. "What are you telling me?"

"I'm gonna put you on the phone with a federal agent," I told him. "He'll explain everything. And I need you to talk to your daughter. She's freaking out."

"Let me call you right back."

I handed Jeff the cell phone and went outside to locate Jenna.

There was a glow in the eastern sky behind the San Jacinto Mountains. A new day was coming, and many of the neighbors were in their yards wearing robes and pajamas, wondering why their street was suddenly infested with law enforcement. Jenna's ranting had flushed them from their homes like a stick poked in an ant hole.

I spotted my crazed fiancée at her neighbor's place, bawling on the shoulder of a woman she'd known since she was in high school.

"Jenna, your dad's on the phone," I called from a safe distance.

"Get away from me," she spat, pointing a warning finger at me.

"I'm not going near you, okay? But he wants to talk to you. Phone's in the house."

She rushed past me and back through the front door. I followed her inside, but she was already gone when I entered the living room.

"She went that way," said Jeff, pointing down the hall.

Jenna was in the master bedroom's walk-in closet behind a closed door. I could hear snippets of conversation as she cried to her father.

"Fucking cops . . . turning over the house . . . George is a rat . . . want to take us away . . ."

Whatever Bill said to his daughter worked, because when Jenna emerged from the closet, all the anger had drained right out of her. Now she just looked completely spent. When she spotted me in the bedroom she paused to study me like I was some curious abstract painting. There was no recognition behind those eyes. It was as if my fiancée was gazing at a complete stranger. And I suppose that wasn't far from the truth.

And now she had fifteen minutes. Fifteen short minutes to leave her life behind and start over with a man she no longer knew.

This imposter.

This motherfucking snitch.

Without a word Jenna drifted like a zombie without direction into the hallway. The female deputy corralled her and led her toward the nursery.

"Do you have kids?" I heard Jenna say. Her voice cracking. Sad and lost. "I don't know what to take. What would you take?"

"Anything you'll need for the baby," replied the deputy. "Take enough clothes for a week. Anything else we'll get to you later."

"We have a dog," said Jenna wearily. "We have birds and a rabbit. I think we have a cat. I just want to lie down. I want to lie down and sleep."

Together they packed the portable crib, a changing table, the stroller and the car seat, along with all the baby clothes from the shower the week before. Then they hauled it out to the minivan and loaded it inside. Last to go was little Sierra, wrapped in a blanket and half asleep. Still wearing her VOL pajamas and a pair of flip-flops, Jenna carried her daughter to the van and strapped her into the car seat.

"I haven't brushed my teeth," was the last thing Jenna said to the deputy.

"No time," came the reply.

Jenna tucked her pregnant belly behind the wheel of the Caravan while I climbed into my truck just ahead of her. We had two black and whites and two undercover escorts as the parade began to roll, headed across town to round up Old Joe.

When the escort arrived at Shooter's place, my buddy was waiting outside the trailer with his bag packed and ready. He walked to my truck, slung the bag into the cab and climbed in after it.

"Think I was going to leave you behind?" I grinned at him.

"Well, the thought did cross my mind," said Joe. "But I'm sure glad to see you."

With Joe now aboard, the procession began rolling again. But doing an about-face in the cul-de-sac at the end of Shooter's street created a clusterfuck. The cops didn't know which way to turn. Eventually they got it straightened out, though, and the circus rolled out of town at last.

We headed north on Highway 79 toward the range of hills known as Lambs Canyon. The undercover cars soon dropped off, and three more county cruisers joined the parade through Beaumont, the town where John and I had met for all those Friday meetings at the Little Luau Hawaiian BBQ.

Guess no more chicken katsu.

It was about 7:00 a.m. and the sun was rising over the mountains when our five-car escort fell away and a California Highway Patrol cruiser led us onto the interstate. At that hour the I-10 heading west toward Los Angeles should have been bumper to bumper with morning commuters. But every lane was empty. There wasn't a vehicle in sight. Just my truck, Jenna's minivan and the Highway Patrol.

It was fuckin' weird, man.

The trooper stayed in front of us for a mile, then turned off as a second CHP cruiser picked us up. Like clockwork, the same thing happened a mile later. This relay continued all the way down the I-10, the Highway Patrol passing us off like a baton from trooper to trooper.

As I'm driving along the interstate my cell phone is blowing up with voice mails and text messages from the Hemet Vagos. At first the messages voiced concern; "Are you alright, George? Did they get you too?" But at some point the Vagos had figured things out and the messages turned nasty. Now it was "Where the fuck are you, George?" and "We know you did this, you motherfucking rat." I even got a voice mail from my ex-girlfriend Christie, who warned, "They'll get you for this, George. You're gonna die."

At that point I stopped reading and listening.

Then came a number on caller ID that I recognized. It was Jenna ringing from the minivan.

"I need to talk to you," she said the moment I picked up.

"I promise I'll tell you everything when we get to where we're going."

"Where's that? Sierra keeps asking."

"I don't know, Jenna. Let's just get to where we're going and we'll talk then."

From the I-10 we turned onto the I-5 and went into the San Fernando Valley, where we pulled into a Walmart so Jenna could buy herself some clothes and ditch the pajamas. Then our escort led us west again to a Simi Valley motel that ATF had booked. There we waited for Charles to show up with the room keys.

If I thought the night of the takedown was hell for me, it had been nothing compared to what my fellow CI had been through in the High Desert. As I'd been fidgeting at church in JB's garage, Charles had been on his way over to Tramp's place, having been summoned to an urgent meeting by his lordship. Charles hadn't had a clue what that meeting was about, but with the takedown just hours away, he'd feared the worst.

When he arrived in Hesperia, there were several Vagos chapter officers waiting inside Tramp's house. As it turned out, they weren't there for an ambush. Apparently one of the Victorville patches was splitting from Psycho to form a chapter of his own called Death Valley, and he wanted to take Quick Draw, aka Charles, with him. In order to do that, Charles was required to pay Tramp a change of chapter fee.

Gotta hand it to Tramp, man. That ol' rascal sure knew how to keep food on the table and a slot machine fed.

Anyway, Charles had paid the fee and gotten out of there alive in fifteen minutes—about ten times longer than it was taking him to bring me the fucking motel room key. I wanted that dude to hurry his ass up because Jenna was peppering me with questions in the parking lot—questions she had every right to ask but that I preferred answering in private. When she realized she wasn't getting anywhere with me, she took her frustrations out on Old Joe, who was in my truck minding his own business.

She flung open the door and demanded, "Did you know?"

"Know what?" said Joe coyly.

"Cut the shit, Joey cakes. You know what I'm talking about."

Joe nodded and said contritely, "Yeah, I knew."

Wrong answer.

"You fucking knew all this time and you didn't tell me? How could you sit there in my house and let me think George hooked up with someone else and I'm driving around at night looking for him and—what the fuck, Joe—all those times I asked what was going on and you never said a thing?"

"I couldn't tell you, Jenna," he said quietly. "I'm sorry, but I just couldn't."

Jenna vented on the phone to her father next. She wanted to go home to Daddy, but he wouldn't allow it. Going to Nana's place was out of the question too. Bill told his daughter she was safest in my company. And the man was right too, because for months after the takedown, Bill and his wife would hear the rumble of Harley-Davidsons cruising past their home.

Not long after Jenna hung up with her dad, Charles pulled into the parking lot with the room keys.

"Who is he?" Jenna wanted to know.

"The other guy," I told her as I moved toward the car.

"Hey, bro, that was some crazy shit, man," I greeted Charles as he stepped from the car.

We hugged and shook hands and swapped stories until Jenna complained she had to pee. So we retired to our rooms, Charles a few doors down and Old Joe in the same room with us. There were no complaints from Jenna this time. I think at that point the girl was beyond caring.

I asked Joe to take Sierra for a walk while Jenna and I talked. No sooner had I pressed the door shut than my fiancée asked the million-dollar question.

"Okay. Why?"

I sat her on the bed and related my story from David's disappearance to the meeting in Bee Canyon with John Carr.

"Uncle John?" she asked.

"Yeah. Uncle John."

"He's a fuckin' cop." She said it matter-of-factly, finally able to make sense of it all. "I thought maybe you were gay. I wish that was it. At least I could deal with that."

She met my eyes with sudden intensity.

"You lied to me, George. The person I thought I was in love with was a lie. And it wasn't just a big lie. It was a life lie."

"If I'd told you the truth, what would you have done?"

Jenna didn't respond. She didn't have to. We both knew the answer to that. I stood from the bed and walked into the bathroom with my shaving kit.

"I went to high school with some of those people," she said behind me. "Some of them were good people. They didn't do anything wrong."

"If they didn't do anything wrong, they wouldn't have been arrested."

"And what about you?" she said.

"What about me?"

"You think you're some kind of angel? What gives you the fuckin' right? You're lucky no one ever went undercover on your ass."

I stripped down and said nothing.

"And how come I'm not locked up, huh?" Jenna continued. "I've sold pills, I've sold weed. I've transported across the border. I should've been busted too, shouldn't I? Fuck, George. You should hear the messages the girls left me."

She was quiet a long moment, then said listlessly, "I can't hang out with my friends anymore."

"They weren't friends, they were pill users," I told her. "They used to talk shit about you all the time."

I ran the shower.

"They were friends, George. They were friends and they'll get married and have kids and I'll never see them or have my kids play with theirs." She paused a moment. "Things will never be the same. Things will never be even close to the same."

She laid on her side and curled up against her pregnant belly.

We didn't speak again that day. I took a shower, then shaved off my beard and moustache, rediscovering my chin for the first time in fourteen years. I didn't recognize the man in the mirror, and that was the whole idea. I was preparing to say good-bye to George Rowe. Course I still had the 22 behind one ear and Green Nation splashed across the back of my head. But I'd deal with those tattoos later.

Jenna didn't bother opening her eyes when I collapsed in bed facing her. Either she couldn't bear to look at me or the girl was as exhausted as I was. Pure adrenaline had kept me going for the past thirty-seven hours. Now, all of a sudden, I had nowhere to go and not a damn thing to do: no trees to trim, no club runs to go on, no church meetings to attend, no guns to buy. I felt like I'd just finished a monthlong meth jag and now it was time to crash.

I rubbed Jenna's swollen belly until I drifted off into a deep sleep. You could have run a locomotive through that motel room and I would have snored right through it.

Finally, it was over.

Operation 22 Green was history.

VAGOS MOTORCYCLE CLUB TARGETED IN SOUTHERN CALIFORNIA CRIME SWEEP *

The Associated Press
March 10, 2006

Rancho Cucamonga, Calif.—Twenty-five leaders and associates of the Vagos motorcycle club were arrested following one of the largest coordinated law enforcement probes ever conducted in Southern California, authorities said.

Thursday's operation involved 700 personnel from the Bureau of Alcohol, Tobacco, Firearms and Explosives and local police and sheriff's departments.

"The Vagos are a ruthless criminal biker gang that virtually held our communities hostage" by dealing in "guns, drugs and death," said John Torres, a special agent in charge with the ATF.

"Operation 22 Green," as it was called, targeted Vagos associates in five Southern California counties. Green is the club's chosen color and 22 corresponds to V, the 22nd letter of the alphabet. More than 80 search and arrest warrants were issued and 25 people were taken into custody Thursday on federal or state charges that included firearms and drug violations. Another five people already were in custody.

Arrestees Thursday included seven chapter presidents, one vice president, one secretary, one treasurer and seven sergeants at arms. The vice president, Ryan Matteson, 29, was arrested for investigation of murder in connection with a home invasion robbery in Lucerne Valley where three people were robbed and one was killed, authorities said.

In a statement, Torres said investigators seized 95 illegal firearms, some illegal drugs, $6,000 in cash and two stolen motorcycles. San Bernardino County District Attorney Michael A. Ramos said the sweep effectively "dismantled" the club, which he estimated has several hundred members. Torres said he anticipated that many of those arrested will have their cases incorporated into a federal racketeering case against the club.

An e-mail message seeking comment from the club was not immediately returned. However, leaders in the past have said that Vagos is a social club, not a criminal enterprise, and frequently have complained of being subjected to witch-hunts.

"It's about riding motorcycles together. Spending time as a family, a pack, a club, a tribe," James Cross, 34, former president of the Placer County Vagos told the *Sacramento Bee* in comments published Wednesday. "The club frowns on criminal activity," said Cross, who is one of three people accused of conspiring to kill a fellow member.

23

Vanishing Act

He'd been straight-out crazy dealing with the aftershocks of Operation 22 Green, but John Carr finally arrived at our motel a few days after the takedown. When I answered his knock, he thought he'd come to the wrong room until he realized that the clean-shaven baby face staring back at him was mine. John laughed and shook my hand, then I turned to introduce him to Jenna.

Holy shit!

It was like staring into the eyes of the Medusa. I mean, if a look could kill a man, Special Agent Carr would have been stone-cold dead on the floor.

"Hi, I'm Uncle John," he said, gamely proffering his hand.

Jenna ignored it.

"No, you're not," she snapped at him. "You're a fucking cop."

A slow smile crept across John's face.

"I always knew you were going to be a handful."

Jenna smirked back. "Whatever you say, Fabio."

Fabio. Guess that was a slight aimed at John's shoulder-length hair. That's what Jenna would call John Carr from that day forward and every chance she got—just to bust his balls. In her view, that ATF special agent was just as responsible for her predicament as I was.

John had come to the motel to talk about WITSEC. The U.S. Marshals Service had given a thumbs-up and were allowing us to enter the program, so John wanted to explain to Jenna what she could expect once she got on board . . . *if* she got on board. He told her we'd be given a place to live, that she could go back to school on the government tab and study to be a nurse (a bad idea Jenna wanted to pursue) and that I could learn how to operate the big cranes, something that interested me. But the entire time John was talking, Jenna's face remained scrunched up like someone in the room had farted.

"I can tell you're not really hip to the program," John said after finishing the pitch.

"What was your first clue, Fabio?" was her snarky response.

"I know you don't like me, and that's okay," said John. "I get that. This isn't the life you chose, and you're not happy about it. But you don't have many options here, Jenna. If you choose to split with the program and go off on your own, well, that's your choice. No one can force you to do this. But you and George have been together for almost three years, and you know as well as I do that the Vagos will think you knew what was going on. I really think you need to consider WITSEC as your best alternative."

Jenna sat tight-lipped and refused to look at him. After a moment John and I left the room together.

"I'll have a marshal come talk to her," he said as we started down the second-floor walkway.

I nodded and paused at the top of the stairwell to light a cigarette.

"What's going on with Billy?" I asked.

"If your fiancée gets on board, I'll talk to him and see if he'll sign off on the kid. But there's no point getting the process started until Jenna makes up her mind."

"I think she'll do it," I told him. "She's just a little pissed off right now."

"A little?" John chuckled. "If that's a little, I'd hate to see her when she's really ticked."

"It ain't pretty," I said.

John smiled at this, then said, "Start getting your things together. We're moving you and Charles up to Oxnard this afternoon. There'll be more room there. You'll need it with the baby on the way."

"We'll be ready."

"And I'll need your cell phone when we get there. Jenna's too. Just precautionary."

"Understood."

John paused to look out over the parking lot.

"You know, George. To be honest, with all the crazy shit we've had to deal with, I'm amazed we pulled the fucking thing off."

"We did, didn't we?" I smiled, and we shook hands.

John headed down the stairs and I tossed my cigarette and returned to the room. I found Jenna crying when I stepped through the door.

"I hate you for what you did," she said, choking back angry tears.

"I know you do," I replied. "But this is where we are . . . for better or worse, huh?"

She looked at me with scorn.

"Do you really think I'd marry you now? After what you've done?"

"That's up to you," I told her as I opened one of the bureau drawers and began pulling clothes. "Right now we need to get our shit together. They're moving us again."

"Oh, let me guess. And Joe's coming with us."

"Joe's coming, yeah."

She shook her head and wiped her eyes.

"Maybe you should fuckin' marry *him*," she said sarcastically.

I kept my mouth shut and dumped a load of clothes on the foot of the bed.

"You know," said Jenna quietly, "there was this one moment when we were driving away from the house that I thought, George could have left and I never would have seen him again. But he came back for me.

I'll finally have him all to myself. We'll be just like a real family—just the four of us."

She gave a mocking laugh.

"And then I saw Joe standing outside that trailer and I thought, George, you motherfucker. Nothing's changed at all. This is how it will always be. George then Joe . . . then me."

"Well, you'll be happy to know—"

"I don't want to hear it," Jenna snapped as she rolled from the bed. "Go fuck yourself, George. You've ruined my life, you rat fucking bastard."

She stormed into the bathroom and slammed the door so hard it woke Sierra.

John Carr was right. It would have been so much cleaner had I never let that crazy woman into my life. The hard truth was, I could shave the beard and change the name, but my past would continue to haunt me as long as Jenna remained . . . dragged from place to place like the chains of Marley's ghost.

Charles and I were resettled at a Residence Inn in the city of Oxnard, about an hour's drive west of Los Angeles. Old Joe even got a room of his own. A few days later, true to his word, John brought in a coordinator from the U.S. marshals who explained the WITSEC program to Jenna all over again. And this time she listened. I guess as long as it wasn't Fabio doing the talking, she was willing to climb aboard the WITSEC train . . . especially once she learned Old Joe wouldn't be coming with us.

A few days later John Carr called Jenna's ex and explained to Billy the situation with Sierra and witness protection. I don't know how the hell John sold it, but I suspect that absentee father never really gave a shit whether his little girl was in his life or not. So he did the right thing for once in his fucked-up existence and signed away all rights to his daughter.

The three of us were now free and clear to enter WITSEC. We were just waiting on the arrival of the fourth, and ten days after the takedown he decided to join us. Unfortunately the baby's timing couldn't have been worse. Jenna and I hit the Ventura Freeway during the morning commute and crawled eastbound toward the medical center in Woodland Hills. As anyone who's ever traveled the 101 during rush hour knows, nothing moves. Drivers, stuck in their cars, are applying makeup, reading the newspaper and brushing their fucking teeth.

I couldn't bear to look over at Jenna beside me. The contractions were coming fast and furious, and she was kicking the door and biting the shoulder strap screaming in agony, "They're every two minutes now!"

I'm not sure how, but we made it to the emergency room with that baby still inside her. Per government instructions, Jenna was admitted as patient Jane Doe. As I walked Jane up and down the maternity ward, trying to jog the kid loose, the family members started arriving. It was a small group. First Bill showed up with Jenna's younger sister, then Charles and Old Joe came in with little Sierra. And that was it. When the time came to deliver, Jenna climbed onto the bed, the curtains were pulled and our little boy began punching his way out while an ATF special agent stood guard outside the door.

When the baby's head popped out, I think I tripped over my jaw. I'd never witnessed anything as amazing as a child entering the world.

My child.

Fuck Todd and all those other wannabes. This was my kid, goddammit.

As the baby's shoulders popped into view, Jenna grabbed hold and pulled him the rest of the way out, laying him on her chest. It was fuckin' amazing.

He was the most beautiful thing I'd ever seen.

"Would you like to cut the umbilical, Mr. Rowe?"

"Huh? What?"

"Cut the cord?" explained the doctor, extending the scissors.

"Hell, no," I said.

That kid just got here. I didn't want to fuck him up right out of the chute. So the doctor snipped the umbilical himself.

And that's how Baby Doe entered the world and witness protection. That was the little booger's name: Baby Doe. Seemed only fitting for a family about to vanish into anonymity.

That boy was healthy as a horse too. To Jenna's everlasting credit, except for an occasional joint, she'd stayed clean and sober through all nine months of pregnancy. It just showed me what that girl could do when she really put her mind to it. Of course, a few weeks after pushing the kid out, she was right back at it again.

The feds call it "downtime." I called it purgatory because you're stuck in limbo, caught between one world and the next. We spent two months hiding and going stir crazy at the Oxnard hotel, waiting for the U.S. marshals to get their shit together so we could get on with our lives. Jenna breast-fed the baby for a couple of those weeks, then got into alcohol and quit nursing. She started spending the hours down in the hotel lounge with Old Joe, drinking beer and wine on the government tab.

Not long after the baby was born, Jenna started warming up to me again. When I overheard her talking to Sierra one night, I knew she'd finally come around. The little girl was asking why she couldn't see her friends back in Hemet anymore.

"Some of the people we thought were nice guys had been very bad and they got in trouble for it," Jenna said, kneeling in front of Sierra.

"Is Daddy in trouble?"

"No, Daddy isn't in trouble, but he had to help put the bad guys in jail. And some of those bad guys are mad because Daddy told the truth about them. That's why you can't see your friends for a while."

"Because the bad guys are mad at Daddy?"

"That's right."

Fuckin' A right, little girl. The bad guys are pissed as hell at Daddy.

While we twiddled thumbs waiting on the marshals, my fiancée got back to abusing whatever she could lay her hands on. When ATF moved us from Oxnard to Lake Isabella out near Bakersfield, she fell in with an old friend and recovering heroin addict. Jenna got into that girl's methadone and before you knew it—whoopee! It was zero to sixty in two seconds. Within days she was slamming dope. In a month she was strung out.

From Lake Isabella the ATF relocated us to Oceanside, but that didn't stop my Jenna. Hell, no. When I prevented the girl from leaving the house to buy heroin one day, she called the cops and told them I'd beaten her. I was arrested and taken away in handcuffs.

John Carr had to bail me out.

Occasionally during our time in hiding I'd catch bits and pieces of news from the old hometown. The Vagos knew where Bill Thompson lived, and they made a point of cruising past his property, hoping Jenna and I might show our faces. Bill bought himself a gun and mounted security cameras outside the house. But he and his new wife never felt safe, and eventually they sold their home and left Hemet for good.

The Vagos were never prosecuted under the RICO Act. The reason, according to John Carr, was the U.S. Attorney's Office lacked the man-power to handle the number of defendants Operation 22 Green had generated. For that reason most of those greenies were processed by the state of California, which wasn't necessarily a bad thing because they all got slapped with the dreaded S.T.E.P. gang enhancement penalties. When all was said and done, and the evidence gathered during the raids was acted upon, forty-two Vagos and their associates were charged for crimes ranging from drug and weapons violations to first-degree murder.

Big Roy Compton pled guilty to felony possession of a firearm while a member of a street gang and was sentenced to twenty-four months in prison. Big Todd got thirty months for felony possession and street gang membership. Apparently I was never going to get a fighting shot at either one of those fuckers in their cells, though. John Carr couldn't make it happen.

In hindsight I figured that was never in the cards anyway.

Jack Fite, the baddest of the bad, was facing a felony conviction for possession of a controlled substance for sale and looking at an automatic twenty-five years to life under California's three-strike rule. He died of complications from hepatitis while awaiting trial, ending his days behind bars just like everyone always said he would. I don't figure many tears were shed for that evil sonofabitch.

The Hemet chapter that I'd gone undercover to drive out of town had been completely gutted, with most of those boys bagged on criminal street-gang-related charges. One year after the takedown, only Loki was holding down the fort, and that Vago was barely hanging on by his fingertips.

In the early spring of 2006 came the news I'd been waiting for.

John was on the line again. It was time to go into WITSEC.

"You ready?"

"Hell, yeah," I told him. "Let's do this."

As instructed by the U.S. marshals, Jenna and I packed one suitcase each. There were no personal photos allowed, no paperwork, nothing of any kind that might link us to the past.

Old Joe and I spent our last day together fishing on Oceanside pier, talking about the time we'd spent together, the people we'd met and the experiences we'd shared along the way. The two of us had been partners for almost twenty years, sticking together through thick and thin. He relied on me as much as I did on him. Without that big gangly bastard I'm not sure I could have made it through those years undercover. We were brother tight, Old Joe and I, and now I was leaving that brother behind. It was one of the hardest things I ever had to do.

"Am I ever gonna see you and the kids again?" he wanted to know.

"Don't know, buddy," I said. "I honestly don't."

Joe had grown especially fond of my son. He once told me he didn't want to get attached to any more kids because they grow up too fast and move away. I think my boy was a bittersweet reminder of the two sons he hadn't seen in years. Now Old Joe was being forced to say good-bye all over again, and that gentle man could hardly bear it.

"I was thinking maybe this day wouldn't happen," he said as he fished. "I guess maybe I was hoping it would never happen."

"Lately I've been thinking the same thing, partner."

Joe turned with a questioning look.

"What are these people really gonna do for me, anyway?" I said to him. "I mean, I don't know where I'm going. Hell, I don't even know who I'm supposed to be."

"Well, whoever you are, I'm gonna miss you."

I grinned, then fell silent and listened to the waves lap against the pilings.

"Funny the shit you remember. This reminds me of a day I spent with my dad when I was a kid. He wanted to fish from this wooden bridge that ran out to an island in the middle of a lake. So I held the poles with one hand and held on to my father's neck with the other, and he swam us out there. I was seven years old. Man, things were so much simpler then."

I glanced over at my friend.

"What the fuck did I do, Joe? I used to think my life was gonna be Ozzie and Harriet, you know? Boy, was that a fuckin' joke."

Old Joe looked out toward the Pacific. "Brother, all I know is, I feel like the loneliest person in the world right now. And you're not even gone yet."

John Carr arrived in his SUV shortly before dark. Our luggage was thrown in back and Joe attached the car seat. Then he strapped my son inside, kissed him on the head and closed the door.

I cried tears of sorrow twice in my life. Like I said, tears were reserved for anger, and that always meant victims. But I cried from the
heart when my father passed away, and I cried that afternoon when I
said good-bye to Old Joe at the curb in Oceanside.

My friend was crying too.

"Love you, brother," he told me, clasping my hand.

"Guess I'll see you when I see you," I said, and turned away.

As we drove off toward the airport, I glanced back. Old Joe was in the
street watching us. He was still standing there as we turned the corner.

At Los Angeles International Airport we were met in the terminal
by three U.S. marshals, two men and a woman. After John turned us
over to their care, I had another good-bye moment with my longtime
shepherd.

"Been quite a ride, huh, buddy?" I said to him. "I just hope you're
not disappointed."

"Why would I be disappointed? Hey, listen. You did good, George.
The Vagos are out of Hemet. That's what you got into this for, right?
You should be proud."

I shrugged. "Yeah, but we didn't get rid of all of them."

"Dude, that was never going to happen. These gangs are like cancer. You can cut 'em out but they always come back again. So we'll just
keep going after the bastards. That's what we do, right?"

He proffered his hand and I shook it. But I felt the moment deserved something more. So I pulled that special agent into a hug and
slapped him on the back.

"Hell of a job, Uncle John."

"You too, George. Take care of yourself."

"Will do."

I lifted the bags, Jenna held the baby with one arm and Sierra's
hand with the other, and we followed the marshals through a side door
that bypassed gate security. As the female marshal led us down the
gangway, she made a half-assed attempt to connect with Jenna.

"I know this must be hard for you," she said, tucking her badge away.

"You want to act like you care?" snarled Jenna.

Oh, shit. Here we go.

"This is your day job, bitch. You're going home to your family to-night. This is my fucking *life* we're talking about."

Man, those marshals couldn't get us on that plane fast enough.

Our commercial flight from Los Angeles took us to an airport in Washing-ton, D.C., where we were met by yet another U.S. marshal dressed like we'd interrupted his weekend of fly-fishing. He wore a tan cotton vest covered with small pockets and a firearm holstered at his side. The man was all business as he directed us into a box van with blacked-out windows, then drove us on a long haul to a military base that I can only assume was Langley.

The first stop in the WITSEC program comes belowground. The marshal maneuvered the van through a sally port and down into a cement bunker with a heavy metal door that closed behind us. From there we were escorted through the bunker's cement bowels, led down corridors lined with doors numbered like any aboveground hotel. Only this Hilton had no windows, the staff never smiled, and room service offered nothing but frozen dinners and microwavable pizza.

Jenna called it the Bat Cave. For me it was purgatory all over again. We were back in limbo, waiting for new identities and our next destination.

The medical staff gave the whole family physicals, including a vaginal for Jenna and an attempt by the doc to poke his finger up my ass, which I politely declined. After that came fingerprinting and paperwork, including the documents establishing our new WITSEC identities. We each had the chance to submit four names—first, middle and last—filled out like a multiple-choice exam. Jenna wanted Sierra to choose her own, but the kid kept opting for names like Lightning, Thunder and Snow, so Mommy chose one for her. Apparently our youngest was exempt from all this. Baby Doe could keep his given name because he was born into protective custody, a child of witness protection.

A serious-minded young marshal with burn scars on his face gathered the paperwork.

"You understand that from this point on, you won't be able to contact anyone who might have known you in the past," he explained.

"Yeah, we get it," I told him.

"In twenty minutes you'll be taken back to the airport and flown to your final destination. Upon arrival you'll be met by your handler. You'll be given twenty-five hundred dollars to get you started and a new place to live."

"And where will that be?" I wanted to know.

"You'll find out when you get there," replied the marshal as he exited the room.

With George Rowe now consigned to history, I downed a few slices of shitty frozen pizza and told Jenna I was heading out to the patio for a much-needed smoke.

"George?" she said before I could leave.

When I turned she looked like she was about to cry.

"I know I've been an angry bitch. But I want you to know I love you. I always will. If it wasn't for you I doubt I'd be alive right now." She paused a moment, then added sadly, "I just wish you had set me free."

EPILOGUE

I'm on a sniper-proof patio surrounded by concrete walls fifteen feet high. I can't see a damn thing from here except the patch of twilight above, and every now and then a jet fighter goes blasting through it, flying so low I can smell the exhaust. In a few minutes the U.S. marshals will escort my family back to the airport and we'll fly off with our new names to a new place and a new life courtesy of the United States government. But as I draw on my cigarette, watching those fighters scream overhead, I'm not thinking about the future. I'm thinking of the road that led me here—to this fortress three thousand miles from home. And I'm asking myself . . .

Man, what the fuck happened?

Life was pretty damn good before I shook hands with the ATF. Now it's all gone to shit. The man with nothing to gain and everything to lose lost everything: a son I'd never see grow up, my home, my business, my friends, the town I risked my neck to defend. Hell, even my own identity—all of it gone like a fart in a fuckin' hurricane.

Not that I expected anything in return. I knew the deal going in. But what exactly did those three years buy me? A federal agent has his retirement, an informant gains his freedom. But for me there was no reward. No thank-you speeches. No key to the city. Just a slap on the back and a boot in the ass that landed me in witness protection, left with one suitcase, two kids and a crazy old lady.

Don't get me wrong, I love those children to death, and Jenna's great when she's not using, but fuck's sake, how did things get so complicated? Used to be just me and Old Joe when this whole thing began. Hell, we could have gone into the program as gay lovers. That would have been easy. But this . . .

Damn it, George. What the hell did you do?

Ah, well. They say no good deed goes unpunished. Maybe this is just some kind of karmic payback for all the sins I've committed— God's way of spanking my naughty ass.

Maybe it's what I deserve.

I drag on the Marlboro and think back to that day John Carr and I first met in Bee Canyon. And I wonder, given a second chance, would I still shake his hand? I mean, knowing the destination, understanding the price, would I take that journey again?

Another jet screams overhead. I toss my spent cigarette and crush it underfoot.

Time to move on.

AFTERWORD

Six years after our police escort out of Hemet on that deserted I-10 freeway, there's not a day goes by that I don't think of my old hometown or ask God's forgiveness for the pain I caused there. And that includes the shit I did but can't remember.

As for the people I left behind, well, thanks to WITSEC I've lost touch with most of them. Occasionally I'll speak to John Carr. He and Koz are still busting motorcycle outlaws for the ATF. But my old friend Detective Duffy is gone. Few years back Kevin checked into a Motel 6 and shot himself. ATF Special Agent Jeff Ryan was another casualty of the profession, committing suicide in 2011. Charles, aka Quick Draw, got a taste for life undercover and continued working as an informant-for-hire. Bubba, the biker cop with the L.A. County Sheriff's Department, retired after twenty-eight years on the job and went back to the real world.

Old Joe? Well, John Carr kept his promise, taking my buddy under ATF's wing and relocating him to a safe place. Jenna relapsed into heroin a few months after entering federal protection, told me she'd fallen out of love and went to work as a stripper. Took a few years, but once she climbed down off the pole, she went back to school, found a job in a professional field and was eventually reunited with Sierra.

And the Vagos? Contrary to claims that the club had been "dismantled" following Operation 22 Green, the "Nation" is thriving—by some accounts nearly doubling in size since the takedown in 2006. Vagos chapters are now found in Hawaii, Canada, Mexico, Nicaragua, Costa Rica and on the far side of the world in New Zealand and Japan.

And, yes, there's even a chapter back in Hemet.

I'll let someone else handle that one.

Rhino, the former international sergeant at arms, was charged with murder in the execution of "Shorty" Daoussis and is serving seventy-five years to life in state prison. His accomplice, Kilo, is doing fifty. "Twist" Foreman from the Victorville chapter, who murdered Little Jimmy in that botched robbery in Lucerne Valley, got life behind bars after his partner in crime, Victorville VP Ryan Matteson, testified against him.

So much for brotherly love.

Terry the Tramp, the "God" of Green Nation, was ousted as the Vagos international president in 2010, but not before the man had squandered over a million dollars of the club's money. When the feds finally busted Tramp and sent him to prison for failure to pay taxes on all that loot, there was a measly sixty-five bucks left in the account. Almost every cent had gone to the mortgage, the utilities and the casinos.

Big Roy did his prison time, then got the hell out of Dodge. With two felony strikes against him, and one more triggering an automatic twenty-five-to-life sentence, he booked for Hawaii, where he and his wife opened the latest incarnation of the Lady Luck.

Roy's good pal, Todd, wasn't so fortunate.

The outlaw life finally caught up with Big Todd in August 2010, when three members of the Brotherhood Motorcycle Club ambushed him in Valle Vista and put a bullet in his head.

And what of those other Vagos I helped put behind bars? Except for

Jack Fite, who died in county jail, every one of those boys is back on the street.

Me? I'm serving a life sentence. I'll be watching my back until the day I die.

George Rowe
Somewhere, USA

ACKNOWLEDGMENTS

For their invaluable contributions to this book I'd like to thank ATF Special Agent Jeff Kerr for hooking me up; my agent, Barry Zucker at McGinniss Associates, for his tireless energy and enthusiasm; Matthew Benjamin, senior editor at Touchstone, for believing in my story; and KC Franks, who gave me a voice and helped tell it the way it was.

For their invaluable contributions to my life I'd like to thank Sergeant Pike of the Riverside County Sheriff's Department, who, along with his father, gave me a hand when I needed it most; my adoptive parents, Pat and Dodi, for taking me into their family; and SA Darrin Kozlowski, who was instrumental to the success of 22 Green.

I'd also like to thank Dave Hale for giving me a chance when no one else would; Rick Dean, who brought me into his church; his wife, Peggy, who fought to keep me on the straight-and-narrow; and Jeremy, for that life-altering kick in the ass. Thanks, also, to the foster parent in Buena Park who taught me the importance of family; my old man, who taught me how to survive; and Darlene, who taught me how to love and behave like a man.

Last, but by no means least, my deepest gratitude goes to Detective Kevin Duffy for pointing me in the right direction; ATF Special Agent John Carr, who shepherded me safely through the valley; and my best buddy, Old Joe, who faithfully walked beside me.

Thanks to God, these are the souls who moved in and out of my life and made a difference, but were never fully appreciated until I climbed from the shadows and took that long look back.

To each one of you I am forever grateful.

—GR